Reviewers' comments about the author's

"It takes a pro to teach Final Cut Pro, and Tom Wolsky delivers. His years of TV and film experience make him uniquely qualified to demystify Final Cut Pro and teach good editing techniques. Every editor needs this book."

— Jim Heid, Avondale Media

"If you want to learn editing with Final Cut Pro, look no further. Tom Wolsky brings a depth of experience to digital editing that few others share. He has proven himself an excellent teacher at Stanford University's Academy for New Media, and I will encourage, if not require, future students of the Academy to read this book."

— Phil Gibson, president, Digital Media Academy

"Tom Wolsky's longtime professional career with ABC News in London — and his later teaching position and full-time studio work in California — takes this work far beyond the simple "how to" books that address Final Cut. In Tom's hands, the subject becomes a look into the process of professional editing and project management as well. Because of this, we believe that he knows Final Cut in many ways better than the people that write the program."

— Ron and Kathlyn Lindeboom, founders, creativecow.net

"*Final Cut Pro 3 Editing Workshop* shows off both Tom's complete expertise with FCP and his skill as a writer. He has always written in a clean, understandable manner with the ability to demystify his subject matter."

— Ken Stone, www.kenstone.net

FINAL CUT PRO 4 EDITING ESSENTIALS

Tom Wolsky

CMP**Books**

San Francisco, CA • New York, NY • Lawrence, KS

Published by CMP Books
an imprint of CMP Media LLC

Main office: 600 Harrison Street, San Francisco, CA 94107 USA
Tel: 415-947-6615; fax: 415-947-6015

Editorial office:
4601 West 6th Street, Suite B, Lawrence, KS 66049 USA

www.cmpbooks.com
email: books@cmp.com

Senior Editor: Dorothy Cox
Editor and Layout Design: Madeleine Reardon Dimond
Cover Layout Design: Damien Castaneda

Distributed in the U.S. by: Distributed in Canada by:
Publishers Group West   Jaguar Book Group
1700 Fourth Street   100 Armstrong Avenue
Berkeley, CA 94710   Georgetown, Ontario M6K 3E7 Canada
1-800-788-3123   905-877-4483

For individual orders and for information on special discounts for quantity orders, please contact:
CMP Books Distribution Center, 6600 Silacci Way, Gilroy, CA 95020
Tel: 1-800-500-6875 or 408-848-3854; fax: 408-848-5784
email: cmp@rushorder.com; Web: www.cmpbooks.com

ISBN: 1-57820-227-2

CMPBooks

For Judy and Stan Corwin
With Love and Gratitude

Table of Contents

Introduction

Thanks to modern technology, anybody with even a modest budget can acquire the means of production to make movies. Affordable camera, lighting, editing. and other equipment of professional quality can produce images better than seen on most home television sets, and these are now available to anyone. Simply possessing these professional level tools is not enough. Even I can buy a tool belt with a hammer and a wide range of the electric tools, but I would still not be a carpenter, let alone an artist in wood. The same is true of video production. Acquiring and learning how to use the tools is only part of the process. You have to also learn the craft.

There are many ways to do this. This book, I would like to think, is one of the steps in the process. Another might be a course of study, such as a film school program or the traditional method of apprenticeship, learning from a master. I have been fortunate enough to learn from both, first at the London School of Film Technique (now the London International Film School) and later with master editors. Starting in Stan Hawks' and Arthur Solomon's cutting rooms, I worked with many talented BBC directors and with a many great camerapeople and editors in England on independent productions and at ABC News in London and New York.

Though this book is about editing with Final Cut Pro 4, the essentials of editing don't change when you use different applications. All that changes is how you use the tools to create the effect that you want. This book is intended to cover the editing aspects of working with this powerful application. The animation features, special effects, and other additional applications that are now included with Final Cut are subjects for another book. This book is very much derived from my earlier books, but has been updated to include the newly available features and techniques.

One of the reasons for this book is that Final Cut Pro 4 has a new editing paradigm. A fundamental change has been made at the heart of the way the application controls, organizes, and inter-links media and the clips based on that media that you work with in the application. This new paradigm means that the workflow for FCP4 often needs to be substantially revised from that used in earlier versions.

This is a book about editing, and editing using the Final Cut Pro application specifically. It is not a manual, and is not intended to supersede or replace the FCP manual. If you want to know how every control, slider, and button in FCP functions, a voluminous manual is supplied with the application.

The work is organized as a series of tutorials and lessons. I hope I have written them in a logical order to lead you from one topic to a more advanced topic. The nature of your work with Final Cut Pro, however, may require the information in Lesson 5, for example, right away. You can read that lesson by itself and make that scroll you need right now. There may, however, be elements in Lesson 5 that presuppose that you know something about using the **Viewer** in conjunction with the **Canvas**.

The book can also be read in the more traditional manner, from start to finish as you absorb the material, without doing the lessons. It doesn't need to be read in linear fashion beginning with this page, though for a new user to Final Cut Pro, it might be better if you did.

In this book I offer a good many opinions on how I like to produce, even how I think scripts should be written, scenes shot and finally edited. I want to emphasize that these are only a single individual's views and are not necessarily the best way to work or the best way for you to work. Everybody has different experiences, both in the field and in the cutting room. How you work depends on many factors, not least of which is your experience and the types of projects you're working on. These latter often dictate your workflow. I'm only offering suggestions for a variety of work scenarios. I hope you find one that's beneficial for you.

Who Is This Book For?

This *Editing Essentials* is intended for all FCP users, but primarily those new to the application who want to learn how to edit with it. Because FCP has expanded into a five-headed Hydra of different applications, each complex in its own right, a single book that covered all these subjects would be monstrously large as well as expensive. This volume covers the editing portions: capturing your material, organizing, editing, adding transitions, basic titling and sound techniques, and outputting from the application.

What's on the DVD?

The DVD contains some of the lessons, projects, and clips used in the book. Not all of the lessons require materials from the DVD. For some, such as Lesson 1, you don't need any at all. For others you may want to substitute your own material, clips you want to work with or are more familiar with. I hope you find this book useful, informative, and fun. I think it's a good way to learn this kind of application.

Acknowledgements

First as always my gratitude to all the people at CMP Books who make this book writing process relatively painless, Paul Temme, associate publisher, and Dorothy Cox, senior editor, for their guidance. Many thanks as always are due to Madeleine Reardon Dimond working through the copy editing and layout despite the vagaries of Microsoft Word. My thanks again to Damien Castaneda for his wonderful work on the covers.

Special thanks to Lanny Cotler and Cotler Brothers Productions, for allowing me to use material from their wonderful 1997 independent film *Heartwood* with Hilary Swank, Eddie Mills, and the late Jason Robards.

So many helped in making this book possible: Sidney Kramer, for his expert advice; Peter Barrett for this Replace FCP Prefs X script; Eric Fry, for his Timecode Calculator, and many others who don't even know it, all those wonderful people in the FCP forums such as 2-pop; the Apple Discussion forums; the Creative Cow forums; Michael Horton's LAFCPUG (Los Angeles Final Cut Pro User Group) forum, Ken Stone, and others. The list of names of contributors of ideas and discussions would be endless, but a representative few to single out would have to include Ralph Fairweather, Jerry Hofmann, Philip Hodgetts, Dan Brockett, Charles (Chawla) Roberts, David Bogie, Bret Williams, Walter Biscardi, Marco Solorio, Nick Meyers, and many, many more.

A great many thanks are due as always to my partner B. T. Corwin for her insights, her endless encouragement, her engineering technical support, and for her patience with me. Without her, none of this would have been possible. Finally, again my thanks to the wonderful people of Damine, Japan, who welcomed us into their homes and whose lives provided the source material for these lessons.

Lesson 1

Capturing Your Material

In the Beginning: Planning

Video or film production is based on the notion of time, usually linear time of a fixed length. Whether it is 10 minutes, 30 minutes, one hour, two hours, or more, the idea is that the film is seen as a single event of fixed duration. On the other hand, time within the film itself is infinitely malleable. Events can happen quickly: we fly from one side of the world to another, from one era to a different century, in the blink of an eye. Or every detail and every angle can be slowed down to a far greater length than the true expanse of time—or seen again and again.

Because film and video production is based on the notion of time, the process of editing, controlling time and space within the story, is of paramount importance. This process of editing, however, does not begin after the film is shot. It begins when the idea is conceived. As soon as you are thinking of your production as a series of shots or scenes, you are mentally editing the movie, arranging the order of the material, juxtaposing one element against another.

1

🐾 *Note*_____

Nonlinear Movies? The notion of nonlinear presentation of films and videos that DVD offers is antithetical to the idea of film as a progression in time. Over the years there have been many attempts to make films nonlinear or with variable structures and outcomes, much like a game. None have been really successful. I think the reason is that the movies are about storytelling, and that implies the linearity of presentation. If variability is introduced to the movie, or if the film can be seen in any order, then its ethos as a story disappears. We will all see a different story. We'll no longer be able to say, "Did you like *Casablanca*?" The question would now be, "How was your version of *Casablanca*?" Not quite the same thing, and probably not providing the same sense of satisfaction and fulfillment, which is why I think the attempts at nonlinearity or variability have largely failed except in gaming itself.

The first movies were single, static shots of everyday events. The Lumière brothers' screening in Paris of a train pulling into the La Ciotat train station caused a sensation. Silent, black and white, it still held a gripping reality for the audience. The brothers followed this with a staged comic scene. Georges Méliès expanded this into staging complex tableaux. It wasn't until Edwin H. Porter and D. W. Griffith in the United States discovered the power of editing one shot next to another that the movies were really born. Griffith also introduced such innovations as the flashback, the first real use of film to manipulate time. Close-ups were used to emphasize the moment of impact, wide shots to establish context, parallel action was introduced, and other story devices were born, but the real discovery was that the shot is the fundamental building block of film, and that the film is built one shot at a time, one after the other.

Films and videos are made in the moments when one shot changes into another, when one image is replaced by the next, when one point of view becomes someone else's point of view. Without the image changing, you just have moving pictures. The Lumières' novelty would have never reached beyond the penny arcade. The idea of changing from one angle to another or from one scene to another quickly leads to the concept of juxtaposing one idea against another. It soon becomes apparent that the impact of storytelling lies in the way in which the shots are ordered.

Editing is about three things: selection, arrangement, and timing. Selecting which shot to use, deciding where that shot should be placed, and how long the shot should be on the screen. The first of these, selection, begins in the process of capturing your material. For many editors the process of logging and capturing material is part of the selection process. In days when hard drives were small and very expensive, this was a critical step in the digital editing process. Now, because drives have become relatively cheap and much, much larger and faster, the pressure to capture selectively has been greatly reduced.

Firing Up the Application

Let's begin by launching the application. Double-click on the icon in the *Applications* folder (Figure 1.1), or better yet, make an alias in the **Dock** and just click on that. After a new installation or after you have trashed your *Final Cut Preferences* file, you will first be greeted with the preferences screen in Figure 1.2.

The default setting is **DV-NTSC** with audio at 48kHz. You have a **DV-PAL** option as well as the two **OfflineRT** options, which are used to capture material at low resolution to conserve drive space. Other choices are available. If you click on the little **Show All** checkbox in the upper right of the window, you will have the option to select for a much longer list of options (Figure 1.3).

The second popup makes you choose a scratch disk (Figure 1.4). The popup defaults to your system partition and offers you the choice of any hard drives on your system. You should choose your separate, dedicated media hard drive, not the system drive that holds your operating system and your applications. The system drive is where you save your documents and your project files, but your media should go on a separate large, fast hard drive.

1.1   Application Icon

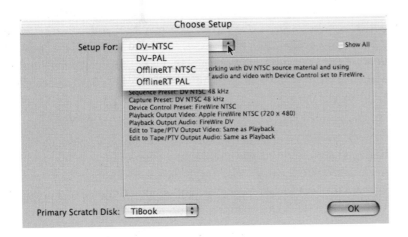

1.2   Start-up Dialogue

Cinema Tools – 23.98fps from DV NTSC
Cinema Tools – 23.98fps from DV PAL
Cinema Tools – 24fps from DV NTSC
Cinema Tools – 24fps from DV PAL
Cinema Tools – DV NTSC NDF
DV–NTSC
DV–NTSC 24p (23.98)
DV–NTSC 24p (23.98) Advanced Pulldown Removal
DV–NTSC Anamorphic
DV–NTSC FireWire Basic
DV–PAL
DV–PAL Anamorphic
DV–PAL FireWire Basic
DV50 – NTSC
DV50 – PAL
DV50 NTSC 24p (23.98)
DV50 NTSC Anamorphic
DV50 PAL Anamorphic
DVCPRO – PAL
DVCPRO – PAL (No Device)
DVCPRO – PAL 48 kHz Anamorphic
NC Device
OfflineRT – DVCPRO – PAL
OfflineRT HD – 23.98
OfflineRT HD – 24
OfflineRT HD – 25
OfflineRT HD – 29.97
OfflineRT HD – 30
OfflineRT NTSC
OfflineRT NTSC 24fps
OfflineRT NTSC 24p (23.98)
OfflineRT NTSC Anamorphic
OfflineRT PAL
OfflineRT PAL Anamorphic
Uncompressed 10–bit NTSC 48 kHz
Uncompressed 10–bit PAL 48 kHz
Uncompressed 8–bit NTSC 48 kHz
Uncompressed 8–bit PAL 48 kHz

1.3 Preset Options

1.4 Scratch Disks

Understanding the Interface

When the application is fully launched, it opens to fill your screen as in Figure 1.5.

The Primary Windows

The screen is divided into four primary windows, with two large empty screens as your principal monitors:

- The **Viewer,** the empty black window in the middle of the screen, allows you to look at individual video clips.

- The **Canvas,** the empty monitor on the right, is the output of your material as you edit it together. The **Canvas** is linked directly to the **Timeline.**

- The **Timeline** for your video is the window with the horizontal bar across the bottom of the screen. This is where you lay out your video and audio material in the order you want it.

- The **Browser** is the fourth window at the top left.

Think of the **Browser** as a giant folder. This is where your project materials are listed. You can nest folders within folders, just like you can on a Mac desktop. This is not where your clips are stored; it is only a list. The data that makes up your clips is stored on your media hard drives. In the **Browser** you can have a variety of different types of files, obviously video files, but also audio files and graphics or still images. You'll also notice in the interface the vertical bars that contain the **Tools** and **Audio Meters.**

Figure 1.5 shows the default configuration, called **Standard,** which is new to Final Cut Pro 4. The former **Standard** arrangement is now called **Two Up.** You can switch to it from the **Windows** menu by selecting **Arrange>Two Up.** You can recall the **Standard** arrangement at any time with the keyboard shortcut **Control-U.**

Windows can be resized by grabbing the edges where the cursor changes to a **Resizing Tool** (Figure 1.6). When you pull with the **Resizing Tool,** the windows will move proportionately, expanding and contracting as needed to fill the available space. You can arrange the windows to your specific needs. You can save these arrangements and call them from the menu **Windows>Arrange**

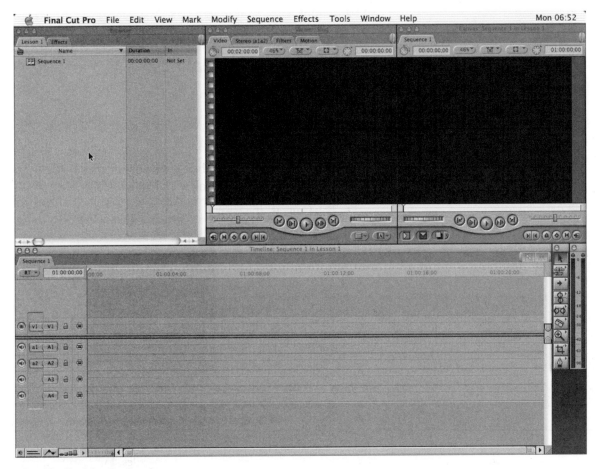

1.5   The Final Cut Pro Interface

(Figure 1.7). Notice that any saved arrangements appear at the bottom of the list with keyboard shortcuts for really fast access.

We will look at these windows in detail in the next lesson, but first we need to get some material captured and into your project. And before we begin that process, we should save our project. This is important because FCP will use the project name to create a folder inside the *Capture Scratch* folder. *Capture Scratch* is where your media will be stored. The application creates it inside the designated scratch disk, which we set up when the application was first launched.

To save the project, go to the **File** menu and select **Save Project As.** Give the project file a name and save it on your system hard drive. It defaults to going into your home *Documents* folder. This isn't a bad place for it. If other users need access, the project file will have to be in the *Shared* folder or in some other location.

Setting up the Application

Digital video editing is divided into three phases:

- Getting your material into the computer
- Editing it, which is the fun part
- Getting it back out of your computer

This lesson is about the first part, getting your material into your computer. First you have to set up your application correctly. In Final Cut Pro, as in most video editing programs, that means setting up your preferences. These fundamentals are absolutely necessary for Final Cut Pro to function properly. Set it up right, get your material into your project properly, and you're halfway home. You cannot overestimate how important this is.

To set up your preferences correctly, you need to understand something about the workflow of video editing and to make some decisions about how you want to work. You have to make a fundamental choice before you start: do you want to work online or offline?

At its simplest level, offline is working with a copy of your material that is never intended to be seen by anyone but the editor, producer, director, and those working on the project. It's the equivalent of a work print in film cutting, which used be to mostly in black and white, full of china graph marks, dust,

> ★ *Tip*
>
> **Window Commands:** There are four handy keyboard shortcuts to navigate your principal windows:
>
> Command-1 is the **Viewer**.
> Command-2 is the **Canvas**.
> Command-3 is the **Timeline**.
> Command-4 is the **Browser**.
>
> This commands will make that the selected shortcut the active window. Also the Q key will quickly toggle you to the **Viewer** and between the **Viewer** and the **Canvas**.

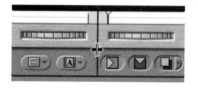

1.6   Window Resizing Tool (above)

1.7   Windows > Arrange (right)

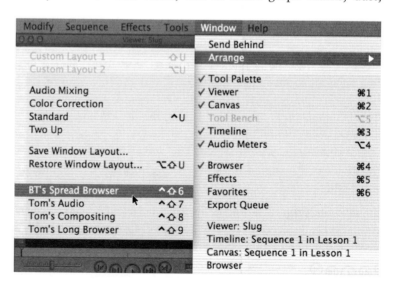

scratches, and tape joins. In video it's usually a low-quality, low-resolution copy of your material. The online version is what is intended to be seen by your audience. Because of the high cost of online equipment, editing a program at finished online quality was cost prohibitive, so most productions were first edited in offline quality. Traditionally the offline was done on a cheap editing system, perhaps even VHS, or at very low quality. This offline produced an Edit Decision List (EDL), a list of every single video and audio edit, and the timecode that defines which tapes and which frames on that tape each edit came from. So offlining is a process of working at low quality on cheap machines, while onlining is the part of the process that changes the quality of the product to its final, finished version. In film days, this was the negative cutter's job; in tape production, it happened in an online edit suite with expensive videotape decks, controllers, mixers, and video engineering equipment.

What is Timecode?

Timecode is a series of numbers that are written on your video tape whenever you make a DV recording or record on a professional device. The numbers represent time and on most consumer cameras begin at 00:00:00:00, zero hours, zero minutes, zero seconds, and zero frames. On professional cameras the start number can be set to anything time you like. A timecode number is assigned to every frames of video—25 frames per second in the European PAL system, 30 frames per second in the North American and Japanese NTSC system.

For NTSC this is a problem, because the true frame rate of all NSTC video isn't 30fps but 29.97fps. Because of this NTSC has created two ways of counting timecode called Drop Frame and Non-Drop Frame.

Non-Drop Frame displays the numbers based on a simple 30fps frame rate. The problem with this is that when your timecode gets to the one-hour mark, one hour of real world time hasn't passed yet. It's still almost four seconds from completing the hour.

Drop Frame uses a complex method of counting that compensates for the difference between 29.97fps and 30fps. No actually frames of video are dropped. DF drops two frames a minute in its count, except every 10th minute. This means that at the one-minute mark, your DF video will go from 59;29 to 1:00;02. There is no 1:00;00 or 1:00;01. Notice the semicolons. The convention is to write DF timecode with semicolons, or at least one semicolon, while NDF is written only with colons.

The DV standard uses Drop Frame timecode as its counting method, though some prosumer and all professional cameras can be switched between the two.

↘ Note

Offline Confusion: Confusion about the term offline has been compounded because FCP often uses the word to mean a clip that's in your **Browser** or **Timeline**, but whose source file is missing or deleted from your hard drive. When I speak of offline and of OfflineRT (real time), I mean the workflow and not the missing media.

In nonlinear editing, *offline* has come to mean the process of digitizing your video material at low resolution, thereby conserving drive space, while allowing the editor access to a huge amount of material. After editing the offline material, an EDL is again produced. The EDL is used to redigitize the material in an edit suite capable of finished resolution quality. In Final Cut Pro, the process remains within one edit suite. FCP is both the offline and the online suite. This simplifies the process and allows greater capabilities because you have the full resources of the application available to you, which you don't when exporting to an EDL. After the material has been redigitized at its high, final resolution, the finish work is done, tweaking the color and effects so that every shot is as perfect as can be.

So this is the decision you have to make when you first set up your preferences: will you start by working in offline, capturing your material at low resolution first and then recapturing at high resolution, or will you capture at your final resolution from the beginning?

System Settings

Before we can bring material into the computer, we should set up our system controls. There are now three separate sets of

---

Preferences Folder:

Once you've worked with your system a little bit and decided you really do like these preferences, it's a good idea to save them. This also saves any **Favorites** you create. So after you've made a few transitions or effects settings that you like, back up your prefs again. If you have problems with FCP, one of the first remedies anyone will suggest is to trash your *Preferences* file. If there is a problem with your system, it's often your preferences that will corrupt. It's easy enough to back up the *Prefs* file. The best way is a great little shareware AppleScript written by New Zealander Peter Barrett. It's in the *Extras* folder on the DVD. Run Replace FCP4 Prefs, and you can archive your preferences, replace your existing preferences with archived copies, or trash your preferences. It also does other system clean-up work. Keep a copy handy on your desktop or an alias in your **Dock**.

If you need to trash your preferences manually, there are three files you have to throw away. The first is inside *Users/Home/Library/Preferences* and is called *com.apple.FinalCutPro.plist*. The other two are inside the same *Preferences* folder in another folder called *Final Cut Pro User Data*. You need to discard the *Final Cut Pro 4.0 Preferences* file and the *Final Cut Pro POA Cache* file. These should be dragged to the **Trash**, and the **Trash** emptied.

Preferences in Final Cut Pro 4, all under the **Final Cut Pro** menu. Some are in a new location. There are the **User Preferences**, which let you set up your computer to your taste, and there are also the **System Settings** and the **Audio/Video Settings**. Let's start by looking at the newly created **System Settings** panel, which brings the **Scratch Disks** panel from **User Preferences** and adds some new options.

Open **System Settings** from the **Final Cut Pro** menu, or use the keyboard shortcut **Shift-Q**. This brings up a tabbed window with five panels beginning with **Scratch Disks** (Figure 1.8).

Scratch Disks

Let's look at the lower portion of the window before we tackle setting the disks. Except for some specialist systems, make sure that the **Capture Audio and Video to Separate Files** box is left unchecked. This box is primarily a legacy of older systems that worked better with separate files on separate drives. If yours is one of the few capture cards that prefers this option, check this box. In all other cases, particularly for DV, leave it unchecked. For DV material the same drive should always be used for both video and audio. For high-resolution work at high data rates, setting audio to a different disk drive helps achieve better performance because the heads need to serve only video or audio, not both. With multiple tracks of audio in a sequence, the drive-handling audio has a great deal of work to do. Having a separate drive deal solely with the high data rate video portion of the signal makes it easier on the system to achieve playback without dropping frames.

The *Waveform Cache* and the *Thumbnail Cache* default to the drive that you set when you first launched the application. This would be the drive you set as your media drive when you first launched the application. These should be reset to the internal drive of your computer. The *Autosave Vault* probably should remain on your dedicated media drive. The reason many recommend this procedure is that if your internal system drive fails, your backups will still be preserved. Similarly if your media drive fails, your main project file, being on a separate drive, will still be available to you.

Minimum Allowable Free Space On Scratch Disks defaults to 10MB. Arguably this low setting will cause the hard drive to become heavily fragmented and slow down. Some go so far as to say that you should leave 25% of your drive free. For large drives, this seems a bit excessive. If you have a large single partition above 50GB, perhaps you could set this number to 1G.

Unless you have a particular reason, you should leave **Limit capture/export segment size to** unchecked. This feature limits the size of segments FCP can capture or export. If your drives have been initialized as HFS+, this should not be a problem. FCP should capture large size clips without segmentation.

The **Limit Capture Now To** box makes it easier to use **Capture Now** by improving the application's performance. Without it FCP would check the available hard drive space before it started **Capture Now**. This could take a long time while the application rummaged through your assigned drives. This box allows you to limit the amount of space FCP will search for. The default is 30 minutes, or about 6G of file space at DV settings. FCP can search through this space quickly.

Let's get back to the main body of the **Scratch Disks** window. Here you assign scratch disks for your captured material and for your render files. Normally you set your project's video, audio, and render files in the same location. Set each drive you want to capture to, and the application will fill that drive and then move on to the next. You can set up to 12 separate drives or partitions.

By default, FCP assigns separate render folders for audio and video. When you click the **Set** button, a navigation window allows you to select the location for these files. Usually I pick the drive I want to use for a project. I used to create separate folders for different projects, but FCP does this internally with the *Capture Scratch* and *Render* folders. Apparently this structure will never change, so I gave up trying to tame it and yielded to its work flow.

When you set the drive, FCP creates these folders: the *Capture Scratch* folder, the *Render Files* folder, and the *Audio Render Files* folder. *Render Files* contains the video renders; *Audio,* the audio renders. As you capture or digitize material, it is stored in *Capture Scratch.* Within each of these folders will be separate folders for each project using the project's name.

✎ Note_____

Naming Drives and Partitions: It's not a good idea to use a numbering scheme like 1, 2, and 3 for drives or partitions. Nor is it a good idea to name drives or partitions Blue, Blue 1, Blue 2, etc. Some FCP users seem to have trouble with drives that use a name that is included in part of another name. The application seems to be much happier with unique drive names such as Larry, Mo, and Curly.

Memory & Cache

The **Memory & Cache** panel is new (Figure 1.9). It allows you to control memory allocation to Final Cut Pro. Normally the application takes all memory available when it's the active application. However, if you have a lot of RAM available and you want other applications to do work in the background, you can reduce the amount of RAM dedicated to FCP, giving some to other uses. You can also control the percentage of memory allocated to working with still images. You may want to raise the number if you're working with very large still files for animation.

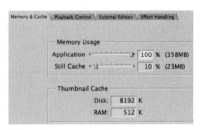

1.9 Memory & Cache Panel

The **Thumbnail Caches** work fine at the default settings unless you like to work in large icon view in the **Browser** or with thumbnails turned on.

Playback Control

This gives you access to real-time playback controls (Figure 1.10). All these functions are available directly in the **Timeline** from the small **RT** popup in the upper left corner (Figure 1.11), where they're more usefully accessed.

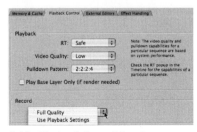

1.10 Playback Control Panel

1.11 Timeline RT Popup

1.12 External Editors Tab

Here you can set **RT** to **Safe** or **Unlimited**. **Safe** will give you assured playback without dropped frames, your system and drives permitting, while **Unlimited** allows you to play back more real-time but with the possibility of dropped frames.

Video Quality can be set to **High, Medium,** or **Low**. The lower the settings, the poorer the image quality, but the greater the real-time playback capabilities.

Pulldown Pattern is the one function not available from the **RT** button in the **Timeline**. This allows you to set the real-time pulldown playback when working with film shot at 24fps dubbed to tape at 29.97fps.

Record lets you set output to either **Full Quality** or **Use Playback Settings**. This is a new feature that allows you to record out to tape at low resolution for a quick dub as an edit check—for client approval, for instance.

External Editors

Next is the **External Editors** tab. Here you can define which applications are used to work on different types of files outside of FCP (Figure 1.12).

This allows you to launch an application to alter a clip from either the **Browser** or the **Timeline**. Select a clip and hold down the **Control** key, and from the shortcut menu choose **Open in Editor**.

This will launch the application that you specify in this preferences panel. After you edit the clip—such as a still image in Photoshop—those changes will be reflected in FCP.

You can set **External Editors** for stills, video, and for audio. Be aware, though, that if you set the QuickTime Player as your editor for video files, choose Peak DV as your editor for audio files, and then select **External Editor** for the audio portion of a sync sound clip, FCP will open the QuickTime Player, not Peak DV. FCP thinks of the audio track as part of a single video clip and so uses the QT Player. Single audio files, even if the creator type is QuickTime, will still open with the separate audio editor, such as Peak DV.

Changes in Photoshop: Sometimes changes made to a file in Photoshop, particularly to the layer structure and opacity, will cause the file to appear to be offline, bringing up the dialog in Figure 1.13. Select **Reconnect** and navigate to the PS file on your hard drive. If the dialog does not come up and the file still appears to be offline, select it in the **Browser**, and from the shortcut menu chose **Reconnect Media**.

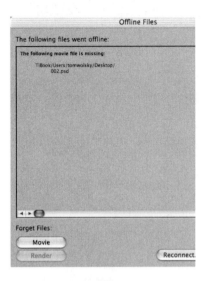

1.13 Reconnect Dialog

Effect Handling

This is a new panel to FCP 4 (Figure 1.14). This panel allows you to set other codecs to handle effects recording for various settings. Some third party codecs can be used for specific formats. This lets you set third party hardware cards to process effects in real time.

Audio/Video Settings

The key to setting up your **Audio/Video Settings** correctly is to start with the tape. To capture your material you have to make sure that the **Capture Presets** in the **Audio/Video Settings** preferences you use match exactly the tape you're capturing from. If the material is DV shot in the North American television standard of NTSC with an audio sampling rate of 48kHz in the widescreen format, then your capture preset should be **DV-NTSC 48kHz Anamorphic.** If the material is analog and you're using a digitizing card like an Aurora Igniter, or if it's digital video that needs to be captured via SDI (Serial Digital Interface) using a board like a Pinnacle CinéWave, then you would use the capture presets that come with that hardware. After the capture presets are fixed, you should make the **Sequences Settings** match your capture presets. When all these components are right, you're ready to begin capturing.

The **Audio/Video Settings** are called up from the **Final Cut Pro** menu or by using the keyboard shortcut (**Command-Option-Q**). This brings up the **Summary** tab (Figure 1.15).

As the name indicates, this window summarizes the other four tabbed windows. Each popup gives the settings for that window, settings you define in the other windows. The names you assign appear here, and you can change easily from one preset to another.

1.14 Effect Handling

1.15 Audio/Video Summary Tab

The **Summary** panel lets you switch your preferred setup. After you've made your selections, press the **Easy Setup** button at the bottom of the panel. These preferences are saved in the *Customs Settings* folder in your system's *Library*, inside *Application Support*, inside *Final Cut Pro System Support*.

You can evoke **Easy Setup** quickly from the **Final Cut Pro** menu or with the keyboard shortcut **Control-Q**. The dialog box it brings up is basically the same one that you see when you launch the application for the very first time. In it you can choose any of your presets to switch quickly from one to another.

Tip

Custom Settings: FCP has four standard settings: DV-NTSC48kHz, DV-PAL 48kHz, OfflineRT-NTSC (Photo-JPEG), and OfflineRT-PAL (Photo-JPEG). To make your presets one of the standard selections, move them from their current location to a special location inside the application package. It's best to do this with the application closed. The default location is inside the system *Library*. Go to *Library/Application Support/Final Cut Pro System Support/Custom Settings*. In this folder you'll find your *Easy Setup* saved settings. To make your preset one of the default startup settings, you want to move it to a folder inside the application. **Control**-click on the Final Cut Pro application in the *Applications* folder. From the contextual menu, select **Show Package Contents**. This will open a folder containing one item: *Contents*. The folder you're looking for is *Contents/Resources/English.lproj/Final Cut Pro Settings/Hardware Settings*. Add your *Easy Setup* to this folder and follow the name with an asterisk (*). It will now appear as a standard preset in FCP. If you reinstall the software, these will be lost, of course.

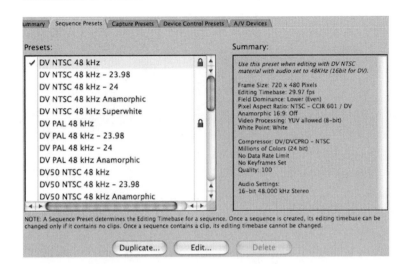

Sequence Presets

In FCP4 Apple has returned to giving **Sequence Presets** options with a whole list of setups in addition to the four locked presets: DV-NTSC 48kHz, DV-PAL 48kHz, OfflineRT NTSC (Photo-JPEG), and OfflineRT PAL (Photo-JPEG). In Figure 1.16 you see only a few of the available options. If you want to use a preset other than what you have from Apple you can create your own. Hardware manufacturers often create their own presets, which may be installed for you when you install the software that goes with your specific hardware.

If you're working in DV material, you'll probably want to use one of the DV presets, unless all your material was shot with the audio at a different sampling rate from the default 48kHz. Then you'll want to create a new sequence preset with that sampling rate.

To create your own custom preset, start off by duplicating either the existing DV-NTSC or the DV-PAL preset.

When the preset has been duplicated, the preset editor opens up. (Figure 1.17). As it opens, the **Name** panel is highlighted for you to rename your preset. You can also edit the description for the **Summary** panel.

Here are controls for all the possible audio and video parameters to set up a sequence exactly the way you need it to be.

OfflineRT

Normally DV material is captured at its full resolution, 3.6MB per second, less than five minutes per gigabyte. **OfflineRT** allows an editor to capture DV material at low resolution first, saving drive space. The material is captured using the DV format, but the computer transcodes it to Photo-JPEG as it captures. It requires a fast computer to do this, a G4/500 or better. The material has a frame size of 320x240 and is quite heavily compressed, down to 660k per second. It looks like VHS material, quite soft and not too blocky and pixilated as you might expect. Working in **OfflineRT** allows you to have nearly 10 times as much material on your hard drive, 40 minutes per gigabyte.

There are two ways to get to work with **OfflineRT**. If your computer is fast enough, you can capture directly to OfflineRT from tape, which of course will save you a great deal of drive space. If your computer isn't fast enough to capture the DV material and convert it to Photo-JPEG on the fly, which is what the OfflineRT process does, then you have to capture in DV and use **Media Manager** to recompress to OfflineRT. We'll look at how to work with **Media Manager** on page 63 in the next lesson. After the material has been reduced in size, the DV media can be thrown away to recover the drive space. You may have to do this in chunks if you're pressed for drive space. Next you edit in **OfflineRT**. Once you've got you're material cut down, you go to **Media Manager** and make everything offline. That frees up your drive space again. You now have to recapture everything that you need for your final edit from the original DV tapes, based on your offline sequence. That's the process of offlining. Obviously, if you have the drive space, it's much easier to work with the original DV material and not bother with the whole offline process at all.

1.17 Sequence Preset Editor

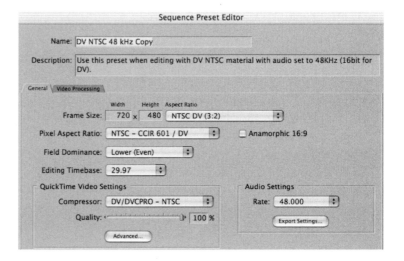

```
                    Capture Preset Editor

       Name: DV NTSC 48 kHz Copy

 Description: Use this preset when capturing NTSC material for DV FireWire input and output using DV

            Width    Height  Aspect Ratio
 Frame Size:  720 x   480   NTSC DV (3:2)         ▲▼      □ Anamorphic 16:9

 QuickTime Video Settings

   Digitizer: DV Video           ▲▼   Compressor: DV/DVCPRO – NTSC       ▲▼
      Input: DSBK–1803           ▲▼      Quality: ◀─────────────────▶ 100 %
                                              FPS:  29.97    ▲▼
                                        □ Limit Data Rate         0 K    ( Advanced... )

 QuickTime Audio Settings

     Device: DV Audio            ▲▼
      Input: First 2 channels    ▲▼       Rate: 48.000 kHz  ▲▼  ( Advanced... )

 ☑ Capture Card Supports Simultaneous Play Through and Capture
 □ Remove Advanced Pulldown (2:3:3:2) From DV–25 and DV–50 Sources
 ☑ High-Quality Video Play Through        ( Cancel )   ( OK )
```

1.18 Capture Presets

Capture Presets

The next tab in the **Audio/Video** panel is **Capture Presets**, which opens with a set of options similar to those in the **Sequence Preset** panel. For DV you should use one of the DV presets, either **DV NTSC 48kHz** or **DV PAL 48kHz**, unless your material was shot at 32kHz, what camera manufacturers call 12-bit audio. If your camera was shooting at 12-bit, you need to create a new preset using a sampling rate of 32kHz.

Again, if you want something other than the standard presets, you're best off to start by duplicating one of the locked items, probably the **DV-NTSC** preset (Figure 1.18).

Like in the **Sequence Preset**, you can give a name and description to your new settings. Like in the **Sequence** tab, you set the parameters to match those of your tape, the frame size and flag whether your material is in 16:9 format. There are **Video** and **Audio** sections were you can set the capture codec as well as the audio sampling rate.

To change to 32kHz, use the **Rate** popup in the **QuickTime Audio Settings** portion of the panel.

Device Control

This panel opens with another stark set of options. Most users will want to have device control, which is pretty simple to set up.

What is 16:9 anyway?

16:9 is widescreen video. Though they have not caught on much yet in the United States, widescreen televisions are fairly common throughout Japan. Consequently, Japanese manufacturers have added this capability to many DV camcorders. The camera squeezes the pixels electronically (so everything looks squashed, as though it's tall and narrow) to fit into a 4:3 frame and then unsqueezes them for playback on a widescreen TV. This is a bit of a kludge. True widescreen is done with an anamorphic lens that distorts the image that's recorded onto the tape.

The problem is that many people want to do 16:9 but don't have the equipment to do it properly. To monitor it, you need a widescreen monitor or one can switch between 4:3 and 16:9. FCP will output the correct 16:9 display if the presets are correct, but you won't see it correctly without the right monitor. You will not see a letterboxed version. Some fairly expensive decks will take a 16:9 image and output it as letterboxed 4:3. You can also place your 16:9 material in a 4:3 sequence and force it to render out the whole thing. You'll then have letterboxed 4:3.

Most DV camcorders will flag 16:9 material as such. FCP will read this regardless of whether the 16:9 checkbox is applied. If you are shooting true 16:9 with an anamorphic lens, the checkbox will force FCP to treat it as widescreen material, even though it doesn't get the DV flag. So be careful. Don't check this box when your material is not 16:9.

If you are capturing from an analog deck like VHS through a convertor box, you should set the preset to **Non-Controllable Device.**

If you're working in DV you want to use either **FireWire** or **FireWire Basic,** unless you're using a professional deck controlled by a different protocol such as RS-422. All Sony cameras use the **FireWire** protocol, while all Canon cameras use **FireWire Basic.** Other manufacturers use a mix, some models using one, others the other.

To set up a new device control preference, again start by duplicating one of the locked presets. Duplicating the **FireWire** preset will bring up the window in Figure 1.19.

Here you use six popups to define the type of device control you're using and how you're connecting to your deck. You also have a new popup where you can set how **Audio Mapping,** which controls how the audio from your timeline will be sent out to a device that is capable of assemble or inserting multiple tracks of audio simultaneous. You can send out up to eight tracks to a record deck such as Digital Betacam that can handle eight audio channels.

1.19 FireWire Device Control Preset

The sixth popup is for **Default Timecode**. Normally this is set to **Drop Frame** because this is the standard for DV. However, there are cameras, such as the Sony PD150 and most professional cameras, that allow you to set either **Drop Frame** or **Non-Drop Frame** when you are shooting. Hence the need for this popup. Though Final Cut will sense whether the timecode is drop or non-drop, it may take it a few moments to do. If you know what format of timecode your source material is using, it's safer to set it here.

Capture Offset and **Playback Offset** allow you to calibrate the accuracy of your deck. This only works if the deck is consistently ahead or behind the capture point or edit point you specify. This is used to calibrate frame accurate decks.

Note the **Autorecord and PTV** box that allows you to automatically put your deck in Record mode when using **Print to Video**. It will automatically start your recording device, such as a camcorder, and record after a specified number of seconds.

A/V Devices

The last tab in **Audio Video Settings, A/V Devices** (Figure 1.20) gives you a group of popups that let you set the way you view material during playback and while recording. If you're working in DV, select the default **FireWire** option. If you're working in other formats with a third-party board, other options will also appear here.

1.20　External Video Panel

For **View During Recording,** it's simplest to set it to **Same as Playback.**

Once this last window is done, your preferences are set. Go back to the **Summary** window and see what your settings look like. If everything is okay, save it as an **Easy Setup** setting in your *Custom Settings* folder of the system, *Library/Application Support/Final Cut Pro System Support/Custom Settings.*

Log and Capture

Once you have your preferences set, you are ready to capture your material. Go to **File>Log and Capture (Command-8).** This brings up the **Log and Capture** window (Figure 1.21).

1.21　Log and Capture Window

The window is divided in two. On the left is a viewer like the standard FCP **Viewer**, but this is a viewer for your tape deck or camera. The **Viewer** has controls at the bottom for playing the tape (Figure 1.22), a play button, buttons for fast forward and rewind, as well as a jog wheel on the left to inch your tape and a shuttle slider on the right to control forward and backward motion.

1.22 Log Viewer Controls

Keyboard Shortcuts

The buttons aren't the only way to control the tape. You also have the keyboard, which is usually the most efficient way to work in FCP. Press the spacebar to play the tape. To pause, press the spacebar again. Spacebar to start, spacebar to stop.

Another common way to play the tape is with the **L** key.

- **L** is play forward.
- **K** is pause.
- **J** is play backwards.

On your keyboard they're clustered together, but you're probably thinking, Why not comma, period, and slash? There is reason to the madness. **J**, **K**, and **L** were chosen because they're directly below **I** and **O**. **I** and **O** are used to mark the In and Out points on your tape. Marking the In point defines where you will begin capturing material on your tape. Marking the Out point defines where the capture will end. They are probably the most commonly used keys on the editing keyboard. Hence **J**, **K**, and **L**, positioned conveniently for the fingers of your right hand with the **I** and **O** keys directly above them.

You can view your video at other speeds. You can play your clip fast forward by repeatedly hitting the **L** key. The more times you hit **L**, the faster the clip will play. Similarly, hitting the **J** key a few times will make the clip play backwards at high speed.

In addition to your keyboard shortcuts for **Mark In** and **Mark Out**, you also have buttons and timecode displays at the bottom of the **Viewer** for these functions.

The two inner buttons mark the In and Out points, **In** on the left, **Out** on the right. The timecode window on the bottom left displays the In point, while the timecode window on the bottom right shows the Out point. Of the buttons on the far outside, the

Tip

L&C Size: The size of the **Log&Capture** window is determined by your window arrangement. If you want a large display for **L&C**, set your arrangement to **Two Up** before you start up **L&C**. If you want a smaller screen on your computer monitor, set the arrangement to **Standard** before you launch the capture window.

left one will take the tape deck to the assigned In point, and the far right one to the assigned Out point.

At the top of the **Viewer** are two other timecode displays (Figure 1.23). The timecode in the upper right of the **Viewer** is the current timecode on your tape, and the timecode display on the upper left is the duration you set between your In and Out points as you mark the tape. Note the display that shows you your available drive space as well as equivalent amount of time for video and audio captured at your current settings.

On the right of the **Log and Capture** window is a tabbed window. The farthest tab on the right is the **Capture Settings** tab (Figure 1.24). Two popups and a button access the preference settings you have already created. **Device Control** and **Capture Settings** let you set the preferences based on the settings available to you. The **Scratch Disks** button takes you directly to the **Scratch Disks preferences** window so that you can change the assigned drives if you wish.

Let's now take a look at the middle tab in the window, **Clip Settings** (Figure 1.25). The top part of the panel allows you to change settings for your clip, to alter the **Hue, Saturation, Brightness, Contrast, Black Level,** and **White Level** of your clip as it is being digitized. This gives you useful control for images that have not been shot well or shot under less than ideal conditions. Fixing

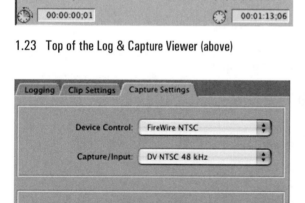

1.23 Top of the Log & Capture Viewer (above)

1.24 Capture Settings Panel

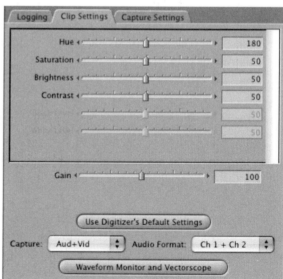

1.25 Clip Settings Panel

the levels here means that you won't have to fix them later and consequently have to rerender all your material.

However, if you are working in DV, this entire top part of the window will be grayed out. Why? Because your material has already been digitized. It happened when the camera was recording. All you can do now is capture your material, which is basically copying the digital information off the tape and onto your hard drive. You are making a clone of your tape material, and if you don't process it any further with effects and record it back into the tape, it will be an exact copy of the original material.

Below the video controls is the **Gain** slider. It allows you to control the audio levels of your material. You should check for every series of shots in which the audio levels change. Digital audio is completely unforgiving; there is no headroom. If you hit the red, the audio will immediately and obviously distort. Analog audio is far more forgiving, allowing a fair amount of headroom. Watch the meters carefully and keep the levels within the green range of the meters. Unfortunately, the metering is not active during capture.

The **Use Digitizer's Default Settings** button (below the meters) is a reset button that returns the capture levels to their standard settings.

1.26   Capture Select Popup

Below the audio meters are two popups (Figures 1.26–1.27) that let you set the tracks you want to record:

- Video
- Audio
- Which audio tracks in what combination

For DV your choices are **CH1 + CH2** or **Stereo**. No selective channel recording or mixdown is possible during capture. Generally Stereo is easier to work with. It gives you two tracks that function in unison.

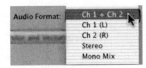

1.27   Audio Format Popup

CH1 + CH2 allows you to record separate channels and discard one if they are identical to save track space in the **Timeline**. With an analog digitizing card, you have the option of selecting channels individually as well as doing a mono mix.

Below that is a button that calls up FCP's **Waveform Monitor and Vectorscope** (Figures 1.28). These allow you to ensure that your video levels are correctly set.

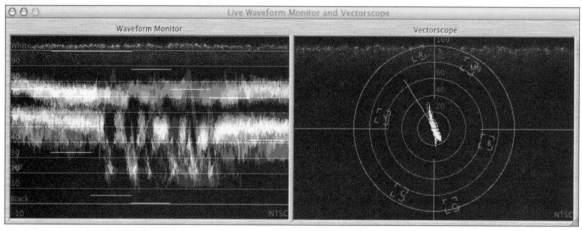

1.28 Waveform Monitor and Vectorscope

Strategies for Capturing

1.29 Capture Buttons

A new tape has been inserted in the VTR. You may wish to change the Reel setting.

OK

1.30 Tape Change Warning

There are basically three strategies for capturing or digitizing material, and you choose the one you want to use with the buttons at the bottom of the **Logging** window (Figure 1.29).

The options you have are:

- Clip
- Now
- Batch

Whichever way you decide to work, it is critical that you properly number your tape reels and enter the assigned number into the reel number panel of the **Log and Capture** window. The reel number becomes part of the data in the QuickTime media file together with the timecode. This is the only way you'll be able to recapture material, should you ever need to. Every clip must have a reel number assigned to it. This is so important that FCP starts with a reel assigned as 001. Every time you change a tape in a deck that is device controlled, the application will sense it and put up the warning in Figure 1.30.

Capture Now

This is the simplest way to work, but it gives you least control. It also requires that your material is properly shot without video breaks. These can cause havoc with any capture, particularly a

Now capture. FCP4 can now capture across timecode breaks, but it will still lose audio/video synchronization if it comes across a section of unstable video or a section of tape with no video at all, even if timecode is present.

Final Cut Pro 4 has a user preference that allows you to set how the application treats timecode breaks. You can set it to create new clips whenever it encounters a break. You also have the option to abort capture on timecode breaks. If there a timecode break on the tape but the timecode continues getting higher, a new clip will start at the break, but the same reel number will be maintained. If the timecode resets to zero at the break, the reel number will be changed and incremented as well as making a new clip. This will treat each portion of the tape where the timecode resets to zero as a separate tape. Avoid having breaks in your timecode if you can. It will make your life easier.

Capturing large chunks of video with **Now** is a common work strategy. Before you initiate the capture, you first need to name the clip. Enter a name in the **Description** box of the **Logging** window as well as any other information in the **Shot/Take** box or the other note areas. In previous versions of FCP, you could name the clip after you captured it, but in FCP4 the clip has to be named first because it immediately appears in the **Browser** with the designated name. If none is given before, the clip is called *Untitled*, which is also the name of the media file on your hard drive.

To use **Capture Now,** put the deck in play and click the **Now** button. A **Capture** screen comes up and begins recording as soon as it's checked your drives and found a video signal from your camera or deck.

FCP records the clip on your designated scratch disk until one of three events occur:

- It runs out of hard drive space.
- It hits your preference time limit.
- You hit the **Escape** key and stop the process.

With this method, you bring all your video material into your computer for editing into smaller subclips rather than using your deck to select clips.

Camcorders and FireWire-controlled DV decks are not very responsive to the control commands—start, stop, fast forward, rewind—nor are many of these devices really designed to shuttle and jog tape. This places great wear and tear on your deck's drive

1.31 Logging Window

| Logging | Clip Settings | Capture Settings |

Log Bin: Miyajima

Reel: 001

Name: Miyajima_8_1   Prompt

Description: Miyajima_8_1   ✓

Scene: 8   ✓

Shot/Take: 1   ✓

Log Note: Mark Good

mechanisms, and if you're working off DV with a camcorder, you're putting a lot of strain on these tiny tapes and small mechanisms. They wear out quickly under this heavy use. What tape can't do quickly, i.e., move large amounts of data, computers are specifically designed to do. With **Capture Now** you're working to the computer's strength, using nonlinear, nondestructive editing to its fullest.

FCP4 has a wonderful tool for those working in DV with the **Capture Now** option. This is the ability to automatically mark up shot changes with **DV Start/Stop Shot Detect**. We'll look at it on page 41 in the next lesson.

Batch Capture

For a variety of reasons—because it's a traditional work method, because of available drive space—the more commonly used work method is the batch strategy. This involves logging your tape and selecting the shots you want to capture. To the right of the **Viewer** in the **Log and Capture** window is the **Logging** window (Figure 1.31) where you can enter a whole array of information about your clip.

The clip name is made up of a number of elements that you can choose with the **Prompt** checkboxes. Any checked item will be added to the name. You can make up a name that includes a label, a scene number, and a shot/take number. This is the standard feature film format for logging film clips. Much of FCP's interface draws from that model. Of course, you can name the clip anything that's useful to you.

▶ Tip

Relogging Clips: If you ever need to relog a clip, use this simple method. Drag the original clip from the **Browser** into the **Log and Capture** window. This will load the clip's In and Out points into the window. Change the In and Out points to whatever you want. You can also use the **Go To** buttons to take you to the In or Out button on the tape, making it easier to reset the values.

✎ *Note*_____

No Forward Slashes: Do not under any circumstances include a forward slash (/) in any naming convention you use. The forward slash in Unix, upon which OS X is based, is used to designate a file path. So if there a / in the file name, the system will look for a folder name with the first part of the name, as in LS/Bridges/Trestle. It will look inside your *Capture Scratch* folder for a folder named *LS*, inside which is supposed to be a folder named *Bridges*, where the shot *Trestle* resides, none of which will be found.

You can also add notes and **Mark Good,** another film term, which refers to marking the takes that looked good to the director. In the **Logging** window, you can even add markers and marker comments before your material is captured.

Once you've set an In and Out point for your clip and entered the logging information, you then press the **Log Clip** button. The clip immediately appears in your **Browser** or a designated bin with a bright red diagonal line through it. The red line indicates that the clip has not been captured.

👉 *Tip* _____

Logging Bin: To assign a bin in your **Browser** as your **Logging** bin, Control-click on the bin you want to log into and from the shortcut menu choose **Set Logging Bin**. A little clapperboard icon will appear next to the designated bin.

Rather than hitting the **Log Clip** button, you could also press **F2.** If the tape is rolling while you're playing—that is, you entered the Out point on the fly—something interesting happens. The deck stops, and you get a dialog box to confirm the clip name. As soon as you click **OK** to accept the dialog, the frame after the previous Out point will enter as the new In point, and the deck will be put into play. The clip will appear in your designated logging bin with a diagonal red line through it (Figure 1.32). The clip is, in FCP terminology, considered offline, ready to be batch captured. The F2 method can be very fast and efficient for batching.

The problem with this method of working is that you're putting the onus of the work on the log and capture process. It doesn't take advantage of nonlinear editing's real strengths. I feel that using **Capture Now** makes the whole organizing process much quicker and simpler.

1.32 Offline Clips in Browser

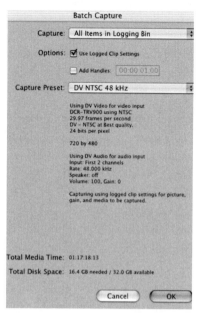

1.33 Batch Capture Dialog Window

If you do use **Log and Capture** to either conserve hard drive space or because you prefer to work that way, you will then need to complete the process by batch capturing your material:

1.   Select the clips in your bin with the red diagonal bar through them, or select the bin itself.

2.   Then press the **Batch** button, which brings up the window in Figure 1.33.

3.   You can also select the clips and choose **Batch Capture** from the **File** menu (**Control-C**).

The popup at the top allows you to select which clips you want to batch capture. There is also a window for setting handles and a checkbox for coalescing clips. If you set handles, coalescing clips can save drive space and time. However, it's dangerous. It combines adjacent clips into one piece of media. You will now have created a single source file that supplies media for two or more clips. You may remove the source file and find you've unintentionally wiped out the media for a clip you still want. It's safest to leave **Coalesce** off. Clicking **OK** will automatically set the deck off, capturing from your tape the clips you've logging into your **Browser**.

Notice the **Total Media Time** and **Total Disk Space** needed information at the bottom of the box. It's useful to double check your batch request to make sure you are capturing what you think you're capturing, as well as having the needed drive space. If something looks odd in the total time, check that you haven't selected more or fewer clips than you intended.

The popup in the middle of the **Batch Capture** dialog lets you select any one of your preset preferences. This is handy if you've captured at low resolution and want to quickly change to capture at high resolution. If you have these different preferences set up ahead of time, you can choose the preference in this popup.

Another method I like is to use an abridged form of logging on tape before batch capture. Here you quickly select In and Out points for large chunks of video on your tape, whole scenes or sections of material, dividing your tape up into four or five pieces, before you perform batch capture.

Clip

The third option in the **Log and Capture** window is the **Clip** button. This functions in the same way as the **Batch** button, except it captures an individual clip immediately after you enter its In, Out, and naming information, and press the **Clip** button. Many people use this as a controlled form of **Capture Now**.

1. Mark an In point near the beginning of the reel and then an Out point near the end.

2. Click **Clip** and let the deck and the computer do its thing.

3. After the clip is captured, it will appear in the **Browser** with your assigned name.

After you've set up your system and captured your material, you are ready to edit. Close the **Log and Capture** window before you start, however. You should not try to play video while **L&C** is open. **Log and Capture** is trying to suck in through the FireWire cable while the **Viewer** is trying to feed out through the same cable. This is the equivalent of northbound 580 being routed into southbound 580 in the middle of rush hour. So shut down **Log and Capture** before you begin editing.

Once you've captured your material, you'll notice that it appears in the **Browser** as a clip with a duration but with no In or Out points defined. **Capturing** only sets the media limit, and FCP assumes you will want to edit the material further, so no In or Out points are designated. The clip has the *de facto* In and Out points marked by the limits of the media; they're not displayed in the **Browser** in the **In** and **Out** columns. If you capture with handles, however, the clips do come in with your designated In and Out points marked and the extra media beyond it.

Tools

FCP4 has some tools to help you after you've captured your material. After you've captured a few clips, it's a good idea to analyze them to make sure everything is all right. Select the clip, and from the **Tools** menu choose **Analyze>Clip**. If you choose **File**, you will get the navigation service dialog window to select a piece of media on your hard drive. **Analyze** will bring up a window that gives you the clip's technical details (frame size, data rate, video and audio track information, etc.) (Figure 1.34). If something seems amiss here—the data rate is too low, or you have odd audio sampling rates or odd frames rates—you'll know something is wrong with your captured material.

Tip
Selecting for Batch Capture: You don't actually have to select each red-lined clip separately. You can just select the whole contents of the **Browser** for batch capture. FCP will then bring up a dialog box asking whether you want to capture all the clips, or just those offline. If you select offline clips only, it will batch capture all the material that is not already on your hard drive.

```
Filename: Temple
Duration: 00:01:39;24
Average Data Rate: 3700k/sec
Audio Shape: Stereo

Video Track 1 (342.5 MB)
  Duration: 00:01:39;24
  Frame Size: 720 x 480
  Color Depth: 24-bit Color
  Codec: DV/DVCPRO - NTSC at Most Quality
  Frame Rate: 29.97 fps
  Average Data Rate: 3512k/sec (117k/frame)

Audio Track 1 (Stereo, 18.3 MB)
  Duration: 00:01:39;24
  Average Data Rate: 188k/sec
  Format: 16-bit, Stereo
  Sampling Rate: 48.000 khz

Timecode Track Source TC
  Timecode: 00:21:38;10
  Reel: 005
```

1.34 Movie Analysis Window

1.35   No Long Frames Detected

A fairly common occurrence when capturing or digitizing video is that the first frame appears as a freeze, producing what FCP calls a long frame. This occasionally happens in the middle of a clip or at a shot change. FCP has a tool that will find these long frames in clips. From the **Tools** menu, select **Long Frames>Mark**. This will scan the clips and place a marker at each long frame. If there are no long frames, you'll see the message in Figure 1.35. In the **Tools** menu, there is also an item that will remove the long frame markers for you, **Long Frames>Clear**.

If there are long frames in your clip, you can twirl open the clip in the **Browser** and see exactly where the long frames are.

The Long Marks on the clip will have timecode In and Out points and a duration for how many frames the long frame extends. It is possible with care to cut these out to patch together your video. You'll also have to adjust the audio to keep it in sync with the picture, which may be more problematic and not always possible.

Importing Music

Importing from a music CD is slightly different from importing video. Audio files on music CDs are AIFF sound files but not at the same sampling rate as that used by digital video. The audio CD format uses a sampling rate of 44.1kHz, while digital video is either 32kHz or, more commonly, 48kHz. While FCP4 can deal with resampling the audio while it plays it back, this requires processor power and may limit your ability to do real-time effects or to play back video without dropping frames, i.e., the video stuttering. This version of FCP also allows you to render at the item level, which we'll see in Lesson 5. Nonetheless, I still recommend resampling the audio to the correct sampling rate you want to use before importing it into FCP.

There are a number of ways to do this. One way is to use iTunes, which probably will launch anyway when you mount a CD. This requires you changing your iTunes preferences, both your importing preferences and the location where your music is stored. As more and more people use iTunes as their personal jukebox, even in edit suites, it seems impractical to be constantly changing these preference settings.

1.36   Audio Tracks to QuickTime Pro Player

There is a simple way to resample using the QuickTime Pro Player.

1. First, make sure that you have upgraded the standard Quick-Time Player to the Pro Player by activating it with the QuickTime Pro serial number that came with FCP4.

2. Mount the CD on the desktop and drag the track or tracks you want to convert from the CD to the QuickTime icon in the **Dock**, as shown in Figure 1.36. This will launch the QuickTime Pro Player.

3. When the track or tracks have opened, go to **File>Export** or use **Command-E**.

4. Change the **Export** popup to **Sound to AIFF** (Figure 1.37).

5. Click the **Options** button and set the **Rate** to **32.000** or **48.000**, whichever you need. Make sure **Compressor** is set to **None**, **Size** to **16-bit**, and **Use** to **Stereo** as in Figure 1.38.

6. When you are finished with the **Options** window, set your media drive as the location to copy the track onto your computer.

7. Press the **Save** button.

The QuickTime Pro Player will then copy the track from the CD to your designated hard drive location and will resample and convert it to the correct format as it does so.

Back in Final Cut, when you drag the track into your **Browser** or use **Command-I** to import it, the track will appear in the **Browser** appended with the suffix *.aif* and will also be in the correct sampling rate that you changed it to. Your system will be happy that you did this.

Another way that I like to convert audio files to the correct format is to use Compressor, which is one of four applications that come with Final Cut Pro 4. You use the Compressor application to create Droplets, which act as tiny applications for running Compressor tasks. You can leave the Droplets on your desktop ready to be used at any time.

To make a Compressor Droplet, begin by launching Compressor.

1. When the application is open, click on the **Presets** button in the upper left corner on the main window.

2. In the **Presets** window, click on the **+** button and select **AIFF** from the menu (Figure 1.39)

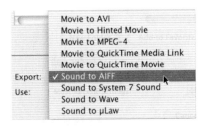

1.37 **Export Popup**

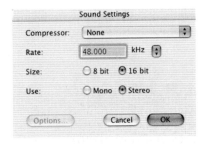

1.38 **AIFF Options**

1.39 **Adding Compressor Preset**

1.40 Compressor Encoder Tab

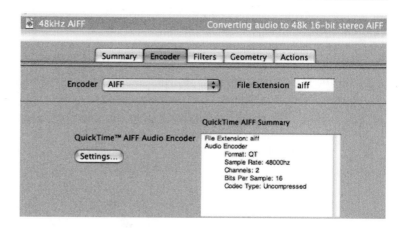

3. Give the new preset a suitable name like *48kHz AIFF*.

4. Go to the **Encoder** tab and click on the **Settings** tab.

5. This will bring up the same window as used by the Quick-Time Pro Player. Again make the settings: **no compression, 48.000, 16-bit, stereo.** When you click **OK**, your **Encoder** tab should look like Figure 1.40.

6. Finally, click the **Droplet** button in the upper right corner (Figure 1.41), set the destination for your results (which gives you limited choices and probably should be your desktop), and then save your **Droplet**.

1.41 Droplet Button

To use your **Droplet** to convert an audio file:

1. First, double-click the **Droplet** to launch it.

2. Drag the audio files you want to convert into the **Source file** window, and press the **Submit** button (Figure 1.42).

This will open the **Batch Monitor** application, where you can watch the progress of your material being converted.

3. Finally, you'll want to drag the converted files off your desktop and onto your media drive before importing them in FCP.

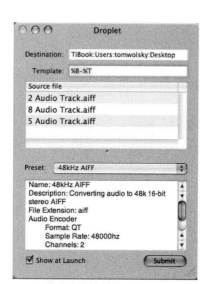

1.42 Droplet Window

Summary

Lesson 1 covers the basics of opening the application, a quick tour of the interface and the process of getting your material captured or digitized into Final Cut Pro, as well as the process of importing music from audio CDs. Next we'll look at how to organize all the material you've brought into FCP, how to work with your clips in the **Viewer** and in the **Browser**.

Lesson 2

Cutting Up Those Shots

Whether you begin the selection process as part of logging and capturing your material, or you wait until your material is captured before beginning to make your selections, you have to begin at some point to make the decisions that will keep some material and reject others. Part of selection process, particularly if you're doing it on the computer, is to organize your material; so this lesson is about selection, and more than that it's about organization. Without organization you can edit a simple 10-minute video, or you can assemble long pieces of a home movies to make a video, but if you want to make a video of a greater length or greater complexity, you and your material have to be organized. That's the subject of this lesson.

There are a number of different ways of working with your material and a few different ways to cut it up. I'll show you a variety of ways that seem to work well in Final Cut Pro 4. Let's begin by loading the material we need for this lesson.

1. Start by loading the DVD that came with this book into your DVD drive. Open the DVD.

You'll see a number of folders, one called *Lesson 2 Media* and another called *Projects*. Inside *Lesson 2 Media* is a QuickTime file, and inside *Projects* are numbered Final Cut project files.

2.   Drag the folder called *Lesson 2 Media* onto your media drive.

You should have a separate, fast hard drive dedicated to holding just your media, while your operating system, applications, and project files are on another.

Copying the *Lesson 2 Media* folder onto your hard drive may take a while. It contains some of the video material used in this book. When you begin any lesson that needs material from the DVD, the first step you should take is to drag the media folder onto the media drive of your computer. The footage included there will play much better and more smoothly from your high-speed drive than from any DVD drive.

3.   When that's finished, drag the *Projects* folder on the DVD onto the system hard drive of your computer. You should probably place it in the *Documents* folder inside your *Home* folder.

4.   Before you open any of the files you copied onto your computer be sure to eject the DVD and put it away.

5.   Open the *Projects* folder from your system hard drive and double-click on the file *Lesson 2*, which will launch the Final Cut Pro 4 application.

The project is empty except for one sequence that is also blank.

The Browser

To get started we need to import some material.

1.   Use **File>Import** (**Command-I**) to import the file called *Temple* from the inside the *Lesson 2 Media* folder on your media hard drive. Or you could also drag the clip directly from the folder on your desktop into your **Browser**.

This is a *master clip*. Every time you import a clip or capture a clip or bring a new clip into the **Browser**, the first instance of that clip is always a master clip. This is a new term in Final Cut Pro 4, and it refers to the new way the application handles media information. In fact, the **Browser** has a new check column that shows you whether or not a clip is a master clip. A master clip can be cut up into smaller clips called *affiliate clips*. Any copy or portion of a master clip has an affiliate relationship to the master. You can no longer cut up a master clip and rename all the pieces. Now all of the pieces, all the affiliates and the master clip, must have the same name. They also must share the same color coded label. If you change one, they all change. So how do you work with your long master clips in FCP4? You have to use different ways of working to accommodate the new way the application handles the media.

☞ *Tip*

_____

Make Offline: To delete a clip from the **Browser**, select it and hit the **Delete** key. This, however, will leave the clip on your drive. If you really want to delete the clip both from your project and get rid of it from your hard drive, select the clip and **Control**-click on it, choosing from the shortcut menu **Make Offline**. This will bring up the dialog box in Figure 2.1, which offers three options, each more final than the next.

Important: If you make a subclip offline, you will delete all the media associated with that clip and all the subclips, master clips, and affiliate clips that share the same media file.

2.1   **Make Offline Dialog Box**

The **Browser** shows you a lot of information about your clips, including the type of video, the type of audio, presence of stereo, frame size, and frame rate (in the case of this clip, 29.97 frames per second, the standard frame rate for all NTSC video), plus a host of other useful information about your material.

As you scroll right along the window, you get more columns where you can type information such as **Description**, as well as the **Scene, Shot/Take,** and **Comments 1** and **2.** You will also see **Offline** and **Last Modified.**

Only the **Name** column cannot be moved. It stays displayed on the left side of the window. You can move any of the other columns by grabbing the header at the top of the column and pulling it to wherever you want the column to appear.

Using Shortcut Menus

Even more information can be displayed in the **Browser** with the **Control** key, one of the most powerful tools in the application. Throughout Final Cut Pro, the **Control** key gives you access to shortcut menus. These menus change according to where your cursor is. If your cursor is above the column headers in the **Browser** and you press the **Control** key while clicking the mouse, you get a shortcut menu (Figure 2.2), a list of just some of the available items in columns, those items that are not already displayed in the **Browser.**

Hide Column
Edit Heading
Save Column Layout...
Restore Column Layout...

✓ Standard Columns
Logging Columns

AudioInfo
LogColumn
VideoInfo

Show Type
Show TC
Show Aux TC 1
Show Aux TC 2
Show Master Comment 4
Show Capture
Show Thumbnail
Show Media End
Show Audio
Show Aud Format
Show Alpha
Show Reverse Alpha
Show Composite
Show Label 2
Show Offline
Show Last Modified
Show Label
Show Source
Show Duration
Show In
Show Out
Show Media Start
Show Reel
Show Good
Show Log Note
Show Aud Rate
Show Length
Show Camera
Show Sound
Show Master Comment 3
Show Description
Show Scene
Show Shot/Take
Show Aux 1 Reel
Show Aux 2 Reel
Show Speed
Show Frame Blending

2.2 List of Browser Column Items

☞ *Tip*

Right Click: Whenever I say **Control**-click, you can also use the right-click of a two-button mouse to call up the shortcut menu. Also note that the scroll wheel on a multifunction mouse works in FCP4. It will scroll any window by placing the mouse over the scroll area.

Notice that you can save and restore bin settings similar to the way you can save and restore window arrangements. These will be saved in a separate folder of your *Preferences* folder called *Column Layouts*. You can also call up saved column arrangements directly from the shortcut menu.

The shortcut menu in the **Browser** header lets you hide a column. It also lets you add even more columns to your **Browser**. You can change the columns from the default **Standard** columns to **Logging** columns, which show:

- **Media Start** and **End** times
- **In** and **Out** points
- **Duration**
- **Good**
- **Description**
- **Scene, Shot, Take,** and **Reel**
- **Log Notes**
- Four **Comments** columns, and much more

Another item hidden in the contextual menu is **Show Thumbnail**. This cool feature brings up a thumbnail that shows the first frame of the video. Grab the thumbnail and drag the mouse. This is called *scrubbing*, and what you're doing is dragging through the video clip itself so you can actually see what's in it. Viewing media like this in the **Browser** can save time. You can quickly scan through a shot to see if it's really the one you're looking for.

You can also change the Poster frame, the frame that appears in the thumbnail. The default is the first frame of the video (or the In point), but if you scrub through the video and find a new frame you would like to set as the thumbnail, press the **Control** key and release the mouse. A new Poster frame has been set. If you change the Poster frame for a clip here or in any other **Browser** window, the frame will change for each instance of that clip anywhere in the **Browser** and will also display as the Poster frame when the **Browser** is set to Icon view.

2.3　Top of Viewer

2.4　Viewer Controls

The Viewer

After you've imported your clip, double-click *Temple* in your **Browser** to open it in a **Viewer**. The **Viewer** is similar to the viewer in the **Log and Capture** window that we saw in the last lesson. Here the **Viewer** is looking at the media on your computer's hard drive rather than at your tape. In Figure 2.3 you see the top of the **Viewer** display. Notice the time display in the upper left corner that gives the duration of the clip as 1:39;24. That's one minute, 39 seconds, and 24 frames. The timecode display on the upper right is the current timecode display. The section of video starts at 21:38;10, a little bit more than 21 and one-half minutes into the tape from which it was captured. We'll be working with this short piece of material in this lesson.

Playing Clips

There are a number of different ways of playing a clip to look at your video very much like the **Log and Capture** window. The most obvious is the big **Play** button in the middle of the **Viewer** controls (Figure 2.4). This time the shuttle slider is on the left and the jog wheel is on the right. If you like working with the mouse, these will be for you, but it is not the most efficient way to work by any means. I'd recommend learning to use the keyboard. It's your friend, and it's really a much simpler, easier way to control your editing than the mouse.

Spacebar

As in the **Log and Capture** window, the simplest way to play your clip is just to press the spacebar. To pause, press the spacebar again. To play the clip backwards, press **Shift**-spacebar.

This method is much quicker and keeps your hands on the keyboard and off the mouse. Using the keyboard, you can play and manipulate clips in the **Viewer** with great efficiency.

> ⭐ *Tip*
>
> **Open Sequence:** Should your project ever open and you don't see any **Canvas** or **Timeline**, it means that there is no sequence open. There needs to be at least one sequence in a project. Simply double-click the sequence in the **Browser**, and it will open the **Timeline** together with its **Canvas**.

As the clip plays, the playhead moves through the *scrubber bar.* The scrubber bar is the white area just below the picture in the Viewer. If you mouse down in this area, you can move forward and backward through the shot by moving the mouse left and right. This moves the playhead, which is the vertical line in the scrubber bar with a small yellow triangle on top of it. There are playheads scattered throughout Final Cut Pro. You can see one in the **Canvas** and another in the **Timeline**. These two are linked together.

Keyboard Shortcuts

As with the **Log and Capture** window, the best way to control your media is with the J, K, and L keys, L to play forward, K to pause, and J to play backwards. These are your VCR controls. As in the L&C window, tapping L multiple times will play forward fast, and tapping J multiple times will play backward fast. These keyboard controls on a fast computer are very responsive. Here too the I key will mark the In point, and the O key will mark the Out point. There are other useful keyboard shortcuts for working with your media. To play a clip one frame at a time, tap the **Right** arrow key. To play it slowly, hold down the key. To play slowly backwards, hold down the **Left** arrow key. Pressing K and L together will give you slow forward, and K and J together, slow backwards.

To go back to the previous edit—the cut prior to the point where you are currently—use the **Up** arrow key. To go to the next edit event, use the **Down** arrow key. To go to the beginning of the clip, press the **Home** key; to go to the end press the **End** key.

Tip

Shortcut Help: If trying to remember all the keyboard shortcuts is shorting out your brain, you can get color-coded special keyboards with keys that display the shortcuts. A great tool, I find, is Loren Miller's KeyGuide, which you can get from Loren's web site http://lormiller. home.mindspring.com. No FCP editor should be without one. He makes them for a number of applications as well as Final Cut.

Table 2.1   Some Principal Keyboard Shortcuts

Play	L
Pause	K
Play backwards	J
Fast forward	Repeat L
Slow forward	L + K
Fast backwards	Repeat J
Slow backwards	J + K

Table 2.1   Some Principal Keyboard Shortcuts (Continued)

Go to previous edit	**Up Arrow**
Go to next edit	**Down Arrow**
Go to beginning	**Home**
Go to end	**End**
Mark the In point	I
Mark the Out point	O
Go to In point	**Shift-I**
Go to Out point	**Shift-O**
Play Around Current Point	\
Play from In point to Out point	**Shift-**
Play from current position to Out	**Shift-P**
Match Frame	**F**
Reveal Master Clip	**Shift-F**
Mark Clip	**X**
Add Marker	**M**

Custom Keyboard Layouts and Buttons

New to FCP4 is the ability to customize the keyboard to suit your
needs and also to make buttons out of any of over 900 functions
within the application. To customize the keyboard, go to the
menu **Tools>Keyboard Layout>Customize (Option-H)**. This
brings up the window in Figure 2.5. Unlock the keyboard with
the button in the lower left, scroll through the list on the right,
and drag the function onto the key of your choice. To find a function, start to type its name in the query box at the top of the list.

Notice the tabs at the top that give you access to all the modifier
key combinations. In the **Keyboard Layout** menu, you can also
Export and **Import** custom keyboards. If you're an Avid editor,
you may want to switch to an Avid-based layout. You'll find an
Avid-based keyboard layout called *AvidKeyboard* in the *Extras*
folder on the DVD. If you want to entirely redo the keyboard, use

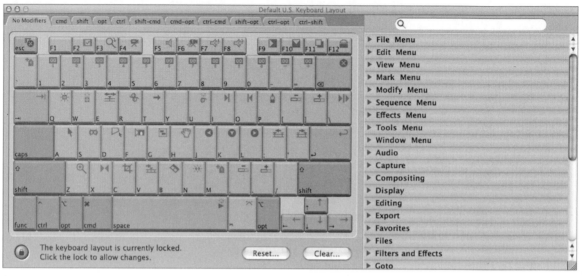

2.5   Custom Keyboard Window

the **Clear** button in the lower right corner. Fortunately, there is also a **Reset** button to return it to its default condition.

FCP4 also has the ability to create buttons which you can place in various windows of the interface. To create new button, drag whatever function or functions you want to any one of the little coffee bean-like holders in the upper right of any of FCP's windows. The little holder (dubbed the *Meaney Bean* by FCP trainer Abba Shapiro after the application's chief software engineer Brian Meaney) can be further customized by adding colors to the buttons, and spacers to group button. You can even color the spacers. Also in the Meaney Bean's shortcut menu (called up by **Control**-clicking), you can save your button configurations for all your windows (Figure 2.6). To remove a button, drag it out of the bean. It will disappear, like an item from the **Dock**, in a puff of smoke.

Creating Subclips

Look through the video. It was shot in the tiny Japanese mountain village of Damine (pronounced Dameenay). Often wreathed in blue wood smoke in winter months, the village is famous for a number of things: their Shinto temple to the goddess Kanon; their ancient annual rice festival, *Dengaku*, held in February; and *kabuki*. They have the only children's *kabuki* troupe in the world. This short video section shows a few shots of the village and the

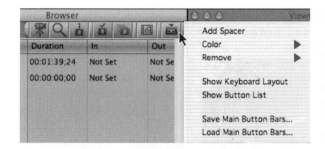

2.6   Custom Buttons and Shortcut Menu

2.7   Master Clips with Segments in Viewer

temple. More and more video editors are working with long sections of material that have not been logged or captured as single shots. Working with single shots may be efficient when capturing narrative material or any carefully controlled and scripted shoot, but for documentary, news, wedding videos, or any other production that's shot quickly without careful slating and marking between shots, it's usually more efficient to do your logging after the material has been captured. FCP affords you some excellent tools to do this.

If you're working in DV, you have the benefit of **DV Start/Stop Detect,** which will automatically segment you material into separate clips at each shot change. This is based on the system detecting the sudden change in time in the metadata that holds the date/time stamp. For this to work, you have to have set the clock in your camera. If you haven't, you won't be able to use **DV Start/Stop Detect.** To use this feature in FCP, select the clip in the **Browser** or the clip in the active **Viewer** window, and from the menus choose **Mark>DV Start/Stop Detect.** This is a new location for this feature in FCP4; previously it was in the **Tools** menu. **DV Start/Stop Detect** will add markers at every shot change based on that date/time stamp. If the clip isn't in the **Viewer,** double-clicking on it will open it in the **Viewer** with all its segments (Figure 2.7).

> ✒ *Tip*
> **Command-D:** This keyboard shortcut is no longer used in FCP4. In earlier versions of the application, it was used for **Deselect All,** which is now **Command-Shift-A.** Because **Command-D** is now available, I use the custom keyboard feature to assign the **DVStart/Stop Detect** function to it.

2.8 Marquee-Dragging before Making Subclips

👉 **Tip**

Moving Shots Out of Bins: To move a shot out of the bin back to the top level of the **Browser**, drag the shot out of the bin and pull it onto the **Name** column header. That puts it at the top level of the project window.

👉 **Tip**

Shortcuts: You can easily move between segments with keyboard shortcuts.

Shift-M (or **Shift-Down** arrow) takes you to the next marker.

Option-M (or **Shift-Up** arrow) takes you to the previous marker.

Option-` to extend the marker.

Command-` or the **Delete** button in the **Marker** dialog box deletes the marker you're positioned on.

Control-` to delete all markers.

Once the material has been segmented, you can twirl open the disclosure triangle in the **Browser** and marquee-drag through all the markers, as shown in Figure 2.8. Then select from the menus **Modify>Make Subclip** or use the keyboard shortcut **Command-U**. Before I do that, I often move the master clip—in this case, *Temple*—into a bin appropriate for its content. To create a new bin, either **Control**-click in the **Browser** and from the shortcut menu choose **New Bin,** or use the keyboard shortcut **Command-B.** I do this so that when I make the subclips from *Temple*, they're already placed in the right bin. Notice in Figure 2.8 that each of the segments has an In point marked, but no duration.

Once your material has been segmented, you can rename the subclips and move them to appropriate bins or organize them however you want. You can do this because subclips are master clips, and though they share the same material as the clip they were segmented from, they do not have a master/affiliate relationship with that clip.

👉 **Tip**

Ordering Columns: If you organize your reels in the **Browser** by **Media Start**, all the shots will get jumbled up from different reels. To get around this, click first in the column header for **Reel**, which will order the **Browser** based on the reel numbers. Then **Shift**-click on the **Media Start** column header to create secondary ordering. Now the clips will be sorted based first on reel number and then on timecode number. And if the reels were properly numbered, you'll see the material exactly in the order in which it was shot.

After you've created your subclips, you can marquee-drag to select the segment markers inside the master *Temple* clip and hit the **Delete** key to remove them, if you wish.

Name	Media Start ▼	Duration
Temple	00:21:38;10	00:01:39;24
wide shot temple grounds	00:21:38;10	00:00:10;16
store	00:21:48;26	00:00:08;14
bowing at incense bowl	00:21:57;10	00:00:17;23
man leaving temple	00:22:15;05	00:00:10;10
wide temple bell	00:22:25;15	00:00:09;08
woman through incense bowl	00:22:34;23	00:00:15;09
woman through incense 2	00:22:50;02	00:00:13;17
woman praying	00:23:03;21	00:00:14;15

2.9   Renamed Subclips in Bin

2.10   Logging Panel in Item Properties

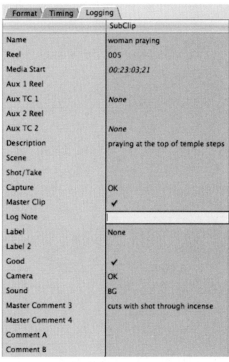

Format	Timing	Logging	
		SubClip	
Name		woman praying	
Reel		005	
Media Start		00:23:03;21	
Aux 1 Reel			
Aux TC 1		None	
Aux 2 Reel			
Aux TC 2		None	
Description		praying at the top of temple steps	
Scene			
Shot/Take			
Capture		OK	
Master Clip		✔	
Log Note			
Label		None	
Label 2			
Good		✔	
Camera		OK	
Sound		BG	
Master Comment 3		cuts with shot through incense	
Master Comment 4			
Comment A			
Comment B			

In Figure 2.9 you can see the renamed subclips in the bin. Notice that the clips are not in alphabetical order. They are sorted according to their **Media Start** time, so they appear in the order they were in the master clip *Temple*. The **Duration** column shows the length of each subclip, based on the length of the segment between markers.

At this stage you're breaking down your material, organizing it, arranging it in bins, renaming clips, adding notes, and so on. This is critical if you're working on a project that's longer than 10 minutes or so or a project with a lot of material, regardless of its finished length. This process of viewing, logging, and organizing should not be skimped, rushed, or dismissed as drudge work; it is crucial to the editing process.

In addition to naming your clips, the **Browser** has many more columns where you can enter information about your material. One simple way to access these is to use the clips' **Item Properties**. Either **Control**-click on a clip or use the keyboard shortcut **Command-9**. At the back of **Item Properties** is the **Logging** panel, where information can be called up as needed. I set my own keyboard shortcut for this, **Command-Shift-L**. It takes me directly to the **Logging** panel of a clip's **Item Properties** (Figure 2.10).

> **✎ Tip**
>
> **Renaming Clips:** Though you can rename your clips and subclips anything you want, be aware that the underlying media that remains on your hard drive is unchanged in any way. Most importantly, its name is not changed. So if you ever need to reconnect the media or recapture it, FCP will want to do it under its original naming convention.

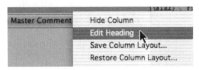

2.11   Editing Column Heading

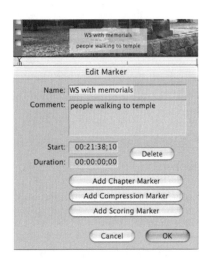

2.12   Marker Dialog Window

The **Tab** key will take you from one description text entry panel to the next. Notice that two items that should be **Master Comment 1** and **Master Comment 2** have been renamed **Camera** and **Sound**. You can change names by **Control**-clicking in the **Master Comment** column header and choosing **Edit Heading**, as shown in Figure 2.11.

Cutting Up Master Clips

If you're working in a format other than DV, you can still cut up your material using subclips. There are a few different ways to do this.

Markers

One way I like is using *markers*. Open your long capture into the Viewer, and add markers as you play the clip—on the fly if you like—by tapping the **M** key or the ` (accent) key. You can create markers with more precision, of course, as well as set up extended markers to segment your material. Try this with *Temple*.

1. Double-click on *Temple* to open it into the Viewer.

2. Set a marker at the beginning of the clip. Do this by moving the playhead to the beginning of the clip with the **Home** key and pressing either the **M** key or the ` (accent) key. That will add a marker to the clip, just like the segment markers that **DV Start/Stop Detect** creates.

3. If you wish, you can label the marker. Press the **M** (or `) key again while sitting over the marker. This brings up the dialog window in Figure 2.12.

4. Change the name of the marker if you wish.

This name will carry over into the name of the subclip. In this case, the subclip would be called *WS with memorials from "Temple"* subclip. You can add something to the **Comment** panel, but this will not carry over when the clip is made into a subclip. However, the comment information will remain with the original clip. Notice also in Figure 2.12 how the marker information displays in the Viewer. This stays with *Temple* and will appear whenever the playhead is over the marker, unless the marker is deleted, of course.

5. Play through the clip either with the spacebar or by scrubbing in the scrubber bar until you find the shot change. Use the

Left and **Right** arrow keys to find the first frame of the next shot at 21:48;26.

6. Add another marker.

You can work your way through the clip, adding markers at each shot change. As with **DV Start/Stop Detect,** the markers can be turned quickly into subclips.

7. Marquee-drag to select the markers from *Temple* in List view and press **Command-U.**

If you're working on narrative film or tightly scripted material, *extended markers* might be useful. When you capture large sections of material, there are often unnecessary pieces: clapperboards, director's instructions, setting the camera, bad takes. You can avoid adding these into your subclips by extending a marker.

1. Start by finding where you'd like the subclip to begin.

2. Add the marker with the **M** or ` key.

3. Play through the shot until the director shouts, "Cut!" or you find the end of the piece you want to make into a subclip.

4. Now extend the marker from the menus by going to **Mark>Markers>Extend,** or extend it even more by using the keyboard shortcut **Option-`** (accent mark).

You can go through your video by markings and extending markers so that the scrubber bar in the **Viewer** might look something like Figure 2.13. The nice thing about this technique is that when you create your subclips by selecting them and hitting **Command-U** or using the **Modify** menu to **Modify>Make Subclip,** the subclips are only for the duration of the extended marker. By extending the markers you've defined the limits of the media available for each shot, basically defined rough In and Out points.

In the *Temple* clip, for instance, there are some camera bobbles, such as right at the end of the second shot, the glass-fronted hut. The start of the third shot also has a reframing zoom. By using extended markers, you can cut these areas out so that they don't appear unexpectedly during a transition. You might also not want to subclip a shot, for instance, the fourth shot in *Temple*. Extend the previous marker to the end of the third shot, and don't add a marker for the fourth shot. This is why there are only seven markers or extended markers in Figure 2.13.

Do not extend markers or define subclips too tightly. This should only be a rough cut covering the entire portion of usable media.

> ⭐ *Tip*
> *Edit Marker:* If you **Shift**-click the **Marker** button in either the **Canvas** or the **Viewer,** it not only sets a marker but also opens the **Edit Marker** dialog, where you can enter information. You can also use **Command-Option-M** to open the **Edit** window for the nearest marker before the current position of the playhead.

2.13   Extended Markers in the Scrubber Bar

FCP will treat the limits of the subclip as the limits of its media and will not allow you to extend the shot farther, so always make the ends of the subclips, the limits of the media, as far as you can without going into another shot or into some rough material, like a swish pan or a quick zoom that you don't want on the screen.

Markers are an excellent tool for entering information about clips, even if you're not using the markers to actually edit your material. Here you can add comments, as well as create *chapter markers* and *compression markers* to use with iDVD or DVD Studio Pro and *scoring markers* to carry over to Final Cut's new music-arranging software Soundtrack. It's important to note that these specialized markers should always be added only to the **Timeline** itself. None of these markers, if added to clips, will carry over into other applications. Markers are also searchable within a sequence, as we shall see.

☆ Tip _____
Removing Subclip Limits: Creating a subclip limits the available media to the length of the shot. If you ever need the rest of the captured material within the original shot, select the clip or clips in either the **Browser** or the **Timeline** and use **Modify > Remove Subclip Limits**. You'll then be able to open the shot in the **Viewer** and access the whole length of the clip, which is still on your hard drive.

Using In and Out Points

Another method of working with media without **DV Start/Stop Detect** is to open the original master clip into the **Viewer** and then mark your shots with In and Out points.

1. If you have placed any markers in *Temple*, delete them so that you have only the long clip itself.

2. Next open *Temple* into the **Viewer** by double-clicking on it, or dragging it into the **Viewer.**

3. Mark an In point at the beginning of the clip with the **I** key.

4. Play through the clip or scrub through it until you find the last frame of the video. Use the **Left** and **Right** arrow keys to find the frame at 21:48;25.

5. Mark an Out point with the **O** key.

Your **Viewer** will look like Figure 2.14. Note the Out point mark in the picture, indicating that the playhead is at the Out point.

6. To make this shot a subclip, hit **Command-U** or use **Modify>Make Subclip**. The clip will immediately appear in the **Browser** with its name highlighted, ready to be renamed.

7. Type in a name.

Switch back to **Viewer,** and you're ready to mark new In and Out points to the master clip to make the next subclip.

2.14 Viewer with In and Out Points
Marked

In previous versions of FCP in which subclips were not handled as
well, this technique presented problems for the user, but with the
new improvements to this key feature, subclipping is probably the
best way to deal with your material.

Edit Points

A note on where edit points occur. The shot change between edits actually takes place between the
frames. That is, you see one frame, and the next frame you see is the first frame of a different shot. So
when you're marking In and Out points, you should know where the shot change is actually taking place.
If you mark the In point for a frame that you're looking at in the **Viewer**, that will be the first frame of the
new clip. The edit will take place in the space before that frame. If you mark the frame you're looking at
as an Out point, that will be the last frame in the clip, and the edit will take place after that frame.

Slicing Up Master Clips

All of the methods described previously—using **DV Start/Stop Detect**, working with markers to define sections of your long clips, or cutting up the long clip by defining In and Out points—use the **Make Subclip** feature of Final Cut Pro, but there are a couple of other ways to work in FCP that allow you to cut up and organize your material without actually creating subclips. I call these methods the Slice methods: slicing up your material, while keeping the entire contents of your long clips. There are a several ways to do this.

Slice 1

The first Slice method is in the **Viewer**. Here we're marking In and Out points but not creating subclips of the material.

1. First open *Temple* from the **Browser** into the **Viewer**.

It will probably have an In and Out point marked. We need to clear those.

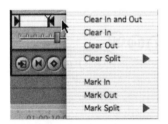

2.15 Clearing In and Out in Scrubber Bar

✦ Tip _____
Clearing from the Browser: If you've opened a clip from the **Browser** and want to clear its In and Out points, you can use the keyboard shortcut **Option-X.** You can use this way to clear In and Out points marked in the **Timeline** also. You can't, however, clear the In and Out from a clip that's been opened from the **Timeline**. A clip that's in a **Timeline** must, by definition, have an In and Out point, a start and end frame, even if it's the first and last frame of the clip.

2. **Control**-click on the scrubber bar at the bottom of the **Viewer** to evoke a shortcut menu.

3. Select **Clear In and Out**. This will—surprise, surprise—clear the In and Out points (Figure 2.15).

4. Let's begin with the second shot in the *Temple*. Find the shot change at 21:48;26.

5. Mark an In point by hitting the **I** key.

6. Press the spacebar to play *Temple*. Use and the **Left** and **Right** arrow keys to find the end of the shot, the last frame of the shot of statue at 21:57;09.

7. Create a new bin in the **Browser** (**Command-B**) and name it *Clips*.

8. Drag the sliced clip of *Temple* from the **Viewer** and drop it into the *Clips* bin. Do not rename this clip; this would rename *Temple*. The new clip still has an affiliate clip relationship to the master clip.

9. Go back to the **Viewer** and repeat the process, marking In and Out points for each shot and dragging them into the *Clips* bin.

As we saw earlier, these clips cannot be renamed because they are all affiliate clips of the master clip *Temple*. However, there is a feature that gets around this problem.

10. Select all the clips you'e created in the *Clips* bin by marquee-dragging through them or by double-clicking on the bin and and using **Command-A** to **Select All**.

11. With the clips selected from the **Modify** menu, use **Modify>Make Master Clip**.

This will turn all of the clips into master clips, allowing you to rename them and organize your material.

Slice 2

The second Slice method is in the **Timeline**. This is where you really are slicing with a digital razor blade.

1. First open *Temple* from the **Browser** into the **Viewer.**

It will probably have an In and Out point marked. We need to clear those.

2. **Control**-click on the scrubber bar at the bottom of the **Viewer** and choose **Clear In and Out** from the shortcut menu or use the keyboard shortcut **Option-X**.

3. If it's not open already, open the empty **Timeline** by double-clicking on *Sequence 1* in the **Browser** and drag *Temple* into it, dropping the clip on **V1**.

When you place a clip in the **Timeline**, the playhead automatically jumps to the end of the clip, ready for you to place another clip in position. In this case, we don't want to do that.

4. Click in the **Timeline** window to make it active (or use **Command-3**), and then press the **Home** key to take you back to the beginning of the **Timeline** (Figure 2.16).

5. Press the spacebar to play *Temple*. The video plays in the **Canvas.**

6. Again use the spacebar to stop and the **Left** and **Right** arrow keys to find the start of the shot of the glass-fronted hut. When you've found the first frame at 01:00:10;16, press **Control-V**.

2.16 Timeline Window

2.17 Timeline Options Popup Menu

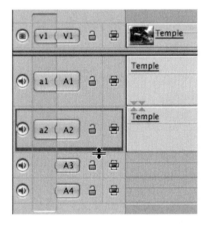

2.18 Adjusting Track Heights

This will cut the video and audio on the clip as though you were cutting it with a knife or a razor blade, which is what was formerly used to cut film, audio tape, and even videotape when it was first edited. What you are doing is the digital metaphor for the same process. When you make the edit, notice the little red triangular marks that appear. They indicate where there is a cut between two shots with contiguous time code. These are *Through Edit* marks that can be switched on and off in the **Timeline Options** panel of the **Sequence Settings** (**Sequence>Settings** menu or **Command-0** [zero]).

In FCP4 the **Timeline Options** functions are available directly from a tiny triangle in the bottom left of the **Timeline** window that acts as a popup menu (Figure 2.17). Here you also toggle on and off the Through Edit marks. This popup also allows you to set track heights as well as save and restore track layout arrangemennts. In FCP4 track heights are customizable by dragging between the tracks in the track header, as shown in Figure 2.18.

7. Now that you've made one cut, find the next shot. Its first frame starts with the quick zoom at 01:00:19;00. Again use **Control-V** to cut the shot.

8. Go through the **Timeline** and slice more clips by using **Control-V** to cut at the first frame of every new shot. (Figure 2.19).

9. After you've cut out the clips you want from the long shot in the **Timeline**, go to the **Browser** and select *Sequence 1*.

10. From the **Modify** menu, select **Modify>Make Sequence Clips Independent**.

11. Drag the clips into a bin in the **Browser**. These clips are all master clips and can be renamed, reedited, and organized. They will have the same master/affiliate relationship as a captured clip, an imported clip, or a subclip.

Edit Points Redux

We talked about where the cut takes place when you're editing, that the In point cuts the space before the frame you're looking at, and the Out point cuts after the frame you're looking at. The **Blade** always cuts on the gap in front of the frame you're seeing in the **Canvas**. So to get the last frame of *the first shot in Temple* when cutting in the Timeline, you have to be looking at the first frame of the shot after it. If you do **Control-V** on the last frame of the first shot, the next shot will have one frame of the previous shot at its head.

2.19 Cutting in the Timeline

Deleting Clips

This process of going through your material to cut it up can also be used to make selections, keeping just the shots you want to work with and throwing away those you don't need.

1. To remove a shot from the edited sequence in the **Timeline,** select the shot and press **Delete,** the large **Delete** key below **F11** and **F12.**

This will remove the clip from the timeline, but it will also leave a gap.

2. So let's undo that with **Command-Z.**

The undo will make the shot reappear in the hole in the timeline. Instead of deleting it, we will do what's called a *ripple delete*.

3. Select the clip, hold down the **Shift** key, and press **Delete.**

In addition to removing the clip, the ripple delete also pulls up all the other material in the timeline, shortening the sequence.

4. Double-click one of your newly created independent clips, either from the sequence or from the ones you dragged into the **Browser.**

Notice that this *Temple* shot comes in with an In and Out point marked, and notice also that the clip contains all the video that's in the original master shot called *Temple*. The upside of this is obvious. Because a sliced clip is a copy of the master clip, you can now access any shot in the reel from inside any sliced clip.

That's the upside; the downside is scrubbing. The master clip is made up of a long length of material, perhaps even a whole reel of film or a roll of videotape, though I would advise against this. It's now difficult to scrub in the **Viewer** because even a tiny movement will move the playhead a long way up and down the scrubber bar.

> **Tip**
>
> *Ripple Delete:* In addition to the keyboard shortcut **Shift-Delete** for for removing a shot and rippling the sequence, on extended keyboards you can also use the **Forward Delete** key to do this. This is the small **Delete** key next to the **End** key.

Razor Blade

In addition to the keyboard shortcut **Control-V** for blading the clip in the **Timeline**, you can also cut it with the **Blade** tool from the **Tools**. The letter **B** will call it up (Figure 2.20). As you move along your clip in the **Timeline**, your cursor will show the **Blade** tool, rather than the **Selector**.

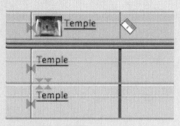

2.20   Razor Blade

Using the **Blade** tool works best if **Snapping** is turned on. So the **Blade** snaps powerfully and exactly to the playhead in the **Timeline**. Snapping can be toggled on and off with the small **Snapping** button in the upper right corner of the **Timeline** (Figure 2.21) or more easily by using the **N** key.

2.21   Snapping Button

The letter **A** is the shortcut that will return you to the **Selection** tool. (Think *A* for *arrow*.) Of course, with the cursor in **Blade** mode, you cannot select a clip. Trying to select a clip will cut it. So to do ripple deletes, you would need to switch back and forth between the **Blade** and the **Selector**. You can do this quickly using **A** and **B**. Or you can leave your cursor in **Blade** mode, and instead of clicking to select a clip, hold down the **Control** key when the cursor is above the clip you want to remove. Holding down the **Control** key will change the cursor from the **Blade** to the contextual menu. Mousing down will open the menu, and from the menu you can select the function **Ripple Delete**. Neat, isn't it?

Slice 3

With the Slice 2 method, you're cutting the pieces you want to keep and moving them into the **Browser**. Let's look at another method of working in the **Timeline**. Here we'll cut away the pieces we don't want to use and leave the good material in the **Timeline**. This method works especially well for narrative fiction or for material that's heavily scripted, material that has rough sections that need to be edited out even before it's organized into bins. It also works very well for news and other material with a quick turn around, material you don't have to store, organize, or log carefully.

1. Begin by deleting everything in *Sequence 1*. **Command-A** will **Select All**, and the **Delete** key will remove everything.

2. Next make sure there aren't any In and Out points marked in the master clip *Temple*. Bring a fresh copy into the sequence by dragging it into the **Timeline**.

3. Press the **Home** key to return to the start of the sequence.

4. Play forward until you reach the beginning of the second shot at 01:00:10;16. We want to remove the second shot from the sequence because we don't need it.

5. Mark an In point in the sequence by pressing the **I** key.

6. Play forward through the second shot and through the zoom at the beginning of the third shot, until about 01:00:21;02. This is all the material we want to cut out, the glass-fronted hut section. We will cut out everything from the first frame of the second shot to and including the frame where the play-head is parked just like we mark In and Out points in the **Viewer.**

7. Press the **O** key to enter an Out point in the **Timeline**, which should look like Figure 2.22.

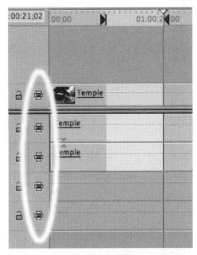

2.22 In and Out Marked in the Timeline with Autoselect Functions

Notice the highlighted area in the tracks. This is the new **Autoselect** feature in FCP4. Tracks can have their selection toggled on and off with the buttons circled on the left in Figure 2.22. This allows you to select some tracks while not selecting others.

8. Now press **Shift-Delete** to execute a ripple delete, removing that section of the video.

🐾 **Note**_____

Important: It is critical that you have nothing selected in the sequence when you use this technique. Anything that is selected—clip, audio, title, anything—will be ripple deleted instead of the marked In and Out section. The simplest way to avoid this is to press **Command-Shift-A** for **Deselect All.** This drops anything that's been selected. A good habit to get into before you execute this technique is to always make the **Timeline** the active window and press **Command-Shift-A**, or if you really like the menus, **Edit > Deselect All**, the opposite of **Command-A, Select All.** Also note that if there is anything selected in the sequence, the autoselect function will not work, and you will not see the highlighting in the sequence.

👆 **Tip**_____

Autoselect Shortcuts: There is a collection of keyboard shortcuts using the keypad of the extended keyboard to toggle off and on the autoselect functions. **Command-1, 2, 3**, and so on will toggle tracks **V1, V2, V3**, and so on. **Option-1, 2, 3, 4**, and so on will toggle audio tracks **A1, A2, A3, A4**, and so on.

This method is a fast, efficient way to cut material quickly. You end up with the shots you want to keep in the timeline. If you do want to organize and rename your material again, running **Modify > Make Sequence Clips Independent** will now separate the clips in the **Timeline** from their master/affiliate relationship. Now you can pull them into bins and rename them if you wish.

Slicing, whether in the **Viewer** or the **Timeline**, has the advantage of quickly and easily accessing all your material while still cutting it up into shots for editing. It has a couple of disadvantages:

- The problem of not being able to scrub easily in the **Viewer**, as we discussed earlier on page 51

- The problem with transitions of accidentally running into material from another shot

🦖 *Note*

Browser and Timeline Clips: This is a good point to explain a bit about the relationship between the clips in the **Browser** and the clips in **Timeline**. Quite simply, there is no relationship—no direct, linked relationship anyway, other than their master/affiliate relationship. Apart from that relationship, which forces them to have the same name and label, they are two separate and distinct items. They may be copies of each other, but they are quite separate clips that share the same media. When you drag the master clip from the **Browser** and place it in a **Timeline**, you are placing an affiliate copy of the master clip. So when you razor blade and ripple delete the clip in the **Timeline**, you are not in any way affecting the master clip that remains untouched in your **Browser**.

Comparison

Let's see how making subclips is different from slicing. Open one of the subclips you created earlier using **DV Start/Stop Detect**. Unlike a sliced clip with its In and Out marking a small portion of the master clip, in the subclips the In point and Out point do not appear at all (Figure 2.23).

2.23 Subclip in the Viewer

The subclip is treated as a separate piece of media, though in reality it's not. Notice the film sprocket holes on the left side of the frame in Figure 2.23. These holes on the left or right edge of the frame indicate that you're at the limit of the media for that clip. Though the subclip is only a portion of the piece of the *Temple* media on your hard drive, it's treated in FCP as a complete, self-contained piece of media. Hence the film sprocket indicator. The advantage to working in the subclip method is that it's easy to scrub the clip, running the mouse along the length of the media.

If you need to access more of the media within that subclip, you can use **Remove Subclip Limits** from the **Modify** menu. When you do this, the clip, if it's in the **Viewer**, will suddenly disappear, and a slug will be loaded in its place. The application has always done that, and I'm not sure why it still does. If you again open that clip after the subclip limits are removed, the clip will revert to its whole length, without In or Out points.

You can also remove subclip limits from a shot or a whole bin of shots directly in the **Browser**. Just select the bin and pull down

Remove Subclip Limits from the Modify menu. All the subclips
will revert to full-length clips.

> ### ☞ Tip
> _____
>
> **Keeping Ins and Outs:** If you want subclips to retain their In and Out points after the subclip limits are
> removed, you need to set In and Out points for them. The simplest way is to hit the **X** key. This will mark and In
> and Out points at the beginning and end of the subclip in the **Viewer**. Now when the subclip limits are removed
> the In and Out will be retained.
>
> The simplest way to do this for a whole group of subclips in the **Browser** is to drag them all into a sequence
> first. Dragging the subclips into a timeline will immediately define In and Out points for the clips. If you then
> delete the original subclips in the **Browser** and drag the clips from the sequence back into the **Browser**, the In
> and Out points for these clips will remain. With **Remove Subclip Limits**, the clips will behave as sliced clips,
> with Ins and Outs defined, but with whole lengths of the media available on either side.

The fact that you can't normally exceed the limits of the subclip is
also an advantage, while being a problem with the slice method
described earlier. The issue is transitions. These take extra media,
extending the shot to create space for themselves. Transitions will
take any available media. In the slice method, that media may
include sudden zooms, garbage frames, or bits of another shot.
These appear as a sudden flash during a transition, barely noticeable, but disconcerting.

Because subclips can't extend the media beyond their duration,
this will never happen with a subclip. The trick to using subclips
is to make sure that you include in your subclip not just the really
good bit of the shot you want to use, but as much extra material
as you safely can without including any garbage or spurious
frames. This means then when you edit down the subclips there
will be room for the transition to extend the material.

Range Clipping

Another technique for slicing or making subclips is to use the
Range tool in the **Timeline**. Some people prefer this method
because it offers a visual display of the In and Out points as you
work. Let's try this.

1. Again, make sure there are no In and Out points in the master clip _Temple_ before dragging it into an empty timeline.

2. Select the **Range** tool from the tools. It's under the second
   icon from the top. You can also call it up by hitting **GGG** (the
   letter **G** three times) (Figure 2.24).

2.24 Range Tool

3.   Position the playhead in the **Timeline** where you want the clip selection to begin.

4.   With the **Range** tool, stroke one section of the clip (Figure 2.25).

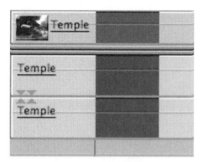

2.25   Range Tool in the Timeline

Unfortunately the **Range** tool, unlike the **Blade**, does not respond to snapping, but the crosshairs let you position the **Range** selector very precisely. As you stroke the clip to make the selection, the **Canvas** will give you a two-up display that shows you the start and end frames as well as the timecode (Figure 2.26).

5.   Now grab the selection from the **Timeline** and drag it to the **Viewer**, where it will load as a sliced clip.

6.   In the previous version of FCP, you could make the selected clip opened from the **Timeline** into the **Viewer** and make it into a subclip with **Command-U.** This is no longer possible in FCP4. To turn the selected clip into a subclip, you have to drag it into the **Browser**, where it can be converted into a new subclip.

Tip

Renaming Clips: As you make subclips from a master shot, you'll probably want to rename the shots immediately. What usually happens, though, is that as soon as you change the name of the subclip, it leaps off somewhere as the **Browser** order is changed. To avoid this, before you go naming the clips, try clicking on any blank column header—**Label**, perhaps—or a column in which everything is the same, like **Frame Size**. Then when you rename the clips, they won't change position in the **Browser** order.

Organizing the Clips

Once you've got your material cut up, you should spend some time getting it put away so that you can find it again. There are no firm rules about this, and I find each project tends to dictate its own organizational structure. Usually I begin with one bin that holds all the master shots. These are usually pretty big chunks of

2.26   Range Selection Two-Up Display in the Canvas

video: 10, 20, 30 minutes, usually not smaller. This master bin holds all the reels of material. I don't like to capture whole reels, though occasionally I do. I usually capture in 15–20 minute blocks, depending on how it was shot and where a natural break occurs. These get stored in the master bin as clip *001a, 001b, 002a, 002b, 002c, 003a*, and so on, the number being the reel number and the letter suffix a piece of that reel.

From the master shots, clips are separated out into bins. Keeping the master shots has the advantage that you can go back to the material in bulk to look through it again. As the project nears completion, I like to do this to see if I overlooked or discarded anything, which can be useful in light of the way the material gets cut together.

The separate bins can be organized in a variety of ways. Tightly scripted projects like some corporate videos and narrative film projects that have numbered scenes tend to have material broken down in scene bins, with sub-bins for different types of shots or characters, depending on how complex the scene. So for a narrative project, you may have a number of scene bins in addition to your master bin, as shown in Figure 2.27.

The figure shows the beginning development of one method of scene organization. In the **Browser** is a *Masters* bin that holds the three master reels captured so far. Three scenes have been shot, and there are three corresponding bins *Scene 7*, *Scene 8*, and *Scene 10*. The *Scene 7* bin is open and has been subdivided into two bins, *Frank* and *Anna*. In each of those bins would be single shots, probably close-ups, of Frank and Anna with their take numbers. Also in the *Scene 7* bin are three takes of the wide shot and a sequence called *Scene 7*, in which the scene is actually edited together from the wide, cover shots and the close-ups.

In the **Browser** you'll also see a bin for *Scene 8*, probably a short bridging scene, with just two takes. It has no sequence of its own.

Scene 10, the open bin at the bottom of the figure, is a more complex scene with a number of bins for characters, covers, cutaways, and for a sub-scene between two characters. There are also two sequences called *Scene 10* and *Scene 10a*, which are the main scene together with a subscene between two characters that may be edited separately and embedded (or *nested* as it's called in Final Cut Pro) within the sequence *Scene 10*.

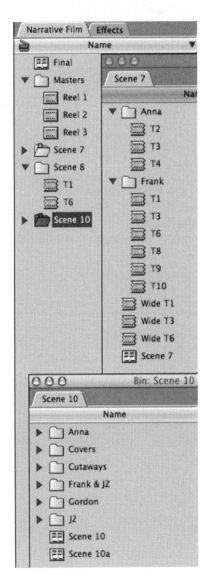

2.27 Narrative Film Organization

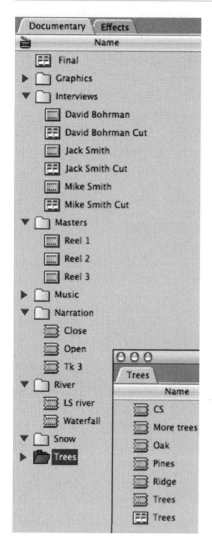

2.28 Documentary Organization

These edited sequences *Scene 7* and *Scene 10* together with the bridging shot for *Scene 8* and eventually *Scene 9*, when it's shot and captured, will all be placed in the sequence called *Final*, which you see at the very top of the **Browser** window.

Documentary projects tend to break the material down into subject matter: a bin for the tree shots, another for river scenes, another for snow scenes, another for all the interviews, another for narration tracks, another for music, another for graphics as in Figure 2.28, which shows part of a documentary organization. There are no hard and fast rules on how material is organized; the organization is usually determined by the subject matter.

Notice that the *Interviews* bin, in addition to having the capturing interview material, also has sequences in which the interviews are edited down into the key soundbites. These are the pieces of the interview that might be used in the *Final Sequence*.

Notice also the open bin *Trees*, inside of which is a sequence also called *Trees*. I like to work with a sequence within the bin. Inside the sequence will be all the shots that are in that bin. In this way I can either look at individual shots that can be searched by FCP's **Finder**, which we'll see in a moment, or I can quickly look through all the shots by scrubbing through the sequence or playing through it at double speed. By putting it in a sequence you get to see what all your choices are, rather than just relying on the find command to locate particular pieces of material. For similar reasons, I like to keep master reels as long clips in separate bins. It allows me to look through the material again in shoot order, as it was the day the cameraperson shot it.

The real trick in organizing your material is to break it down into enough bins so that the material in your **Browser** has a logical structure, but not so many bins that it becomes difficult to find material. As you move clips into bins, add notes—lots of them. The more information you include on the clips, the easier it will be to find them.

FCP provides ways to help you organize your material. Principally you have bins, and bins within bins. But at the most visible level you have color-coded and user-definable labels. **Control-**click on a clip or bin to call up a shortcut menu from which you can select from label colors and names (Figure 2.29). You can set the names however you like in the **Labels** panel of **User Preferences**.

Moving Between Sequence: Keeping a sequence of shots available for a subject allows you to drag a shot from one sequence into a final sequence. A second computer monitor is useful for this to give yourself enough screen real estate. You can also copy shots that are in one sequence and paste them into another. One thing I like about keeping a subject material sequence is that as shots get copied and used in the final sequence, they can be deleted from the sequence to avoid the danger of reusing a shot unintentionally. Or, often better, is to mark the shot as *used*. Go to **Item Properties (Command-9)** and add an asterisk to the name. By marking it used, you don't remove it from the sequence, so if later on you find a place where that particular shot will serve you better, it's still an available shot in your choices, though you may want to replace its earlier use. **Dupe Detection**, which we'll see on page 105, is a big help in finding that other usage of the shot.

The **Browser** or the **Logging** panel of **Item Properties** both give you all the information boxes we saw earlier. Use them. Do not overlook or hurry through the note-taking and entering process. All editors have their own ways of organizing material, loading information into the computer, and keeping it consistent. However you do it, it opens up to you one of computer-based editing's great boons, the computer's ability to search through huge amounts of data almost instantly. But you have to enter the information first. You can enter it either directly in the **Browser** fields, or by **Control**-clicking the clip and selecting **Item Properties>Logging Info**.

What is entered in the **Logging** panel also appears in the **Browser** columns and will be searchable with FCP's search engine.

All these tools are a great help to editors, but nothing helps an editor in long form more than a good visual and aural memory. Simply being able to remember material over perhaps hundreds of reels is a real gift, but even without this talent, looking closely at all your material, making good notes, and having a decent search engine will go a long way toward making your life a lot easier.

2.29 Labels Shortcut Menu

Final Cut has an excellent search tool, which is why adding the notes is so important. You can call up Final Cut's **Finder** with the keyboard shortcut **Command-F** (Figure 2.30). The first popup in the **Find** window lets you search:

- The open project
- All open projects
- The *Effects* folder

It searches anything tabbed into the **Browser**.

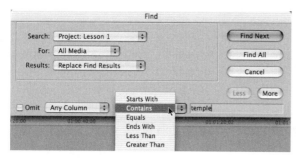

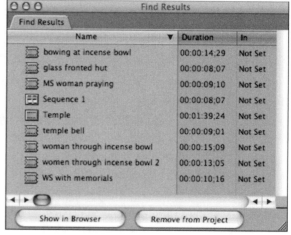

2.30 Find Dialog

2.31 Finder Results

The second popup selects **All Media** or a choice of **Used** or **Unused Media**, while the third popup lets you replace or add to existing results. The two popups at the bottom define parameters. The left one sets where it's going to look, while the right sets the search options.

Unless you have pretty good idea where the information is—for instance, if you're looking for a specific type of file—just leave it on the default **Any Column**.

If you press the **Find All button** rather than the default **Find Next**, the requested clips appear in a new **Browser** window (Figure 2.31). It found these clips because I had typed the word *temple* in the **Scene** name in the **Logging** panel for each shot. Notice also that it found *Sequence 1*, which contains a shot with that scene name.

The two buttons at the bottom let you:

- Show a selected item in the regular **Browser** bins
- Remove selected items from project

This **Remove** is not the powerful **Make Offline** tool we saw earlier on page 35, which lets you delete the media. This one deletes the clip in the **Browser** window.

The key to being able to find something with the search engine is to enter the data correctly to start with, to anticipate how you'll be searching for the material, by subject matter, by type of shot, by words spoken. By anticipating the questions you might want to ask of the material you'll be able to input the right data into the logging columns. With the right data loaded, searching through your material becomes a breeze.

✎ Note

Search Engine: This is the **Browser's** search engine, so unfortunately FCP cannot at this time search through marker screen information. It would be very useful if it could, but as of this writing, it has not been implemented. If you use the search feature in a specific sequence, you will get a more limited search engine, but one that does look for text in the marker screen information (Figure 2.32).

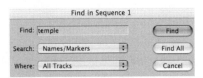

2.32 Sequence Search Window

Look Before You Cut

However you work your video into clips or subclips, what you're really doing is looking through your material. What you should watch for is relationships, shots that can easily be cut together. Getting familiar with the material is an important part of the editing process, learning what you have to work with and looking for cutting points. I think this is one reason why many editors still like to use the batch capture method. It allows them the first opportunity to look at the available material. Many editors now like to look through their material carefully after its been captured, putting the shots into a sequence to look through it.

Look through the master shot *Temple*. It's quite short but it shows a few shots that have obvious relationships. The same woman, in the white woolen hat, appears in four of them:

- In the third shot, as she bows before an incense bowl
- The shot from behind her that looks a little blue, in which she is walking up the stairs
- Another, in quick succession to the previous one, also from behind as she goes up the steps
- In medium shot from the side as she bows and prays

These shots can obviously be cut together to make a little sequence. You might want to put in a cutaway between the shot of her bowing at the bowl and her from behind walking up the steps or at the top of the steps already. From either of those two shots, a direct cut to her bowing would work without problem.

Searching for these relationships between shots is critical as you look through your material. Some editors like to immediately create small sequences and group them together, not finely honed, but roughly laid out, so that first important impression is preserved. You may not use it in your final project, but assembling related shots quickly into a sequence is an efficient way to make notes about your material. We'll look at assembling material into sequences in our next lesson.

Duplicating Sequences

1. Select the sequence called *Sequence 1* that appeared in the **Browser** when you opened *Lesson 2*.

2. Then go to the **Edit** menu and select **Duplicate**, or use the keyboard shortcut **Option-D**. This duplicates everything currently in that sequence and automatically names it *Sequence 1 Copy*.

3. Rename this sequence something appropriate.

4. Open it by double-clicking on it, press **Command-A** to select everything that may be in the **Timeline**, and press the **Delete** key.

Everything's gone, and you now have a brand new, pristine, empty timeline that you're sure has the right settings for your work.

You can have multiple sequences open at the same time. Timelines normally tab together into one **Timeline** window, but you can pull the timelines apart so that you have two sequences open on the screen at the same time. You can pull shots from one sequence into another. By doing this, you're actually copying the shot from one sequence into the new sequence.

While you edit, you just put together the shots you want to work with—edit them, rearrange them, shorten and lengthen them—how you like. You can just park your edited sequence to be used later, either as an edited group of shots or just as a holding bin for a group of shots, but unlike a simple bin, here the shots are laid out in the specific order you have arranged.

There are many different ways to work, perhaps as many different ways as there are editors. The longer the project, the more variations in work flow. How you organize your material is critical in long-form production. Many people like to work in organized bins; some prefer to work with multiple sequences with very few bins. Those coming from the Media100 editing software often work like this: one or two bins for the major material, then sequences with the shots gathered together by scene or subject matter. The final scene is then made up by selecting shots from multiple open timelines and moving them to the final sequence. This way of working is best with very large computer monitors.

Others prefer to work with multiple bins, all of them open at once, all in Icon view. A second computer monitor is almost a prerequisite for working like this. Others prefer to work with toggled open bins set in list view with the **Comments** and **Log Notes** columns pulled over next to the **Name** column. Others like to use the **Find** tool, leaving found multiple lists open at the same time.

As you become more experienced, you'll find yourself working with some methods more than others. You'll probably also find that on different projects, you work in different ways. Some material lends itself to working with multiple sequences; other material might not. Some workflows are faster than others. Laying out clips in bins that you trim in the **Viewer** and then rearrange as a storyboard might sound good, but cutting up and rearranging material entirely in a timeline is probably a lot quicker for small amounts of material.

Media Manager

At some stage in the editing process, you may want to remove all the excess material from your hard drive and just keep the core material that your project needs. You may do this housekeeping more than once in the course of creating a longer project. You may do it fairly early once you've gleaned out the good material, and you may do it toward the end of the project as you're finalizing it. Or maybe at the very end of the project after everything is edited and reduced to one sequence and its media for archiving purposes. Whenever you decide, in Final Cut Pro you should always try to use **Media Manager** (Figure 2.33).

You select **Media Manager** from the **File** menu. You can apply **Media Manager** to single or multiple sequences or multiple clips or bins. Whatever you select, **Media Manager** will only include those items in the consolidation.

Because of FCP's new master/affiliate architecture, if you wish to Media Manage the contents of a sequence or group of sequences, there is an important procedure you should follow.

1. Select the sequence or sequences to be Media Managed and duplicate them.

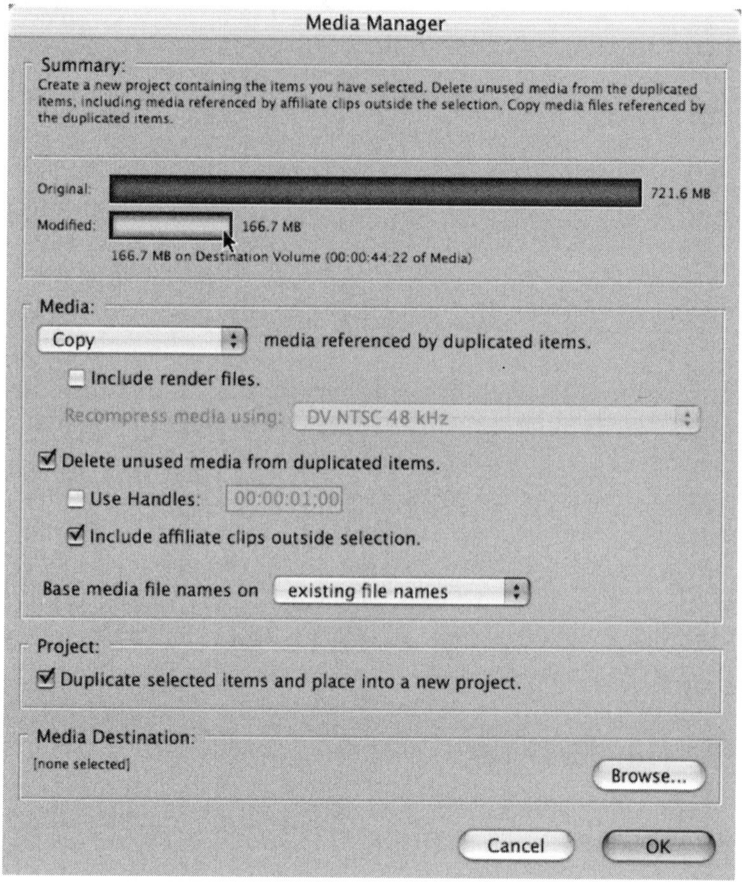

2.33 Media Manager

2.34 Media Manager Popup

2. With the sequences selected, choose **Modify>Make Sequence Clips Independent**.

This separates the clips within the sequences from their master affiliation. With the clips separated, **Media Manager** can deal with the material without needing all the master clip material.

The **Media Manager** window itself is pretty self-explanatory. It lists your options and what the system will do with them. The summary information at the top of the window explains what your options are doing, below that the bar graphs show the amount of media involved, how long it is, and how much your media management will produce.

The **Media** popup offers a number of options (Figure 2.34). The default copies the media to a new location picked with the **Browse** button at the bottom of the window. With the **Copy** process, the media is copied and the unused media deleted or not, as requested, and a new project is created. The new project opens immediately into FCP.

Make sure that you uncheck the box for **Include affiliate clips outside selection** if you do not want the additional affiliated clips associated with that media.

If the clips in a sequence have the same name, which often happens, the names are incremented with a suffix to distinguish them from each other. Notice that in this version of **Media Manager** you are offered the choice to **Base file names on** either the **existing file names** or **clip names** (Figure 2.35). If you choose file names, FCP will use the names given to the media on the hard drive. If you use clip names, the names for the new media will be that given by you within the application.

2.35 Base Files Names on Popup

The **Move** option actually moves the media to the new location. When moving to a different drive or partition, the media will have to copy over, and after the operation is completed, the original media will disappear from the original location. If you use the **Move** option and other clips are associated with the media, a dialog box appears (Figure 2.36).

Selecting **Add** will maintain the link to clips in other projects. Choosing **Continue** will break the link. Because this is undoable, choosing either **Add** or **Continue** will bring up a further warning before you can execute the action.

When media is moved, it's transferred to the designated place and put in a folder named after the project. This folder, in turn, is inside another folder called *Media*. Though the filing system seems convoluted, the process is efficient and works remarkably well. In the **Move** option, unlike the **Copy** option, a new project is not created; the media is moved to a new location specified with the **Browser** button.

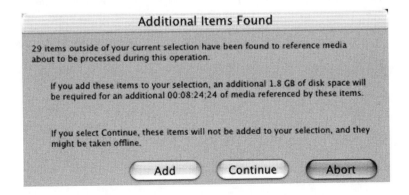

2.36 Moving Dialog

2.37 Recompress to Photo JPEG

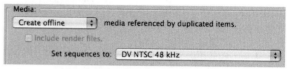

2.38 Create Offline to DV NTSC

The **Recompress** function allows you to convert your material to a different format or codec. This is useful, for instance, if you want to take your existing project and edit it on a PowerBook using **OfflineRT**. You can use **Recompress** as in Figure 2.37 to convert your material to 320×240 using Photo-JPEG or whatever presets you have available. After editing in the Photo-JPEG format, you'd need to use the **Create Offline** function of **Media Manager** and recapture your material at full resolution, perhaps back in the DV format you started in, as in Figure 2.38.

The **Use Existing** option is really the opposite of the **Move** option. While **Move** transfers the material but does nothing to the project, **Use Existing** creates a new project with whatever is included in **Media Manager**. If you have **Delete Unused** selected, it will immediately delete the unneeded portions from your hard drive and replace them with only the media required for the new project. This is fatal and final. I would recommend using this option only if you are pressed for drive space. If you have the space available, use **Copy** or **Move**.

The **Create Offline** option makes a new project with sequences and/or clips as requested in **Media Manager**, but leaves all the clips marked **Offline**, with the red diagonal line through them, ready to be recpatured.

Media Manager defaults to no handles and not moving render files. I would recommend making some handles, especially for **Create Offline**. One second is usually good. Probably dumping the render files is a good idea, unless the project is render intensive. Then it might be worthwhile preserving them to save time later.

Summary

In this lesson we've covered the master/affiliate relationship in FCP4, as well as cutting up media, creating subclips, organizing your material so that you can work efficiently, and consolidating with the **Media Manager**. In the next lesson we'll look at editing sequences.

Lesson 3

Building Your Sequence

Now that you've brought your material into Final Cut Pro and cut it up, we're ready to begin putting it all together. There is no right way to edit a scene or a sequence or even a whole film or video; there are only bad ways, good ways, and better ways. In this lesson we're going to look at some video and edit it.

Loading the Lesson

As in the previous lesson, start by loading the DVD into your DVD drive. When you begin any lesson that needs material from the DVD, you should first drag the needed folders onto the media drive of your computer. The sound and video clips included there will play much better and more smoothly from your computer's high-speed media drive than from any DVD drive. For this lesson you'll also need the folders called *Lesson 3 Media* as well as the project file called *Lesson 3*, which is inside the *Projects* folder on the DVD.

1. Drag the *Projects* folder to your internal system drive. Again, probably the best place for it is in your *Documents* folder.

2. Before opening anything, eject the DVD from your computer.

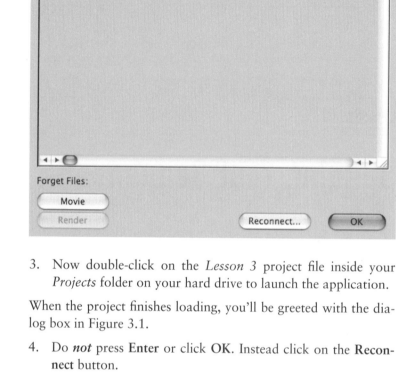

3.1   Offline Files Dialog Box

3.   Now double-click on the *Lesson 3* project file inside your *Projects* folder on your hard drive to launch the application.

When the project finishes loading, you'll be greeted with the dialog box in Figure 3.1.

4.   Do *not* press **Enter** or click **OK**. Instead click on the **Reconnect** button.

3.2   Reconnect Options Dialog Box

Do not click the **Movie** button underneath **Forget Files either**, because the application will do exactly that: forget that it needs the media. After you click **Reconnect**, you will get the **Reconnect Options** dialog box in Figure 3.2.

The computer will now search through your hard drives looking for a QuickTime file called *Food*. When the file is found, you'll get a dialog box that looks similar to the one in Figure 3.3.

5.   If this is the correct file on your media drive, click the **Select** button.

Final Cut will now reconnect all the material for the project and you're ready to go.

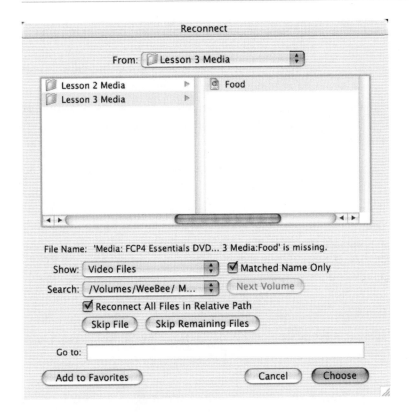

3.3 Reconnect Selection Window

Working with Clips

Inside the **Browser** of your copy of *Lesson 3*, you'll see a couple of sequences:

- *Sequence 1*
- *Food Sequence*

Sequence 1 is empty. We'll look at *Food Sequence* in a moment. In the **Browser** there is also the master clip, *Food*, a bin called *Clips*, and an audio file called *Music.aif*. Open the *Clips* bin and you'll see the shots from *Food* cut up into subclips.

These are the clips we're going to work with in this lesson. Take a quick look at *Food Sequence*. This is where we're going. To begin, let's look at where we're coming from, the material we have to work with.

1. Double-click on the clip called *Food*, which will bring it into the **Viewer**.

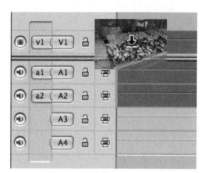

3.4   Dragging into the Timeline

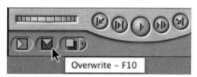

3.5   Edit Buttons

3.6   Canvas Edit Overlay (CEO)

The material is one minute and 17 seconds long.

2. Play through the material.

3. Open the *Clips* bin and double-click on the shot called *Food 1*, which is 6:01 long, six seconds and one frame.

4. Play the shot, let it pan from left to right across the trays of food, let the pan end, give it a beat, and then stop.

5. Enter an Out point.

This is probably around 1:37;01, making the shot about four and one-half seconds in length.

Try it a few times until you get the pacing of the movement down. You might find that the more times you try it, the more you're shaving off the shot. Perhaps you'll feel the front needs to be shortened as well. Instead of beginning right at the start of the shot, enter an In point just before the camera pans right. When you have it the way you want it, you're ready to move it into the **Timeline**.

There are five ways to get material from the **Viewer** to the **Timeline**:

- Drag it there. Grab the image from the **Viewer** and pull it directly into the **Timeline**, dropping it onto **V1** as in Figure 3.4.

- The second way is to press the little red button, the middle button, in the group of three at the bottom left of the **Canvas** (Figure 3.5).

- The third way is use the keyboard shortcut **F10**.

- The fourth method is to drag the clip from the **Viewer** to the **Canvas**, and the visual dialog box in Figure 3.6 appears immediately.

- The final way, which I wouldn't recommend to anybody, is to drag the clip onto one of the edit points.

Poor Playback: One of the most common causes of poor playback (especially frustrating for new users of FCP) is caused by the viewing window not fitting the video. If you look at your DV video in a small frame while the material is set to full size, you're expecting the computer to display only a portion of the video while playing it back. This will inevitably cause stuttering video on your computer monitor and usually cut off playback output to your FireWire connection. You can always tell if the image is too large for the viewing window when you see scroll bars on the sides, as in Figure 3.7. To correct this, select **Fit to Window** from the **Viewer Size** popup or use the keyboard shortcut **Shift-Z**.

3.7   Due To Scrollbars Showing, Image is Too Large

Fit to Window works on all windows. It is one of my favorite shortcuts because it will fit the contents of a sequence into the **Timeline** window, a useful feature because the playhead and the sequence window do not track together while you're playing back your edited material.

Overwrite

Let's look at the **Canvas Edit Overlay (CEO)**. It offers a number of different editing options. The most commonly used is the **Overwrite** command.

1. Drag the clip from the **Viewer** until the box marked **Overwrite** highlights.
2. Drop the clip.

It will overwrite whatever is in the **Timeline** beginning at the point where the playhead is parked.

When you drag a clip onto the **CEO**, or use a button or a keyboard shortcut to execute an edit, the clip is placed in the **Timeline** on the designated destination tracks, in this case **V1** and **A2/A2**. These are the default destination tracks set in the patch panel at the head of the **Timeline** (Figure 3.8).

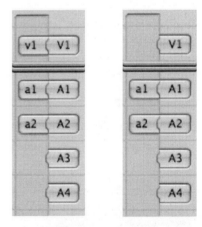

3.8   Patch Panel (above left)

3.9   Patch Panel with Stereo Music (above right)

The number of tracks and the types available as destination tracks are controlled by what is loaded in the **Viewer**. For instance, if you have a still image in the Viewer, only one destination track for video will be available. Similarly, if you have a piece of stereo music loaded in the Viewer, only two tracks of audio will be available as destinations and no video tracks, as in Figure 3.9. In FCP4 you can have one track of video combined with up to 24 tracks of audio. If you load a clip like the one shown in the Viewer, you'll have options for setting destinations for each one of the 24 audio tracks.

The FCP4 patch panel as a number of distinct functions. One of them, **Destination Track** selection, controls how material gets placed into your sequence. **Autoselect** is similar. It controls how edits—like an **Add** edit—are executed, which items are copied, etc. I think of **Autoselect** as controlling how items go out of the sequence, the opposite function from setting the destination tracks in the patch panel.

By marking In and Out points in a clip and editing it into a sequence, you have created what's called a three-point edit. In a three-point edit you're defining three elements required to execute the edit function:

- Where you want the clip to start (by marking an In point)
- Where you want the clip to end (by marking the Out point)
- Where you want to place the clip (by the position of the playhead)

🐎 **Note**

Different In Point: You can also define the In point in the **Timeline** to be a different point from the playhead. Go to the **Canvas** or the **Timeline** window and press the I key to mark an In point (Figure 3.10). This will be the In point for the next edit, and when you drag the clip from **Viewer** to **Canvas** or hit **F10** or the red **Overwrite** button, the clip will drop at the marked In point and not at the playhead's current position.

So that we can look at the functionality offered in the **CEO**, let's quickly drag a few shots into the **Timeline** to see how they work.

🐎 **Note**

Overwrite Constraint: Note that F10 does not overwrite directly from the **Browser**. F10 only works when overwriting from the **Viewer**. If the **Viewer** is closed, F10 will input a slug, a long section of black with a stereo audio track.

3.10 In Point Mark in the Timeline

1. If you haven't already done it, drag *Food1* from the **Viewer** and drop it on **Overwrite**.
2. Then select clips *Food2* and *Food3* in the **Browser** and drag them directly to the **Overwrite** box in the **CEO**.

The clips will appear in the **Timeline** following *Food1* in their bin order. Note that every time you place a clip in the **Timeline**, the playhead automatically leaps to end of the clip, ready for the next edit event, and the **Canvas** displays the last frame of the sequence. Also notice that in the **Timeline**, *Food2* and *Food3* will appear with **Through Edit** markings. This happens because the shots have contiguous timecode.

Insert

If **Overwrite** is the most commonly used of the **CEO** features, then the next most used must be **Insert**. This is where an NLE system shows its power.

1. Move the playhead to the edit between *Food1* and *Food2*.

As you move the playhead onto the edit point, it should snap strongly to the join and display on the tracks the marks in Figure 3.11. If you don't see the snap marks, **Snapping** is turned off.

2. Press the **N** key. Try it several times, toggling the **Snapping** function on and off.

The **N** key may become one of your most often-used keys in Final Cut Pro. You'll find as you work with the application that you'll be constantly changing from one mode to the other.

Now with snapping on, you should have the playhead parked between the clips.

3. Grab *Food5* directly from the **Browser** and drag into across to the **Canvas**, calling up the **CEO**.

4. Drop it on **Overwrite** to see what happens.

Food5 wipes out all of *Food2* and some of *Food3*.

5. Quickly undo that with **Command-Z**.

6. This time, instead of dragging *Food5* onto **Overwrite**, drag it onto **Insert**.

Immediately the **Timeline** rearranges itself. *Food5* drops into the **Timeline**, appears between *Food1* and *Food2*, and pushes everything further down in the **Timeline**, as shown in Figure 3.12.

Insert will move everything down the track regardless of a clip's position. So if you insert into the middle of the clip, the clip will be cut, and everything on all the tracks will be pushed out of the

3.11 Snap Markings

The Magic Frame

If the playhead moves to the end of the last clip in a sequence, the **Canvas** displays the last frame of the clip with a blue bar down the right side. This is the Magic Frame, because the playhead is actually sitting on the next frame of video—the blank, empty frame—but the display shows the previous frame. Try it.

1. Place a clip in an empty sequence and use the **Up** and **Down** arrow keys to move back and forth between the beginning and the end of the clip. You see the first and last frames of the clip.

2. Now, leaving a gap in the **Timeline**, place another clip in the sequence.

This time when you use the **Up** and **Down** keys to toggle, at the beginning you see the first frame of video, but at the end you see the first frame of black, the empty space. This is important to remember that the playhead is always sitting at the start of the video frame, despite what the Magic Frame shows you.

3.12 **The Insert Edit**

way. This applies to all tracks, including music or narration, which you may not want to cut.

Track locks are useful in these circumstances. For instance, to prevent an Insert edit from slicing into a music track, lock the track or tracks. All the other tracks will move, but the locked tracks will remain stationary.

Let's try this and see what happens.

1. Undo the Insert edit you did when moving *Food5* into the **Timeline.**

2. In the **Browser,** grab the icon for the audio file called *Music.aif.*

3. Drag it directly into the **Timeline** and place it right at the beginning of tracks **A3** and **A4.** It's a stereo pair of music tracks.

4. Move the playhead back between *Food1* and *Food 2.*

5. Execute the Insert edit with *Food5.*

You'll notice that immediately not only is the video and audio for *Food5* being inserted into the sequence, but the music track is actually being cut with the Insert edit.

6. Undo this edit with **Command-Z**.

7. Just click on the track locks (Figure 3.13) at the head of each track. (Remember to lock and unlock both tracks of a stereo pair.)

8. Redo the Insert edit, and you'll see that the video moves to accommodate the clip, the music track now does not.

9. Before we go any further, let's undo the Insert edit and remove the audio on **A3** and **A4**, bringing the **Timeline** back to just the three clips, *Food1*, *Food2*, and *Food3*.

You could use the **Control** key and the shortcut menu to do a ripple delete of *Food5* (Figure 3.14), or just ripple delete with **Shift-Delete**. You can also ripple delete using the **Forward Delete** key, sometimes marked as **Del**, on an extended keyboard.

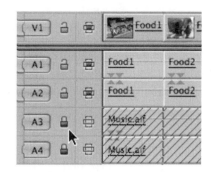

3.13 Track Locks

👉 *Tip* _____

Keyboard Shortcuts: As usual in FCP, there are keyboard shortcuts for locking and unlocking tracks. To lock a video track, press **F4** and the track number. To lock an audio track, press **F5** and the track number. If you want to lock all the video tracks, use **Shift-F4**. For all the audio tracks, **Shift-F5**. These key commands are toggles: unlocked tracks will lock, and locked tracks will unlock.

Sometimes it's handy to lock all the video or audio tracks except one. Use **Option**-click on the lock, and that track will remain unlocked while all the other tracks of that type, video or audio, will lock. Do **Option**-click on the track again to unlock everything.

3.14 Shortcut Menu > Ripple Delete

Alternative Overwrite and Insert

Overwrite and **Insert** are the primary functions in the **CEO**, but let's look at another way to do them.

Drag *Food5* directly from the **Browser** to the **Timeline**. As you drag it onto the edit point between *Food1* and *Food2*, a little arrow appears, indicating how the edit will be performed. If the arrow is pointing downward as in Figure 3.15, the edit will overwrite. If the little arrow is pointing to the right as in Figure 3.16, you will be doing an Insert edit, which will push the material out of the way.

3.15 Overwrite Arrow (right)

3.16 Insert Arrow (far right)

You'll notice also that in addition to the arrow indicators, the clip colors change. In **Overwrite**, the track color changes to the highlighted brown color. In **Insert**, the track has an outline box.

We'll skip **Overwrite with Transition** and **Insert with Transition** for a later lesson and look at:

- Replace
- Fit to Fill
- Superimpose

Replace

Replace is remarkably sophisticated in the way it works. It will replace a clip in the **Timeline** with another clip either from the **Viewer** or dragged from the **Browser** to the **CEO**. The trick to understanding how **Replace** works is to understand that it works precisely from the point at which the playhead is positioned.

Let's do a replace edit.

1. Start with your base three shots in the **Timeline**, *Food1*, *Food2*, and *Food3*.

2. Place the playhead at the edit point between *Food1* and *Food2*, right at the beginning of *Food2*.

3. Open *Food5* into the **Viewer** and make sure the playhead there is close to the beginning of the clip.

4. Drag the clip from the **Viewer** into **Replace** in the **Canvas,** or use the keyboard shortcut **F11**. *Food5* will immediately replace *Food2*.

The **Viewer** and the **Canvas** will show the same frame because Final Cut has taken what was in the **Viewer** and placed it in exactly the same frame position as the shot it's replacing in the **Timeline**. It's extending the shot that was in the **Viewer** forward and backward from the point where the playhead was to fill exactly the duration of the shot it's replacing.

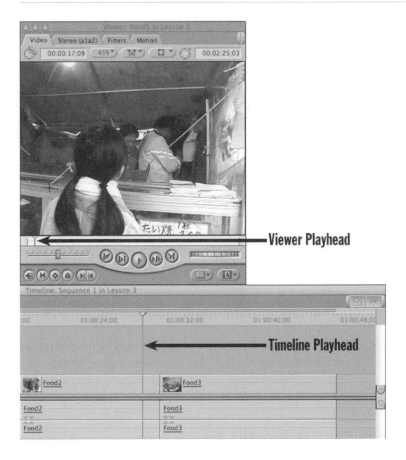

3.17   One Clip Trying to Replace
Another

Take a look at the clips in Figure 3.17. The clip in the **Timeline**, *Food2*, has the playhead parked near the end of the shot. I want to replace it with the clip *Food5*. In the **Viewer** *Food5* has the playhead near the beginning of the shot. The current position of the playhead in *Food5* is indicated. I won't be able to replace *Food2* with *Food5* even though the new clip is much longer than the clip it's replacing. Why? Because FCP calculates the replace edit from the position of the playhead. There just aren't enough frames in front of the current position of the playhead in *Food5* to replace all the frames in front of the current position of the playhead in *Food2*.

If you tried to do a replace edit now you would get a error message saying *Insufficient content for edit*. Whenever you see this message, it means that FCP cannot execute the edit or function the way you asked it to, usually because there isn't enough media available to perform the function.

3.18   Ins and Outs in the Timeline

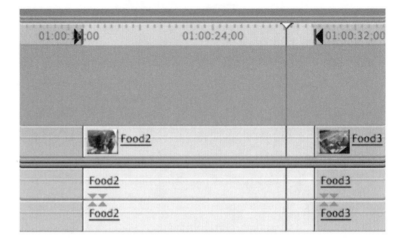

If you're having trouble doing a replace edit, try this simple way to get the clips to line up. Take both clips, the one in the **Timeline** and the one in the **Viewer**, back to their In points and do a replace from there.

Another way is to use **Overwrite** after first defining the limits of the shot you want to replace. That's easy to do in FCP. With the playhead parked over the shot, press the **X** key. This sets In and Out points on the timeline that are exactly the length of the clip, as in Figure 3.18. If you now do an Overwrite edit, it will effectively replace the shot in the **Timeline**.

Fit to Fill

Fit to Fill functions similarly to **Replace** except that it's never hampered by lack of media. **Fit to Fill** adjusts the speed of the clip to match the area it needs to occupy. This is a great tool for putting into the **Timeline** still images or titles that you want to be a specific length. Because stills aren't real video FCP can produce the frames very accurately and quickly. It's a little more problematic when using it with video where it can raise some serious problems.

1. To see how this functions, first undo the last edit so that you're back to having just *Food1*, *Food2*, and *Food3* in the **Timeline**.

2. Insert *Food5* into the **Timeline** between *Food1* and *Food2*.

3. Open the clip *Food6* in the **Viewer**.

Food1	Food6 (45%)		Food6 (45%)	Food2
Food1	Food6 (45%)		Food6 (45%)	Food2
Food1	Food6 (45%)		Food6 (45%)	Food2

3.19 Slow Motion Clip in the Timeline

You can see by the duration in the upper left corner of the **Viewer** that *Food6* is quite a bit shorter than *Food5*. *Food6* is 7;23, while *Food5* is 17;09.

4. With the playhead parked over the middle of *Food5* in the **Timeline**, drag the *Food6* from the **Viewer** and drop it on the **Fit to Fill** box, or use the keyboard shortcut **Shift-F11**.

The clip will immediately drop into the **Timeline**. Unless it is exactly the same size as the clip it's replacing, a colored bar will appear at the top of the **Timeline** above the clip, red if your system is not capable of playing back a speed change in real time and green if it is. The red or green line indicates that the section of the **Timeline** needs to be rendered at some point before output. If the line is red, the clip will have to be rendered immediately to be viewed, if it's green you will have real-time preview. This section needs to be rendered because of the speed change to *Food6*, which is now in slow motion to accommodate the **Fit to Fill** edit. The clip in the **Timeline** also shows the speed change, in this case, 45% of real speed—pretty slow (Figure 3.19).

Notice also the dark green bar that appears inside the audio portion of the clip. This indicates that the audio will also need to be rendered as well before final out. The audio too is slowed down together with the video.

Let's check the speed.

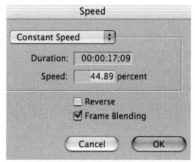

3.20 Speed Dialog Box

5. Select the clip in the **Timeline** and hit **Command-J**, which calls up the **Speed** dialog box (Figure 3.20).

The speed displayed in the **Timeline** isn't quite accurate. The real speed of this clip is 44.89%.

Modify>Speed (**Command-J**) is where constant clip speed changes are made, to make a clip in slow motion as **Fit to Fill** is doing here, or to speed the clip up. The real problem with speed changes is that it is difficult to create smooth motion, particularly at odd speeds such as 44.89%. This may not be always be noticeable, but you can often get some nasty stuttering effects, particularly if

⭐ *Tip* _____

Changing to Slomo: When a speed change is done in a sequence, a ripple edit is performed, i.e., the contents of the **Timeline** shift, based on the new length of the clip. This is usually good, but sometimes you just don't want that to happen. If you're speeding up the material, the easiest way is to go to the head of the clip in the **Timeline** and press the **F** key to match back to the clip in the **Browser**. Mark an In point and use **Command-J** to call up the **Speed Change** dialog. For example, change the speed to 200% and then **Overwrite** back into the **Timeline**, cutting away what's left of the clip that you don't need. If you're slowing down the material, it's slightly different. Again use the **F** key to match back and then mark an In point. Execute the speed change to 50%, and now drag the clip to **Replace**. The slomo will be the duration of the clip it's replacing without rippling the sequence.

the clips are speeded up. In slow motion we get some unpleasant-looking artifacts because it becomes difficult for the application to make sensible intermediate frames. The program needs to extrapolate and create frames that don't exist and blend them together at the correct frame rate of 29.97fps. It's better if you want to do slow or fast motion to use simple multiples: 50%, 150%, 25%, or 200%. These are much easier to calculate and generally produce better results. **Fit to Fill** calculates an absolute number and, as you can see, usually a bizarre one.

Frame blending can help, but it will slow down render time. The default is to have **Frame Blending** turned on. With **Frame Blending** off, FCP merely duplicates or drops frames as necessary to make up the right speed. For slow motion you usually want to have **Frame Blending** turned on, but for clips being speeded up, it works better to have it switched off.

Rather than using **Fit to Fill**, if you do want to slow down or speed up a shot to fit a gap in your sequence, I recommend the following procedure:

1. Place the clip on the track above the gap you want to fill.

2. Use **Command-J** to change the speed, lengthening or shortening the clip as necessary, using a common increment such as 150%, 200%, 50%, or 25% so that it covers the gap.

3. Then trim the clip to fit the hole.

I think this will make the smoothest **Fit to Fill**, especially for interlaced video.

Superimpose

Superimpose is used primarily to place titles on the track above a piece of video. It works a bit like **Replace**. The clip you're superimposing takes its duration from the clip below. Drag the clip from the **Viewer** to **Superimpose**, and it will be placed above the clip where the playhead sits.

Let's ripple delete the **Fit to Fill** shot in the **Timeline** so that we're left with only *Food1, Food2,* and *Food3*.

1. Place the playhead somewhere over the middle of the *Food2*.

2. Drag *Food5* from the **Browser** to the **Canvas** and drop it on the **Superimpose** box, or use the keyboard shortcut **F12**.

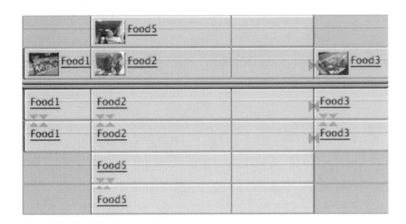

3.21 Superimpose Clip

The clip appears in the **Timeline** directly above the destination track (Figure 3.21), while the audio goes below the destination audio tracks onto **A3** and **A4**.

Making a Sequence

Now that we've gone through the principal means of going from **Viewer** to **Canvas**, let's edit in the **Timeline** itself, trimming and adjusting the clips. We'll edit together a quickly paced sequence of shots.

> ✎ **Note**
>
> **Superimpose:** There is often some misunderstanding about the term *superimpose*. In FCP it is used to mean placing a clip on the track above the current destination track. It does not mean what many people expect in the sense that the super-imposed image will appear partially transparent and the underlying image will still be visible beneath it.

> 👍 **Tip**
>
> **Finding Buttons:** If you like using the buttons at the bottom of the Canvas, you are not limited to the three normally visible. You can also have Superimpose, Fit to Fill, and the transition edits. Mouse down on the Replace button, and the others will appear as in Figure 3.22.

Rather than working on the clips in the **Timeline**, let's start afresh with the first clip.

1. Delete everything in the **Timeline**. With the **Timeline** window active, press **Command-A** to **Select All** and then use the **Delete** key to remove everything from the sequence.

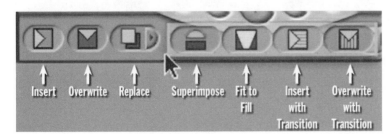

3.22 All the Edit Buttons

Storyboarding

Some editors like to build storyboards in bins. Working in Large or Medium Icon mode, you can:

- Trim and set the clips
- Set the Poster frame
- Arrange the layout order of the shots in the **Timeline**.

To set the Poster frame of a clip when you're in Icon view, either:

- Open the clip into the **Viewer**, find the frame, and use **Marks** > **Set Poster Frame (Control-P)**, or
- Hold down **Control-Shift** on the icon in the bin. This will let you scrub the clip. Hold down the two modifier keys and release the mouse over the clip where you want to set the Poster frame.

Storyboarding is a fast, easy way to move the shot order around, to try different arrangements and sequences. Though you can't play the clips back as a sequence, you can make a quick arrangement of shots in your bin. Then marquee through the shots and drag them into the **Timeline** (Figure 3.23).

The shots will appear in the sequence in the order they are in the bin. Notice the shots in the **Timeline** in Figure 3.23 follow the bin order as they are laid out, left to right, top to bottom. Be careful with the row heights: clips that are placed higher up in the bin will appear earlier.

3.23 Storyboarded Bin and Shots in the Timeline

2. Double-click on *Food1* in the **Browser** to open it into the **Viewer.**

3. Scrub through to the point where the camera starts moving from left to right.

4. Find the beginning of the movement and mark the In point.

5. Now find the end of the movement and mark the Out point. We can leave the shots a little loose at this stage.

6. After you've marked the In and Out points, drag the clip to **Overwrite,** or press **F10.**

I'm not sure which part of the second shot, *Food2,* I'll use at this stage, but I'll probably use something.

1. Take *Food2* from just before the zoom starts and let it run almost to the end, leaving the hands turning the skewers.

2. Again **Overwrite** to the **Timeline.**

Food3 is a little more complex. I want to use more than one part of the shot.

1. Start by marking the In at the beginning of the shot.

2. Mark the Out just before the small pull back.

3. **Overwrite.**

Because the shot in the **Viewer** was loaded from the **Browser,** it is not the shot that I just placed in the **Timeline.** By putting the shot in the **Timeline,** I made a copy of the shot that's in the **Viewer.** So now I can set new Ins and Outs in the **Viewer** without affecting what I've already done to the shot in the sequence.

Marking Edit Points

Many editors like to mark their Out points on the fly. This has the advantage of allowing you to judge the pace of the shot and of the sequence, to do it almost tactilely, to feel the rhythm of the shot. After a few tries you'll probably find you're hitting the Out point consistently on the same frame. If you're not, perhaps it isn't the right shot to be using, or perhaps you should look again at the pace the sequence is imposing on you. It's possible the shot doesn't work where it is.

Marking the In point is a little different because usually you want to mark the edit point before an action begins, but judging how far in front of the action to begin on the fly is difficult. Some editors like to mark the In point while the video is playing backwards. By playing it backwards, you see where the action begins, and you get to judge the pace of how far before the action you want the edit to occur. Sometimes you want the edit to happen in the middle of the action. Then you might make the In point cut while playing forwards. We'll look at cutting on action in Lesson 7 on page 219.

1. Set a new In point just before the pan left begins.

2. Let the shot carry over to the steaming kettle, until about the 2:00;02 mark. Put in an Out point.

3. Add that to the **Timeline**.

Let's take a third section from that clip.

1. Mark an In point just before the camera tilts up.

2. Put the Out point shortly before the shot ends.

3. Edit that into the sequence on the end.

Food4 might fit nicely before the close-up of the steaming tray.

1. Position the playhead in the **Timeline** between *Food2* and *Food3*.

2. Mark an In point at the beginning of *Food4* and an Out point just before the pan to the right, around 2:10;23.

3. Drag the clip to **Insert**, or use the shortcut **F9**.

We might be able to get another piece out of *Food4*.

1. Mark an In point around 2:13;03, just before the static portion of the shot of the man hunched over his soup.

2. Mark an Out point just before the camera pans left around 2:17;11.

3. Move the playhead in the **Timeline** in front of the first portion of *Food4*, to the edit point that separates *Food2* and *Food4*.

4. Execute an Insert edit to move the shot from the **Viewer** into the **Timeline**.

Let's look at *Food5*. It's the most human part of the material, the little girl at the food stall. My thought is to use it as bookends: the little girl at the beginning of the sequence and at the end.

1. Make the first part of the shot one clip, basically until after she hands the vendor her money.

2. Mark an In point near the beginning of the shot and an Out point around 2:30;19.

3. Make sure the playhead is at the start of the **Timeline**, then drag to **Insert**.

4. Make the second part of *Food5* begin shortly before the vendor reaches for the biscuit, around 2:32;18. Mark an In point there and let it go until just before the end.

Food5	Food1	Food2	Food4	Food4	Food3	Food3	Food3	Food6	Food5
Food5	Food1	Food2	Food4	Food4	Food3	Food3	Food3	Food6	Food5
Food5	Food1	Food2	Food4	Food4	Food3	Food3	Food3	Food6	Food5

3.24 Before the Swap Edit

5. Move the playhead to the end of the **Timeline** with the **End key.**

6. Drag the second half of *Food5* from the **Viewer** to **Overwrite,** or use **F10.**

We want *Food6* before the last shot.

1. Open up *Food6* in the **Viewer** and play it.

2. Start it with an In point near the beginning.

3. End it with an Out point after the move with the biscuits, around 2:45;13.

4. In the **Timeline** the playhead is probably at the end of the material. Use the **Up** arrow to move backwards one edit.

5. Now drag the clip from **Viewer** to **Insert,** or use **F9.**

The total duration of this little sequence should be roughly about 45 seconds, depending on how tightly you cut the shots. Looking through it, it's obvious it needs to be tightened up as well as have the order rearranged.

Swap Edit

There are three pieces of *Food3* in the sequence. Let's begin by moving *Food1*, which is now the second shot in sequence, between the first two pieces of *Food3* in the **Timeline**. This is called a *Swap edit*. Figure 3.24 shows the sequence of shots before the Swap edit.

1. Grab the shot and start to pull it along the timeline.

2. After you've started the movement, hold down the **Option key.**

It has to be after you've started to move the clip while you're already in mouse-down mode. As you move, a downward hooked arrow appears on the clip (Figure 3.25). You'll also see a number displayed. This tells you how far in the sequence you have moved the clip.

3. When you get to the edit point between the first and second portions of *Food3* in the sequence, drop the clip.

☞ *Tip*

Timecode Location: To go to a specific timecode point in either the Canvas, the Viewer, or the Timeline, tap out the number on your keypad—in this case, *24513*—and press Enter. The playhead will immediately move to that point.

3.25 Swap Edit Option Drag Arrow

3.26 After the Swap Edit

3.27 Timeline after Paste Insert

Swap Edit Limit: The Swap Edit function that lets you move clips will only work on one clip at a time. Unfortunately, you can't grab a couple of clips or a small section of clips and do the same thing. It also works best if you have **Snapping** turned on to avoid slicing off a little bit of a shot by accident.

Figure 3.26 shows the sequence after the Swap edit. In the **Timeline** window, you'll see that you've done an Insert edit as well a ripple delete. You've removed the clip from one point on the timeline, placed it somewhere else in the timeline, and pushed everything out of the way to make room for it. I use this great hidden tool often.

You can only move one shot at a time when you do a swap, but there is a handy way to move groups of clips. Look at the two pieces of *Food4* followed by the first part of *Food3*. These should be moved together right after *Food5* at the head of the **Timeline**. This would make them the second, third, and fourth shots in the sequence. I could just move *Food2* after them, but let me show you a way to move groups of clips.

1. Start by selecting the clips.

2. Next cut them out not with the usual **Command-X**, but with **Shift-X**.

Shift-X performs a **Ripple Cut** instead of a simple Lift edit that leaves a gap in the track. This not only cuts the clips out of the timeline, but also closes the gap the missing clips leave behind.

3. Now go to the edit at the end of *Food5*, between *Food5* and *Food2*. You want to place the clips and use **Shift-V**, which will paste the clips as a **Paste Insert** edit. **Command-V** would also paste, but as an Overwrite edit.

Your timeline should be laid out something like Figure 3.27.

👍 *Tip*

Gaps and Syncing: FCP defines a gap as a space in the **Timeline** that extends across all tracks. So if you have a music track on **A3** and **A4**, for instance, FCP will not see the space between the shots on the video tracks as a gap. This is where the ability to lock tracks really helps. If you lock those music tracks, you can then close the gap. Or use **Option**-lock to lock all other tracks, and again you can close the gap.

Besides the shortcut menu, there are two other ways to close a gap in the track:

- With the playhead over the gap, press **Control-G**
- Click on it to select the gap and then press the **Delete** key.

Be careful, though, with closing gaps like this. It can throw shots out of sync with elements on other tracks like music or narration tracks.

The sequence is getting better, but there are still a few edits I don't like and quite a few shots that need trimming. We'll get to trimming in a moment, but let's rearrange a few more shots.

In the first shot, I like the way the camera moves around the girl at the beginning, and I like the way she hands over her money with her fingers splayed out. I don't care for the hesitation in the middle. What I'd like to do is move *Food2* right into the middle of that first shot. I know *Food2* is too long; we'll get to trimming it shortly.

1. Scrub or play through the beginning of the timeline to find the point just after the camera finishes moving around the girl, around 2;17 into the sequence.

2. Use **Control-V** to slice the clip in the sequence.

3. Play or scrub forward in the timeline to find the point just before the vendor reaches his hand out for the money, around 2;28.

4. Press **Control-V** again. You have now isolated a short section to cut out.

5. Ripple delete it either by **Control**-clicking to call up the shortcut menu or by selecting it and pressing **Shift-Delete**.

You could also have done this by using the **Add Edit** function with **Control-V**, marking an In and Out point in the **Timeline**, and ripple deleting the short section.

👍 *Tip*

Moving the Playhead: Shift-Left or **Right** arrow will move the playhead forward or backward in one-second increments.

Jump Cuts

The sequence as we've laid it out so far has the most obvious form of jump cut, which is any abrupt edit that jars the viewer. This is generally considered a *faux pas*. The most common cause is placing side-by-side shots, such as the two halves of *Food5*, that are very similar, but not the same. You get this disconcerting little jump, as though you blacked out for a fraction of a second. It suddenly pulls the viewers out from the content of the video as they say to themselves, or perhaps even out loud, "What was that?" You can also get a jump cut if you put together two very different shots, such as the shot of a long street with the small figure of a person in the distance, cutting to a tight close-up. It's disorienting because the viewer has no reference that the close-up belongs to the person seen in the far distance in the previous shot. These are jump cuts. The general rule is to avoid them if you can. Or use them so often that it becomes your style. Then it's art.

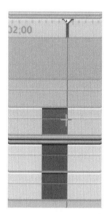

3.28 Range Tool Selection in the Timeline

A third way to do this would be to use the **Range** tool (**GGG**), which we saw in the previous lesson. Here, instead of using it to select a portion of the clip to save, you can also use it to select a portion of the clip to ripple delete, a feature that's new to FCP4 (Figure 3.28). You may have to switch off **Snapping** to make such a short edit. While you're dragging with the **Range** tool, you'll see a two-up display in the **Canvas** showing you the start and end points of the edit (Figure 3.29).

There is obviously now a jump cut in that first shot between the two pieces. So let's take *Food2* from further down in the sequence and do a Swap edit to move it in between the two cut pieces in *Food5*.

The arrangement is almost right, but I don't care for the very last shot. Just after the vendor puts the biscuit in the bag, the camera jiggles. I'd like to remove this. So let's do this in the **Timeline**.

1. Scrub or play the timeline to the frame when the biscuit just disappears into the bag behind the counter.

3.29 Two-Up Canvas Display

3.30 Timeline after Last Edit

2. Mark an In point in the timeline.

Right after this the camera is jostled.

3. Move further down the timeline to where the vendor is about to reach forward with the bag, as his hands separate, and mark an Out point here with the **O** key.

4. To make sure nothing is selected in the sequence press **Command-Shift-A** (**Deselect All**), and then use **Shift-Delete** to ripple delete the middle portion of the shot.

Now we have the same problem we had in the first shot.

This time we're going to move the last portion of *Food3* from its earlier position. This is the shot of the tilt up from the kettle.

5. Drag *Food3* with **Option** and drop it between the two halves of *Food5* that you just split to do a Swap edit.

6. I also cut out from the sequence the second portion of *Food3*, the pan from the steam tray to the kettle.

7. Your timeline should look like Figure 3.30.

If you look through the sequence, you'll see that the shots are in the order we want, but we still need to tighten it up quite a bit, trimming the shots to make them faster paced, which we'll look at next.

👍 *Tip*_____

Timeline Scaling: You can change the scale of the **Timeline** to zoom in and out with the tabbed slider at the bottom of the window. Pulling either end of the tab will change the scale of the **Timeline** window. At the bottom left is a little slider that will adjust the scale (Figure 3.31).

3.31 Scaling Slider and Tabbed Slider

My personal favorite is to use the keyboard shortcuts **Option-** = (think **Option-** +) to zoom in and **Option-** − (that's **Option** minus) to zoom out. What's nice about using the keyboard shortcuts is that, if nothing is selected in the sequence, it leaves the playhead centered in the **Timeline** as you zoom in and out. If a clip is selected in the **Timeline**, the scaling will then take place around that rather than around the playhead. You can use **Command-** + or **Command-** − to scale in any other active window, but **Option-** + and **Option-**— will scale the **Timeline** regardless of which window is active.

3.32   Trim Tools

Trimming Your Sequence

The trim tools—**Roll** and **Ripple**, **Slip** and **Slide**—are clustered in the fourth and fifth buttons (Figure 3.32).

The first two trim tools, **Ripple** and **Roll**, change the duration of clips, while the second two, **Slip** and **Slide**, leave the clip duration intact.

A *ripple* edit moves an edit point up and down the timeline by pushing or pulling all the material on the track, shortening or lengthening the whole sequence. In a ripple edit, only one clip changes duration, getting longer or shorter. Everything else that comes after it in the track adjusts to accommodate it. In Figure 3.33 the edit is being rippled to the left, and everything after it moves to accompany it, just as in a ripple delete.

A *roll* edit moves an edit point up and down the timeline between two adjacent shots. Only those two shots have their durations changed. While one gets longer, the adjacent shot gets shorter to accommodate it. The overall length of the track remains unchanged. In Figure 3.34 the edit point itself can be moved either left or right.

A *slip* edit changes the In and Out points of a single clip. The duration of the clip remains the same, and all the clips around it remain the same. Only the In and Out of the slipped clip change. If more frames are added on the front, the same amount are cut off the end, and vice versa, if some are added to the end, an equal amount are taken off the beginning. In Figure 3.35 the contents change by changing the clip's In and Out points, but neither its position in the timeline nor either of the adjacent shots are affected.

3.33   Ripple Edit Left

3.34   Roll Edit Directions

3.35 Slip Edit Directions   3.36 Slide Edit Directions

A **Slide** edit moves a clip forward or backward along the timeline. The clip itself, its duration, and In and Out points remain unchanged. Only its position on the timeline, earlier or later, shortens and lengthens the adjacent shots as it slides up and down the track. In Figure 3.36 the central clip *Food4* can slide up and down the timeline. The shot itself isn't altered; only the two adjacent shots are.

The Ripple Tool

We're first going to work with the **Ripple** tool. Press the fourth button and extend the popout to select the tool as in Figure 3.37. You can also call it up by pressing **RR**; that's the R key twice.

Let's use it on some of the shots we want to work on. Start with the first edit between shots *Food5* and *Food2*. Take the tool and place it near the edit. Notice it changes direction as you move it across the edit as in Figures 3.38 and 3.39.

When the tool is on the right side, it will ripple the second shot; when it's on the left side, it will ripple the first shot.

In this case, we want to ripple the second shot. As you grab the clip on the right side of the edit point, you will get a small two-up display in the **Canvas**, as shown in Figure 3.40. Pull the shot until you have trimmed off the beginning zoom, all the way until just before the hands come into the frame to turn the skewers. You might want to trim some off the end as well, rippling the left side and pulling the shot a bit until just as the hands leave the frame. It might be easier to do this if you toggle **Snapping** off, which you can do with the **N** key.

3.37 The Ripple Tool

3.38 Ripple Tool Right

3.39 Ripple Tool Left

3.40 Ripple Canvas Display

A word of caution about rippling: If you're working with material that's cut to narration or music, rippling will easily upset the timing of the sequence, because it's pulling and pushing the entire track and its sync sound. So what's working for you at this moment in the edit may be ruining something else further down the timeline. In these cases, the **Roll** tool may work better for you.

The Roll Tool

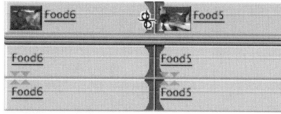

3.41 The Roll Tool

The **Roll** tool is also under the fourth button in the tools as in Figure 3.41. It can be evoked with the **R** key. Like the **Ripple** tool, it can be used in the **Timeline**, as shown in Figure 3.42.

The **Roll** tool acts on both shots, extending one shot while shortening the other. While the **Ripple** tool changes the enter length of the sequence by moving everything up and down the line, the **Roll** tool only affects the two adjacent shots.

A good candidate to try with the **Roll** tool is the edit towards the end of the sequence between *Food6* and *Food5*. As you roll to the left, a two-up display will again appear in the **Canvas** as in Figure 3.43. I rolled the shot back a little to the point in *Food5* just before the girl looks up at the vendor.

Using **Roll** and **Ripple**, tighten up some of the shots in the sequence.

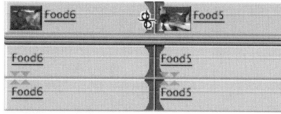

3.42 The Roll Tool in the Timeline

3.43 Roll Canvas Display

Ripple and Roll Shortcuts: You can also use the **Ripple** and **Roll** tools incrementally with keyboard shortcuts in the **Timeline**. Select the edit point by moving the playhead over it and pressing the **V** key. Now, by using the **U** key, you can toggle through **Ripple Right**, **Ripple Left**, and **Roll**. Whichever edit you have selected, you can now move incrementally with the less-than bracket **<** and the greater-than bracket **>**. (Actually, it's the comma and period, but most people think of them as **<** and **>**.) Each tap will move the edit one frame left or right in the direction the bracket is pointed. **Shift-<** and **Shift->** will move the edit for the duration you have set for **Multi-Frame Trimming** in your **User Preferences**. This also works if you select a clip in the **Timeline** and choose either the **Slip** or **Slide** tools.

Extend Edit

Final Cut's **Extend Edit** is another nice way to perform a roll edit. It's a simple way to move an edit point, even one with a transition.

1.   Choose an edit and click on it to select it.

2.   Find your new edit point in the **Timeline** (or in the **Canvas**) and hit **E** or select **Sequence>Extend Edit**.

If the selection is dimmed or you hear a system warning, it's because you don't have enough media to perform the Extend Edit.

The Slip Tool

Let's look at **Slip** tool, which works in the **Timeline** and the **Viewer**. **Slip** is one of my favorite tools. You can select it from the fifth button in the **Tools**, as shown in Figure 3.44. You can also call up the **Slip** tool with the **S** key.

3.44   The Slip Tool

One shot that you might want to slip is the first of the two *Food4* shots in the sequence. Grab the clip in the sequence with the **Slip** tool and start moving it from side to side as in Figure 3.45. What you're doing is slipping the media for the clip up and down its length. The overall duration of the clip remains unchanged but the section of media for that duration is adjusted. The **Canvas** shows you a two-up display. The frame on the left shows the In point, the first frame of the shot, while the frame on the right is the Out point, the last frame of the shot. The two-up display will help keep you from slipping the clip too far into some unwanted material.

Food2	Food5	Food4	Food4	Food3	Food1
			+00:01:05		
Food2	Food5	Food4	Food4	Food3	Food1
Food2	Food5	Food4	Food4	Food3	Food1

3.45 The Slip Tool in the Timeline

It is also possible to slip in the **Viewer**, which can be especially beneficial when you're adjusting a clip before you bring it into the **Timeline**.

1. To slip in the **Viewer**, double-click the clip to load it into the **Viewer**.

2. Hold down the **Shift** key as you grab either the In point or the Out point and drag. This way you will drag both points together and maintain a constant duration.

You are slipping the In and Out points of the clip, and what you see in the display is the start frame in the **Viewer** and the end frame in the **Canvas** as in Figure 3.46. It doesn't matter which end you grab to pull. The display is always the same: start in the **Viewer**; end in the **Canvas**.

3.46 Slipping in the Viewer with the Canvas Display

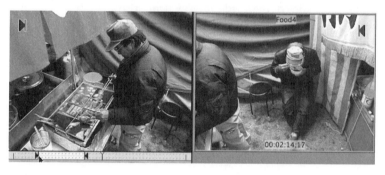

3.47 The Slide Tool

The Slide Tool

Let's look at the last trimming tool, the **Slide** tool, also in the fifth **Tools** button (Figure 3.47). The **Slide** tool can be brought out with **SS** (S twice).

It works only in the **Timeline**, unlike the **Slip** tool. The **Slide** tool doesn't change anything in the clip you're working on; it grabs the clip and pulls it forward or backward along the **Timeline**, wiping out material on one side, extending the material on the other side, as shown in Figure 3.48.

You're not moving just one clip. You're also affecting the two adjacent clips. That's why they're highlighted with boxes in Figure 3.48.

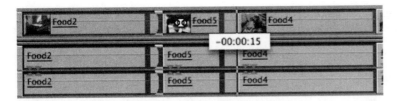

3.48 The Slide Tool in the Timeline

The two-up display in the **Canvas** (Figure 3.49) shows you the two adjacent shots that you're displacing. On the left, the end of the shot before the one you're moving. On the right, the beginning of the shot after the one you're moving.

You are limited in how far you can slide a clip by the amount of media available in the adjacent shots.

The Trim Edit Window

If you're going to be doing a lot of trimming, you can call up a separate **Trim Edit** window (Figure 3.50) where you can work with the **Ripple** and **Roll** tools as well as still having access to the **Slip** tool.

1. You open the **Trim Edit** window by moving the playhead to an edit point and using the menu **Sequence>Trim Edit** or the keyboard shortcut **Command-7**.

Notice the bars on the top of the windows in Figure 3.50. They're colored green in the application. The green bars indicate what mode you're in. When a green bar appears over both sides, as in Figure 3.51, you're in Roll mode. By clicking on one side or the other, you can either ripple the outgoing shot as in Figure 3.52 or the incoming shot in Figure 3.53. To get back to rolling the edit point, click on the space between the two frames. You can also toggle between the **Ripple** and **Roll** tools in the **Trim Edit** window with the **U** key. This is very handy but can be slightly deceptive because the cursor doesn't change, just the marking on the clip.

3.49 The Slide Tool Canvas Display

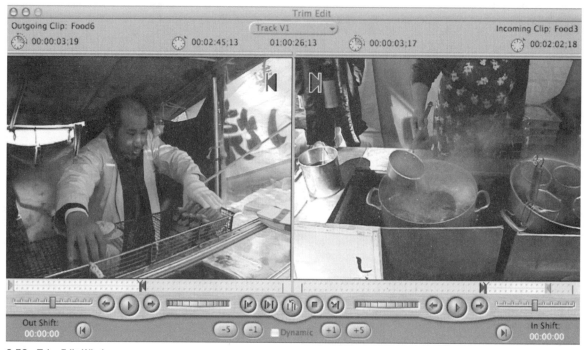

3.50   Trim Edit Window

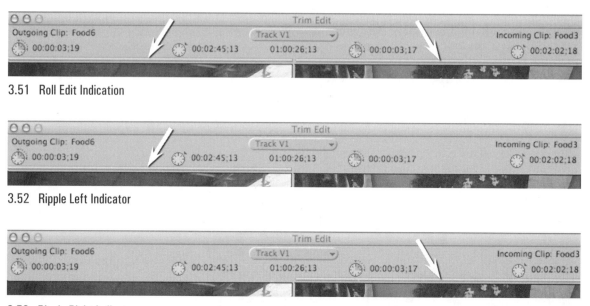

3.51   Roll Edit Indication

3.52   Ripple Left Indicator

3.53   Ripple Right Indicator

There's a lot of useful timecode information at the top of the **Trim Edit** window (Figure 3.54):

- The number to the far left is the duration of the outgoing shot (*A* in Figure 3.54).
- The next timecode number is the Out point of the outgoing shot (*B* in Figure 3.54).
- The center number under the track indicator is the current time in the sequence starting at one hour (*C* in Figure 3.54).
- The next number displayed is duration of the incoming shot (*D* in Figure 3.54).
- On the far right of the window, the number is the current In point of the incoming shot (*E* in Figure 3.54).

You can play either side of the **Trim Edit** window with the **J, K,** and **L** keys. Which side plays is not determined by the green bars, however. The side that plays is determined by the position of the cursor. If the cursor is over the left or outgoing side, that side will play. If you execute an edit however by pressing either the **I** or **O** keys, the edit function will be controlled by the green bar display regardless of which side is playing. Normally you're playing and editing the same side.

The **K** and **L** keys serve an interesting function when the cursor is sitting over the **Timeline** portion of the screen. The L key acts in looped play-around mode. It will play around the edit point again and again so that you can view it repeatedly. The **K** key will pause. The spacebar will do the same thing, starting and stopping looped play-around mode. To play either side slowly, or to have slow looped play-around, hold down the **K** key together with the **L** key. The amount of play-around, how much before the edit and how far after the edit, is controlled in **User Preferences** under **Preview Pre-Roll** and **Preview Post-Roll**. The default is five seconds before the edit and two seconds after. I usually set it down to two or three seconds before and two after.

3.54 Timecode Displays in the Trim Edit Window

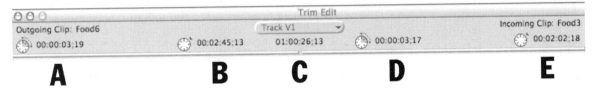

How Long is Long Enough?

A static shot, either close-up or medium shot, needs to be on the screen a much shorter time than a long shot in which the audience is following a movement. A shot that has been seen before, a repeat, can be on the screen quite briefly for the audience to get the information. Though there is no hard and fast rule, generally shots without dialog remain on the screen no more than six to eight seconds on television with its small screen. In feature films shots can be held for quite a bit longer because the viewer's eye has a lot more traveling to do to take in the full scope of the image. This is probably why movies seem much slower on the television screen than they do in the theater. While a close-up can be on the screen quite briefly, a long shot will often contain a great deal of information and needs to be held longer so that your viewer has time for his or her eye to rove around it. A moving shot, such as a pan, you can often hold longer because the audience is basically looking at two shots, one at the beginning and the other at the end. If the movement is well shot, a fairly brisk move, no more than about five seconds, you can also cut it quite tightly. All you need to show is a brief glimpse of the static shot, the movement, and then cut out as soon as the camera settles at the end of the move.

✎ Note

Trim Edit Shortcut: In the Trim Edit window, in addition to the trim buttons, you can use the keyboard shortcuts [and] to trim plus or minus one frame and Shift-[and Shift-] to trim plus or minus the multiframe trim size. Like the buttons, these will work on the fly while you're in looped play-around mode.

New to Final Cut Pro 4 is the ability to do *dynamic trimming* in the **Trim Edit** window. You'll see a little checkbox at the bottom of the window that activates this function, which can also be turned on in **User Preferences**. This allows you to play in the **Trim Edit** window using the J, K, and L keys. Whenever you press the K key to pause, the edit will automatically execute. This will work in any edit mode: Roll, Ripple Left, or Ripple Right. As soon as you press the pause key, the edit will be executed. Try it. It's pretty slick.

To trim an edit, you enter a new In or Out point. You will change the edit, either as a ripple or as a roll, in the **Timeline**. You can also use the little plus and minus buttons at the bottom of the window to make incremental edits on either side of the **Trim Edit** window. This is also a user-defined function controlled in **Preferences** under **Multi-Frame Trim Size**. You can set it as high at 99 frames if you want.

Fine tune the edit as much as you can, tightening so that the shots move quickly and flow smoothly through the short scene.

Look at your finished sequence. It should look something like *Food Sequence* in the **Browser**. I'm still not happy with the piece, principally because the audio is so abrupt and choppy, marking each cut. The audio needs to be smoothed out, perhaps extending sound from a single clip or adding some constant underlying sound from somewhere else. But that's for another lesson.

Summary

You've learned how to use the **Canvas** editing tools:

- **Overwrite**
- **Insert**
- **Fit to Fill**
- **Replace**
- **Superimpose**

You've learned how to use the various sequence editing tools:

- **Roll** and **Ripple**
- **Slip** and **Slide**
- **Trim Edit window**

In the next lesson we're going to look at how to work with sound, how to get rid of some of those rough patches and smooth out the aural presentation of the sequence.

> ☆ *Tip*
> *Moving Slowly in the Trim Window:* You can move forward slowly by holding down the K and L keys together. To move backwards slowly, hold down the K and J keys together. To go forward one frame, hold down the K key and tap L. Backwards one frame, tap J.

Lesson 4

Using Sound

Film and video are primarily visual media. Oddly enough, though, the moment an edit occurs is often driven as much by the sound as by the picture. So let's take a look at editing sound in Final Cut Pro. How sound is used, where it comes in, and how long it lasts are key to good editing. With few exceptions, sound almost never cuts with the picture. Sometimes the sound comes first and then the picture; sometimes the picture leads the sound. The principal reason video and audio are so often cut separately is that we see and hear quite differently. We see in cuts. I look from one person to another, from one object to another, from the keyboard to the monitor. Though my head turns or my eyes travel across the room, I really only see the objects I'm interested in looking at. We hear, on the other hand, in fades. I walk into a room, the door closes behind me, and the sound of the other room fades away. As a car approaches, the sound gets louder. Screams, gunshots, and doors slamming being exceptions, our aural perception is based on smooth transitions from one to another. Sounds, especially background sounds, generally need to overlap to smooth out the jarring abruptness of the hard cut. As we shall see, dialog poses a special, interesting problem for the editor when it comes to overlapping sound.

101

Loading the Lesson

This is going to sound familiar, but it's worth repeating. Begin by loading the material you need on the media hard drive of your computer.

1. If you don't already have it on your drive, drag the *Lesson 4 Media* folder from the DVD to your media drive.

2. Drag the *Projects* folder from the DVD into your home *Documents* folder if you have not already done so.

3. Eject the DVD and launch the *Lesson 4* project that's on your hard drive in the *Projects* folder.

4. As in earlier lessons, choose the **Reconnect** option to relink the media files when the **Offline Files** dialog appears.

Setting up the Project

You'll find in the project's **Browser** an empty sequence called *Sequence 1* and a number of other sequences that we'll look at during this lesson. There is also a master clip called *Backstage* and another folder called *Clips*, which contains the subclips pulled from the master.

Viewing Your Material

> **Note**
> **Flash Frame:** When you look through the individual clips that are in the *Clips* folder, you may see a flash of another piece of video right at the end of each clip. This is due to a very unfortunate shortcoming in QuickTime. To avoid it getting into your sequence, make sure you do not edit in the very last frame of any of the clips.

In this lesson we're going to look at backstage preparations for a kabuki performance. Before beginning the lesson, it might be a good idea to look through the material, which is about three and one-half minutes long. You can start by double-clicking the shot *Backstage* to open it in the **Viewer** and then playing through the material.

The Split Edit

A common method of editing is to begin by laying the shots in scene order entirely as straight cuts, as we did in the previous lesson. Take a look at the sequence called *Rough Cut*. This is the edited material cut as straight edits. What's most striking as you play it is how abruptly the audio changes at each shot. But audio and video seldom cut in parallel in a finished video, so you will have to offset them. Take a look at the sequence called *Final*. The three and one-half minutes that is *Backstage* has been cut down to one minute and 23 seconds for the *Final* sequence. This is where we're going. Notice how the audio overlaps and the way it fades in and out. When audio and video have separate In and Out points that aren't at the same time, the edit is called a *split edit*, *J-cut*, or *L-cut*. Whatever you call it, the effect is the same. There are many ways to create a split edit.

In the Timeline

Many instructors tell you to create split edits in the **Viewer**, but I think the **Viewer** is the least flexible place to perform this function. Let's set up a split edit inside the **Timeline**. It's a much more logical place to perform this type of work and very effective.

In making split edits, particularly in the **Timeline**, you will be frequently linking and unlinking clips, switching off the link between synced video and audio. You can do this with the little switch in the upper right corner of the **Timeline** window that toggles **Linked Selection** off and on (Figure 4.1). When **Linked Selection** is turned on, the button is green; when it's off, the icon is black.

You might want to switch **Linked Selection** off if you want to move a lot of sync sound clips, splitting the audio and the video. But I don't think that's ever a good idea. I think **Linked Selection** should be maintained at all times and only toggled on and off as needed for individual clips. You might get away with leaving it off

4.1   **Linked Selection and Snapping Buttons**

➤ **Tip**

Missing Buttons: If the Snapping and/or **Linked Selection** buttons are missing, **Control**-click on the bean, and from the shortcut menu select **Restore Default**.

Viewing Rushes

Old habits die hard. I can't get over using the British term for overnight film processing, *rushes*, rather than the American term, *dailies*. Whatever you call them—rushes, dailies, tape, cassettes, reels—this is the raw material that editors work with. Watching this material for the first time, whether it's in a darkened screening room, on a tape deck in a room crowded with humming electronic equipment, in the viewfinder of your camcorder, or even on the **Viewer** in Final Cut Pro—that first moment has a magic of its own. Don't miss it. Use it to grasp those first impressions, to find those visceral moments that affect you. As you watch, think about the relationships between pictures, between moments in time. Think about and watch for those moments that repeat themselves in various forms. This first viewing and listening is crucial to editing. If a piece of dialog is difficult to understand the first time you hear it, then it probably will be for your audience as well. As you work, you'll be hearing it dozens of times more, and by then it will probably seem okay to you. You'll get it; but your audience, unless they're equipped with Replay or TiVo, have only one shot at it. Even with a Replay, they're not going to enjoy backtracking on the program very often.

Backstage01	Backstage06	Backsta	Backstage04		Backstage11	Backstage17	Backstage06
Backstage01	...ge06	Backsta	Backstage04		Backstage11	Backstage17	Backstage06
Backstage01	Backstage06	Backsta	Backstage04		Backstage11	Backstage17	Backstage06

4.2   Duplicated Clips in the Timeline

4.3   Timeline Window Options

most of the time, but one day it will leap up and bite you hard. So for these lessons, let's just leave **Linked Selection** turned on.

Before we begin working on the sequence, it would probably be a good idea to duplicate the *Rough Cut* sequence. Select it and use **Edit>Duplicate** or the keyboard shortcut **Option-D**. This way you can also refer back to the original *Rough Cut* should you ever need to.

Start by double-clicking the copy of *Rough Cut* and take a look at the **Timeline**. You may notice a couple of red lines at the base of two of the clips in the **Timeline**, on the second and the seventh shot, which are circled in Figure 4.2. These red lines indicate where portions of the shot *Backstage06* are duplicated. This is a new feature in FCP4 and can be toggled on and off in the with the tiny triangle popup at the bottom left of the **Timeline** window (Figure 4.3). **Dupe Detection** will go through a number of other colors if clips are used more than once. Its functionality can be controlled in the first panel of **User Preferences**. To remove the duplicate shot from the *Rough Cut copy* sequence, select it and press **Shift-Delete** to perform a ripple delete edit.

The trick to smoothing out the audio for this type of sequence— or any sequence with abrupt sound changes at the edit points—is to overlap sounds and create sounds beds that carry through other shots. Ideally, a wild track was shot on location, a long section of continuous sound from the scene, a couple of minutes or more, which can be used as a bed to which the sync sound is added as needed. Here there was no wild track as such, but some of the shots are lengthy enough to have a similar effect.

Making Split Edits

1. Play through the first three or four shots in the *Rough Cut copy* sequence. The change between the first and second shot is quite noticeable, even more so between the second and third.

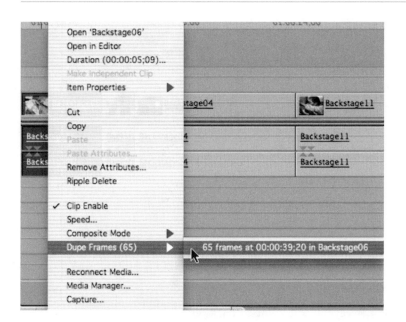

Tip

Find the Duplicate: To quickly find the other duplicate in the **Timeline**, **Control**-click on the **Dupe Detection** indicator. A shortcut menu will tell you where it is (Figure 4.4). If you select the item, it will move the playhead to its location in the sequence.

4.4   Shortcut Menu for Dupe Detection

2. Hold down the **Option** key and select the audio portion of the second shot, *Backstage06*.

3. With the **Option** key still pressed, tap the **Down** arrow key twice. This will move the stereo pair of audio down two tracks. This can be done with any tracks, video or audio, as long as there is nothing in the way, like another clip, that prevents it.

Note

Toggling Linking: Option-clicking the audio (or video) edit point will toggle off **Linked Selection**, if **LS** is turned on. If **Linked Selection** is off, **Option**-clicking the edit point will toggle it on.

4. Again holding down the **Option** key, drag the head of the audio edit point toward the beginning of the **Timeline** (Figure 4.5). While you drag it, a small box will appear. It gives you a time duration change for the edit you are making. If **Snapping** is turned on, it may be helpful to toggle it off with the **N** key.

5. Repeat the process on the other side of the audio. Holding down the **Option** key, drag out the audio so that your sequence looks like Figure 4.6.

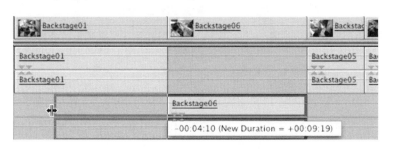

4.5   Dragging Audio to Create Split Edit

4.6 Timeline after Making Split Edits

You have now created two split edits for the clip *Backstage06*.

Adding Audio Transitions

➤ Note

Linear or Logarithmic: FCP has two cross fades, the default +3dB as well as a 0dB transition. The +3dB cross fade that FCP calls an equal power cross fade is generally preferred because it gives a logarithmic roll of sound, which is the way sound really works. The 0dB cross fade is a linear fade. It will often produce an apparent dip in the audio level at the midpoint of the crossover from one track to the other.

We want the sound of the first shot, *Background01*, to fade out before it ends. The simplest way to do this is to apply an audio cross fade.

1. Select the edit point by clicking on it.

2. To add the audio transition, either use the menu **Effects>Audio Transitions>Cross Fade (+3dB)**, or use the keyboard shortcut **Command-Option-T**.

Because the audio is not butted against anything, the application will by default create an end-on-edit transition, as shown in Figure 4.7. We'll look at transitions in much greater detail in the next lesson.

In the Viewer

You can also create a split edit in the Viewer. Let's first set up a new sequence.

1. Begin by again duplicating the *Rough Cut* sequence.

2. Open the duplicate sequence and delete everything but the first shot.

4.7 Cross Fade Transition Applied

Slipping Out of Sync

Sometimes when you move an unlinked audio track it may accidentally slip out of sync with the video material. If that happens, you'll see time indicators in the **Timeline** tracks (Figure 4.8) showing you how far out of sync the clips have slipped. The time slippage shows in a red box. The minus number means that the audio is three frames ahead of the picture. A plus number indicates that the audio is behind the video.

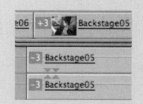

4.8 Out of Sync Audio

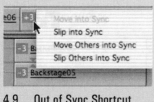

4.9 Out of Sync Shortcut Menu

4.10 Typing in Numeric Value to Move Audio

If the audio does slip out of sync, the easiest way to get it back in sync is to **Control**-click on the red box and choose from the options available in the shortcut menu (Figure 4.9).

You could also nudge the clip back into sync. **Option**-click on the audio to select the audio portion of the clip. If you just click on the audio, you'll select both video and audio even though they are out of sync. With only the audio selected, use the < or > keys to slide the clip forward or backwards.

As it moves, the time displays will update and finally disappear when the clip is back in sync. Every hit of the < or > keys nudges the clip one frame. Holding down the **Shift** key will nudge the clip the trim amount you selected in your **Multi-Frame Trim Size** in **User Preferences**.

You can also select the audio portion of the clip (or whichever portion has free track space around it) and type plus or minus the value in the red box as in Figure 4.10. Then press the **Enter** key to move the clip.

Let's do this with a clip from the **Browser**.

3. Find the clip *Backstage06* in the *Clips* bin in the **Browser**.

4. Double-click on it to open it into the **Viewer**. Because we want to use all the audio, begin by marking a split audio In point at the beginning of the clip. With the playhead at the very start of the shot, either **Control**-click and from the shortcut menu choose **Mark Split>Audio In** (Figure 4.11), or use the keyboard shortcut **Command-Option-I**.

5. Play through the clip till you find the In point for the edit at about 1:23;14.

6. Instead of hitting **I** to enter the In point, hit **Control-I**.

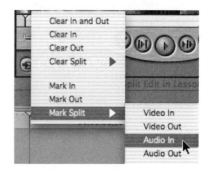

4.11 Marking Split Audio In

4.12 Split Edit in Viewer

Next we'll make the split edit for the Out point.

7. Play forward till you get to the Out point at 1:28;22.

8. Instead of hitting **O** to enter the Out point, hit **Control-O**.

Note the markings in the **Viewer** scrubber bar and on screen in Figure 4.12 that indicate the split edit.

Viewer To Timeline

The simplest way to work with the split edit in the **Viewer** is to drag and drop to the **Timeline**.

4.13 Patch Panel Setting Destination
Tracks

1. Open the sequence called *Split Edit* by double-clicking on it.

2. Reset the destination tracks by pulling the **a2** button down to **A4** and the **a1** button down to **A3** in the patch panel at the head of the tracks as in Figure 4.13.

3. With the playhead at the end of the shot in the **Timeline**, drag the clip from the **Viewer** to the **Timeline**, as in Figure 4.14.

What may happen is that the edit will be performed as in Figure 4.15. This seems to be a bug in the software that has not been fixed as of this writing. Should that happen, grab the clip and slide it to butt up against the first shot, as shown in Figure 4.16.

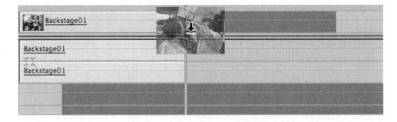

4.14 Dragging Split Edit to the Timeline

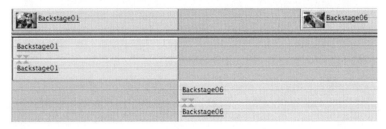

4.15 Displaced Split Edit in Timeline

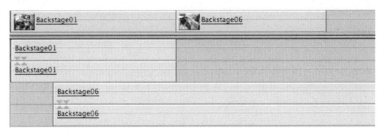

4.16 Correctly Placed Split Edit

Controlling Levels

Next we need to look at how to control the audio levels. This can be done either in the **Timeline** or in the **Viewer**. It's easier and quicker in the **Timeline**, but the **Viewer** controls afford a great deal more precision.

In the Timeline

To work in the **Timeline**, let's return to the first *Rough Cut* duplicated sequence that still contains all the clips. To adjust the audio levels in the **Timeline**, you first need to turn on the **Clip Overlays** button in the lower left corner of the **Timeline** window (Figure 4.17) or use the keyboard shortcut **Option-W.** It's a good idea to leave the **Clip Overlays** turned off when you're not using them, because it's easy to accidentally shift the level line while just trying to grab a clip to move it.

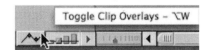

4.17 Clip Overlay Button

4.18 Dragging the Levels Line

4.19 Pen Tools

4.20 Adding a Keyframe

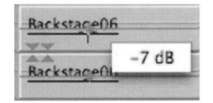

4.21 Lowering the Keyframe Level

When the **Clip Overlays** are turned on, a thin pink line appears through the middle of the audio portion of the clips. This is the audio level control for the clips. Notice also the thin black line that appears at the top of video. This controls the opacity for the video portion.

Play the audio for the third shot in the sequence, *Backstage05*. It's pretty low and adds nothing to the soundtrack except to muddy it a bit. To eliminate the audio, you could select the audio portion of the clip with the **Option** key and delete it. However, if you ever decide you want that audio or if you move the clip to a place where the audio is needed, it's a bit of a nuisance to get it back.

A simpler way is to reduce the audio level to zero. With **Clip Overlays** turned on, move the cursor over the line. It will change to the **Resizing** tool. Grab the line and pull it down to the bottom of the clip as shown in Figure 4.18.

Fading Levels in the Timeline

You usually don't want to reduce the overall levels. More often you'll want to reduce the levels of portions of the sound, raise other portions, or fade in or out. For a simple fade up, you could use the cross fade transition that we saw earlier, or you can do it by fading the level line. To do this you use the **Pen** tool. There are a number of them available in the very last of the **Tools** (Figure 4.19). You can also call up the **Pen** tool with the **P** key.

Let's create a fade in at the beginning of the second shot, *Backstage06*, that's on **A3/A4**.

1. Move the **Pen** over the pink level line in the clip. The cursor will change to a pen nib, allowing you to click on the line to create an audio keyframe (Figure 4.20). This adds a tiny diamond to the levels line.

2. Put a keyframe about one second from the beginning of the shot by clicking with the **Pen** tool on the level line.

3. As you move the cursor to the newly created keyframe it will change into a simple crosshairs cursor. This lets you grab the keyframe and move it up or down. Pull the keyframe down to about −7dB as in Figure 4.21. Notice that because there are no other keyframes on the level line, the volume for the entire clip is reduced.

4. Take the **Pen** tool and grab the very left end of the level line. Pull it down to create a curved fade up ramp (Figure 4.22.)

🐎 *Note*

Stereo Pair: Notice that as you lower the level, both tracks go down together. That's because these tracks are a *stereo pair* of audio tracks, indicated by the inward pointing pairs of triangles you see in the Time-line. Should you have separate tracks for **Mono (a1)** and **Mono (a2)** audio, you'll have to lower each track separately. Should you need to switch from **Mono (a1)/Mono (a2)** audio to a stereo pair or vice versa, select the clip and go to **Modify > Stereo Pair**, or use the keyboard shortcut **Option-L**.

4.22 Fade Out in the Timeline

We haven't finished with *Backstage06* yet. We still need to bring the sound up to full level as the shot is introduced, and then fade it out at the end.

5. To bring the level back up first add a keyframe at about the point where the cross fade begins on **A1/A2**.

6. Next, add another keyframe at about the point where the cross fade ends. Push the level line back up to 0dB (Figure 4.23). Because this is the last keyframe on the level line, everything after that point will come back up to full volume.

7. Finally, we want to fade out the audio at the end. With the **Pen** tool, add a keyframe to the level line about two seconds before the end of the clip. Go to the end of the clip, and pull the end of the line all the way down to create a slow fade out as in Figure 4.24.

⭐ *Tip*

No Switching Necessary: If don't want to switch to the **Pen** tool from the standard **Selector** tool, as you move the cursor to the level line and it changes to the **Resizing** tool, hold down the **Option** key and the cursor will automatically change to the **Pen** tool. If you are working with the **Pen** tool and you want to switch to the straight-level line-moving **Resizing** tool, hold down the **Command** key.

Controlling Track Levels

There may be occasions when you want to change the audio level for an entire track—say, of music—to give it a lower base level,

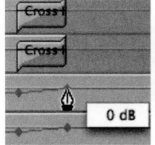 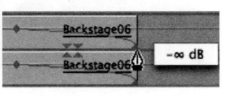

4.23 Ramping Up the Audio (far left)

4.24 Slow Fade Out (left)

Waveform in the Timeline

When you're working in the **Timeline**, it may be beneficial to turn on the waveform display in **Timeline** window (Figure 4.25).

Do this by going to the **Timeline Options** popup on the lower left corner of the **Timeline** window, where we saw **Dupe Detection** earlier, and select **Show Audio Waveforms**, or use the keyboard shortcut **Command-Option-W**.

Because displaying the audio waveform in the **Timeline** takes a good deal of computer processing power (prereading the audio and then displaying it), the redraw ability and video playback capabilities of the computer are markedly slowed down. So it's a good idea to toggle the waveform display on and off as needed with that handy keyboard shortcut.

4.25 Waveform in Timeline

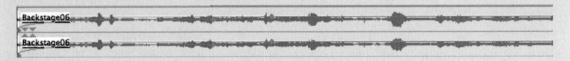

especially CD music, which is often recorded and compressed at maximum audio levels, often too high for use with most digital video systems. You can do this by selecting the track you want with the **Track** tool, the third button in the **Tools** (Figure 4.26).

You can select a single track, multiple tracks forward and backward, a single track forward and backward, or a whole track of audio and adjust its level globally.

4.26 Track Tools

Select the items or the track with the **Track** tool (**T**). Once you have your track or clips selected, go to **Modify>Levels**, or use the keyboard shortcut **Command-Option-L**.

This command calls up a dialog box that allows you to adjust the audio levels of the clips (Figure 4.27). The slider or the value box will change the gain setting for all the clips selected. The **Relative** and **Absolute** popup sets how the gain is affected. **Absolute** will make the level you set affect the whole of all the clips, eliminating any fades. Using the **Relative** setting will change the value of the levels relative to any current settings or fades. This global levels control not only works on audio, but also works on opacity as well on a title or on the video portion of a clip.

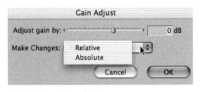

4.27 Level Controls

Another way to change the audio level of more than one clip is to change its attributes. You can copy an audio clip by selecting it and pressing **Command-C**. Select the clips you want by marquee-ing or **Command**-clicking, and then use **Paste Attributes** from the **Edit** menu or press **Option-V**. Then check the attributes you want to paste to the other clips' **Levels** or **Pan** values (Figure 4.28).

4.28 Pasting Audio Attributes

Notice the **Scale Attributes Over Time** checkbox at the top. It defaults to the on position. If you have keyframed the levels in the copied clips, that keyframing will be distributed proportionately onto the pasted clip, based on the relative durations of the clips. If the copied clip is shorter, the keyframing will be spread out; if it is longer, the keyframing will tighten up. If you want to paste the keyframes in the same duration as in the copied clip, uncheck **Scale Attributes Over Time**.

✒ Tip

Changing a Range of Keyframes: You can also change the relative or absolute levels of a group of audio keyframes. Use the **Range** tool (GGG) to select the area that includes the audio keyframes (Figure 4.29). If you then apply the **Levels** function, it will raise or lower the relative or absolute values of the keyframes in the selected area.

4.29 Range Selection of Audio Keyframes

More Fades

Before we look at how to control audio levels in the **Viewer**, let's down some more work on the *Rough Cut copy* sequence.

Take a look at the fifth shot in the sequence *Backstage11*. We need to overlap its audio underneath the adjacent clips.

1. With the **Option** key pressed, select the audio portion of the clip. Still holding down the **Option** key, tap the **Down** arrow key twice to move the stereo pair onto **A3/A4**.

2. Holding down the **Option** key again, drag out the front and end of the audio portion of *Backstage11* so that it overlaps the adjacent clips as in Figure 4.30.

3. The next step is to add a fade out at the end of *Backstage04* on **A1/A2**. Select the edit point and use the keyboard shortcut **Command-Option-T** to put in the default audio transition.

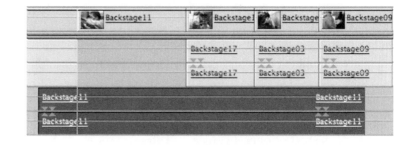

4.30 Backstage11 Overlapping Clips

Backstage17, which immediately follows *Backstage11*, is quite loud and has a pronounced music track. Like you did with *Backstage05* earlier in the sequence, suppress its sound completely by dragging the level line right down to the bottom.

For the next shot, *Backstage03*, I want to fade up the sound, but as so often when working with video, I want the fade to come up before the shot actually begins.

1. Use a roll edit or extend edit to move the audio portion of the shot earlier in the sequence.

2. To do this again, hold down the **Option** key and click on the edit point in the audio portion of the clip.

3. Now either use the **Roll** tool to move that audio edit about a second earlier, or do an extend edit, moving the playhead about one second earlier and pressing the E key to create a split edit that looks like Figure 4.31.

4. To complete the fade, with the edit still selected, press **Command-Option-T** to add the cross fade.

I would like to fade in the overlapping *Backstage11* a little earlier. To do this I need to ripple the sequence to move the overlapping on **A3/A4** so that they butt up against each other. We'll do this with the **Ripple** tool.

1. With the **Ripple** tool, select the left side of the edit between *Backstage04* and *Backstage11*.

4.31 Roll or Extend Audio Edit (above)

4.32 Multitrack Ripple Edit (right)

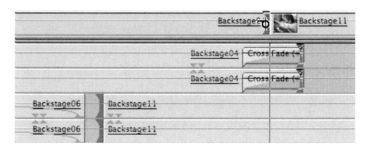

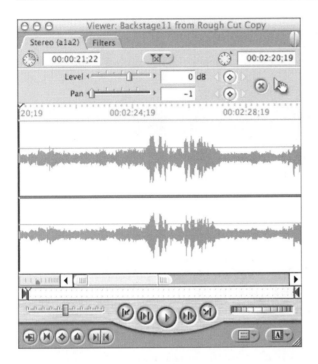

4.33   Audio Viewer (left)

4.34   Decibel Level Change Indicators

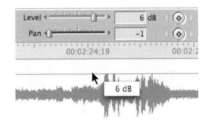

2. Hold down the **Command** key and click just to the left of the audio portion of *Backstage11*, in the empty space between it and the previous shot (Figure 4.32). You'll now ripple the empty space together with *Backstage04*.

3. Pull the edit until the audio tracks collide on **A3/A4**.

In the Viewer

Let's add the fade at the beginning of *Background11* in the Viewer.

1. Hold down the **Option** key again and double-click on the audio portion of the clip. This opens the clip to the **Audio** tab in the **Viewer** (Figure 4.33). Here you see the clip's audio waveform.

Notice the mauve line in the center of the audio track. As you move the cursor over the line, it changes to the **Resizing** tool we saw earlier, which allows you to raise and lower the audio level.

At the top of Figure 4.33 you'll notice the **Level** slider and the **Decibel Indicator** box. It's currently at 0, which is the level at which the audio was digitized or captured.

As you move the line up or down with the cursor, both the Level slider and the Decibel Indicator box at the top move. A small

> ✈ **Tip**
>
> **Real Time Adjustment:** You can adjust audio levels in real time while playing in the **Audio** tab of the **Viewer**. Press **Control- +** to raise the level and **Control- -** to lower it. After a small hesitation, the audio will continue to play. Unfortunately, you can't actually mix like this. These controls only affect the clip's overall level. They won't take audio keyframing into account.

window appears in the waveform as well that shows the amount in decibels that you're changing the audio level (Figure 4.34).

1. To add a keyframe, either use the **Pen** tool or hold down the **Option** key as the cursor approaches the level line. The cursor then changes into the **Pen** tool.

2. Go about one second into the shot in the **Viewer** and add a keyframe.

3. Go back to the beginning of the clip and pull the level line down so that the audio fades up from the beginning of the shot (Figure 4.35).

You can also add keyframes with the little diamond button next to **Level** slider.

4. Click the little button, which will turn green while adding a keyframe to the level line. Go to a different point in time. Then pull the **Level** slider up or down to change the sound volume, and another keyframe will be added.

4.35 Audio Fade In

There are several ways to delete an audio keyframe:

- Grab it and pull it down out of the audio timeline.
- Hold down the **Option** key when you're over the keyframe. The cursor will change into the **Pen Delete** tool (Figure 4.36).
- Use the shortcut menu, by clicking on the keyframe and selecting **Clear**.
- If the playhead is sitting on a keyframe, you can also remove it by clicking the little green keyframe diamond next to the **Levels** slider. This will turn the keyframe button gray and remove the keyframe in the **level** line.

To move the keyframe, grab it and slide it left and right along the line.

4.36 Pen Delete Tool

One of the great features for editing sound in the **Viewer** is that you can do it with great precision, down to 1/100th of a second. To do this you have to zoom into the waveform, either with the scaling tab at the bottom of the **Viewer** window or with the **Zoom** tool (Figure 4.37), which you can call up with the **Z** key. To zoom out, hold down the **Option** key while you click in the waveform. You can also use **Command-+** to zoom in and **Command- -** to zoom out. The black band in Figure 4.37 represents one frame of video, and you can zoom in farther still. Notice the tiny slice of audio that has been cut out of the track, less than one video frame in length.

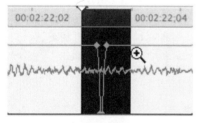

4.37 Zoom Tool in the Waveform with Audio Slice

Middle of the Sequence

Let's finish off the *Rough Cut copy* sequence. There are only a few more levels to tweak. Further along in the **Timeline** is another portion of *Backstage05*. This time we do want to use the sound.

1. Again with the **Option** key, select the audio portion of the clip and move the stereo pair down to **A3/A4**.

2. Extend the front of the sound until it butts up against *Backstage11*, also on **A3/A4**.

3. Next, extend the end of the sound as far as it will go, which isn't that far.

Between *Backstage03* and *Backstage05* are two shots, *Backstage09* and *10*. Both of these shots are quite loud.

4. Marquee-drag or **Command-**click to select the pair of them, and use **Modify>Levels** or **Command-Option-L** to reduce their levels to –9dB.

⭐ Tip

Zoom a Marquee: You can also use the **Zoom** tool to drag a marquee along a section of the waveform to zoom into just that portion of the display. This technique will work in the **Viewer**, the **Canvas**, as well as the **Timeline**.

Fixing Soft Audio

Sometimes audio is just too low to be as forceful as you'd like, even after you crank it up with FCP's level controls. A neat little trick is to double up the audio tracks. Just put another copy of the same sound on the track below. A simple way to do that is to hold the **Option** key to select just the audio. Hold the **Option** key and drag down to see the right-pointing Insert arrow. Now add the **Shift** key to constrain the direction, and change the arrow to the downward-pointing **Overwrite** arrow. Drop the audio on the tracks below. You will have created a duplicate. Now push that audio level up as well. Double your pleasure.

A neat new feature of FCP4 is the ability to merge up to 24 tracks of audio with a single track of video. Normally this is done in the **Browser**. In fact, when you're working in the **Timeline**, the **Merge Clips** function in the **Modify** menu is greyed out. But you can still do it in the **Timeline** to your audio-doubled clip. Select the clip, then **Command-**click the duplicate audio tracks to select them as well, and use **Modify > Link** or **Command-L** to link them all together as a single clip with four or more audio tracks.

Another way to increase really low audio levels is to use nesting. Turn the clip volume as far up as it will go, which is 12dB, select the clip, and use **Sequence > Nest Item(s)** or the keyboard shortcut **Option-C**. This will embed the clip in a sequence of its own. The audio for the nested sequence will be at the 0dB level, and you can raise it another 12dB to further boost the sound. To delete all the keyframes in the audio, click the **Reset** button, the button with the red **X** next to the grab handle at the top of the panel (Figure 4.38).

4.38 Reset Button

Pan Values

In addition to the mauve level line in the **Viewer**, there is also a purple pan line. In a stereo pair such as this material, the pan lines are defaulted to –1. This indicates that the left channel is going to the left speaker and the right channel to the right speaker. By moving the lines up toward zero as in Figure 4.39, the two tracks are centered between the speakers. Going to 1 will make the channels cross over and swap sides. You can also just type in a value in the **Pan** slider box.

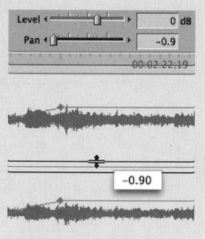

When you have a multitrack recording with separate **Mono (a1)** and **Mono (a2)** sound, the **Viewer** appears with separate tabs, one for each channel. Level and Pan values can then be set separately for each channel, one set to –1 and the other to 1. This allows you to move the audio from one side of the stereo speakers to the other.

4.39 Changing Spread Value

When you're working with separate channels using the pan line, you can shift the sound to come from either the left side or the right side. Moving the **Pan** slider to the left to –1 will move all the sound to the left speaker, and moving the **Pan** slider all the way to the right to 1 will move the sound to the right speaker. Like **Levels**, **Pan** values can be keyframed. The classic example is the racing car that approaches from the left with all sound coming from the left speaker, roars by, and disappears to the right, while the sounds sweeps past to the right speaker.

A little trick to quickly get the channels centered between the speakers is to select the clips in the **Timeline** and use the keyboard shortcut **Control-period** to center the tracks to the zero value.

5. To smooth the transition between *Backstage09* and *Backstage10*, add a cross fade transition between the pair.

6. Add a cross fade transition to the beginning of *Backstage13*, which follows *Backstage05*. Select the edit point at the beginning and press **Command-Option-T**.

7. With the **Pen** tool, add a slow fade out to the end of *Backstage13*. The middle portion of the sequence should now look like Figure 4.40.

End of the Sequence

There is an interesting little problem in the ending portion of the sequence that will again require a ripple edit of empty space.

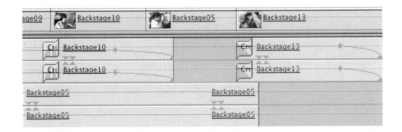

4.40 Middle Portion of the Completed Sequence

1. Pull the audio tracks for *Backstage02* down onto **A3/A4** and extend them front and end as far as you can.

2. For *Backstage16*, which is the second to last shot, just add a cross fade at the edit point.

3. One more stereo pair to pull down onto **A3/A4**, the last shot *Background14*. Bring the audio down to **A3/A4** and extend the front until it meets *Backstage02* on **A3/A4**.

I want to put a cross fade transition between the two shots on **A3/A4**, but I can't because there isn't enough media available on the end of *Backstage02*. I need to ripple that shot back by 15 frames to create enough space for the overlap.

4. With the **Ripple** tool, select the edit at the end of *Backstage02*. Holding down the **Command** key, click just to the left of the beginning of *Backstage16* tracks on **A1/A2**, as shown in Figure 4.41.

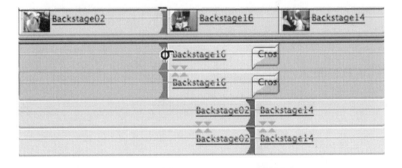

4.41 Selecting the Ripple Edits

5. Pull the edit point to the left so that it moves 15 frames, or edit it numerically (Type *–15* and press the **Enter** key). As you type, a little box will appear at the top of the **Timeline** window telling you that you're rippling the edit (Figure 4.42).

6. Finally, add the cross fade between the two audio clips on **A3/A4**.

4.42 Numerical Ripple Edit

4.43 Audio Mixer

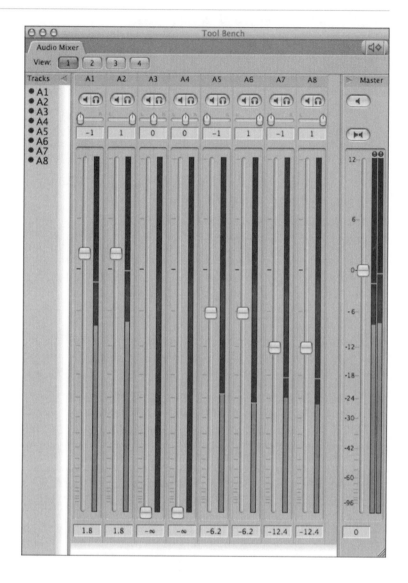

Audio Mixer

New to Final Cut Pro 4 is the introduction of an audio track mixing console. You can call it up directly from the **Tools** menu or with the keyboard shortcut **Option-6**. Better still, from the **Windows** menu, select **Arrange>Audio Mixing**. This brings the **Audio Mixer** into FCP's **Tool Bench** (Figure 4.43).

The numbers of tracks that appear in the mixer is determined by the number of tracks in the active sequence. Switch sequences and the number of sliders changes to match the sequence.

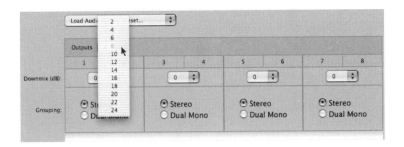

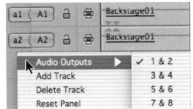

4.45 Selecting Output Channels

When you're working with DV, only two output channels appear on the right edge. In other formats that allow more outputs, more channels will appear. You can output up to 24 channels, if you have the hardware to support it, and edit to tape up to eight channels of output. You can select the number of channels in your **Sequence>Settings** (**Command-zero**) in the **Audio Outputs** panel (Figure 4.44). To set which track goes to which output channel, **Control**-click at the head of the track in the **Timeline**, and choose from the shortcut menu (Figure 4.45).

Though the standard level for digital audio is –12dB and the absolute volume that digital audio can reach is zero, notice that the output meters exceed zero. This isn't because you can go beyond zero as you can in analog audio; it's there to give you an indication of how far over zero your audio is being driven, which the regular audio meters in FCP do not do.

For complex mixing you often don't want to have all the tracks visible at once. You can set which tracks are visible with the patch panel dots on the left edge of the mixer. The **View** buttons above that let you preset different groups of tracks. The patch panel and **View** buttons can be seen in Figure 4.46. **View 1** might be set to show all the tracks, while **View 2** would be only **A5/A6** and **A7/A8** as in Figure 4.46, while **View 3** was only **A1/A2** and **A3/A4**, whatever arrangement you want.

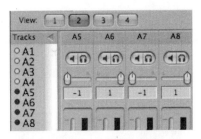

4.46 Patch Panel and View Buttons

The horizontal sliders in Figure 4.46 are pan sliders, letting you control the spread of audio channels. Notice also the **Mute/ Solo** buttons, which let you mute individual tracks, or solo them so that only a single channel or combinations of channels are heard as you need. These **Mute/Solo** buttons are also available in the **Timeline**. You open them by clicking on the tiny speaker button in the far lower left corner of the **Timeline** window, which pops open the array of **Mute/Solo** buttons (Figure 4.47), just like the ones in the mixer. Notice the green **Visbility** (audibility) buttons

4.47 Timeline Mute/Solo Buttons

4.48 Keyframe Button

4.49 Audio Keyframe Settings

at the head of the **Timeline**. The difference between these and the **Mute** buttons is that when audibility is switched off, that track will not play out to tape. If a track is muted, it will still output even though it can't be heard during playback in the **Timeline**.

To control your levels with the mixer, move the sliders up and down as desired. If the audio is a stereo pair, moving one slider will move the pair. It's best to work this mixer by setting levels for individual tracks one at a time. It's only a virtual mixer, and you only have one mouse, not 10 fingers, to move the sliders. Unfortunately, as yet there is no feature that gangs groups of sliders together.

When you set the level with a slider, it sets the level for the whole track from when you mouse down up until you release the mouse. The default is for the sliders to work on the levels for the whole track, but you can automate your slider controls to create keyframes. To do this, you have to activate the **Keyframe** button in the upper right corner of the mixer (Figure 4.48), which can also be toggled on and off with the keyboard shortcut **Command-Shift-K**. When this is on, whatever you do with the sliders will be recorded and appear as keyframes in **Timeline**. There are three settings in the **User Preferences** for the amount of keyframes added to the track (Figure 4.49). The default **Reduced** is a good compromise. **All** can produce thousands of keyframes, while **Peaks Only** is too coarse and produces very long slow ramps.

☞ *Tip*_____

Scrolling Sliders: FCP4 works with a scroll wheel. Wherever you place the cursor—in the **Timeline, Browser, Viewer**—the scroll wheel will function. One great thing about this is that the scroll wheel can be used to control the audio mixer sliders. Just place the cursor over a slider and twirl up or down with your scroll wheel to move the slider.

Audio Peaks

FCP can analyze the audio levels of a clip or a sequence and place markers indicating where the sound exceeds acceptable levels. You can then either pull down the levels or keyframe the area around the overloaded audio and pull it down that way. It's simple to do.

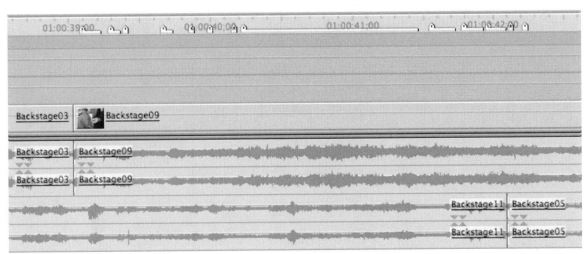

4.50 Audio Marks in the Timeline

Start by selecting the clip you want analyzed, either in the **Browser, Viewer,** or an active **Timeline** window. Then choose from the **Mark** menu **Audio Peaks>Mark.**

The application will quickly look through the clip or sequence and place a marker wherever it detects an audio peak. With sequence markers, the analysis is done quickly, and with waveforms displayed in the **Timeline,** it's easy to see where the peaks are occurring, especially if you zoom into a section of the **Timeline** more closely, as in Figure 4.50.

Notice also that if there are extended portions of peak audio, FCP will place extended markers in the **Timeline.** It may be an idea to bring down the overall levels on some of these clips to make the audio levels acceptable. Lower the levels with the tools we've seen, and run the analysis again.

You can clear audio peak markers either with the standard marker clearing tools (**Control- accent**) or individual markers. To specifically delete audio peak markers, from the **Mark** menu choose **Audio Peaks>Clear.**

Voice Over

FCP has a **Voice Over** tool that allows you to record audio tracks directly to your hard drive while playing back your **Timeline.** **Voice Over** is most valuable for making *scratch tracks,* test narrations used to try out pacing and content with picture. It could be used for final recording, though you'd probably want to isolate

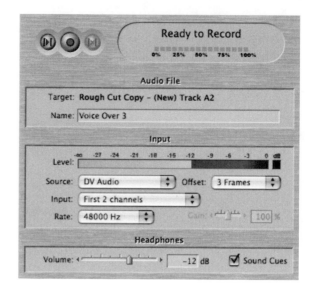

4.51   Voice Over Tool

the computer and other extraneous sounds from the recording artist. Many people actually prefer to record narrations before final editing, so that the picture and sound can be controlled more tightly. Others feel that recording to the picture allows for a more spontaneous delivery from the narrator. However you use it, **Voice Over** can be an important tool.

Voice Over is part of the **Tool Bench**. You can call it from the **Tools** menu, which brings up the window in Figure 4.51.

First you'll have to configure your recording setup for **Source**, **Input**, and **Sampling Rate**.

Source defines where the sound is coming from: the computer mic input, a USB device, a camcorder, or an installed digitizing card.

Input controls the type of signal being received, whether it's line level, balanced audio in, digital audio, or whatever your source device is capable of handling.

Offset adjusts for the delay taken by the analog to digital conversion. USB devices typically take one frame. DV cameras can be three frames or more.

Let's look at some of the controls in this panel:

- The large red button, the middle of the three in the top portion of the window, is the **Record** button. It will also stop the recording, as will the **Escape** key.

⟍ Note_____

More RAM for VO: Because Voice Over works in RAM (storing the sound before recording it to disk), you may need to put more RAM into your computer over and above the minimum requirements asked for by FCP4 because the audio is buffered in RAM as it's recorded. 48kHz audio consumes 6MB per minute. So a half-hour track would take 180MB. After the recording is finished, the audio is dumped from RAM to disk and stored in your *Capture Scratch* folder with the project name.

- The button to its left is the **Preview/Review** button and will play the selected area of your sequence.

- The button to the right is the **Discard** button. Pressing it will delete the just-recorded or aborted file from your hard drive.

- The **Gain** slider, next to the **Input** popup, allows you to control the recording level based on the horizontal LCD display meter. This is fine for scratch tracks, but for finished work, it would probably be better to have a hardware mixer before the input for good mic level control.

- The **Headphones** volume does just what it says. If there is nothing jacked into the headphone output of your computer, the sound will come out of the computer speaker itself. To avoid recording it or the **Sound Cues**, pull the **Volume** slider down to the minimum level.

FCP gives the recording artist elaborate sound cues, which are turned on with the little checkbox. Together with the aural sound cues in the headphones, there is visual cuing as well, which appears in the window to the right of the **Record** button. As the recording starts, a countdown begins, with cue tones as the display, that starts pale yellow becomes darker and more orange until the recording begins. Then the display changes to red. There is a cue tone at 15 seconds from the end of the recording as well as beeps counting down the last five seconds to the end of the recording. Recording actually begins during countdown and continues two seconds after the end of the recording during finishing. Though this doesn't appear in the **Timeline** after the recording, you can just drag out the front and end of the clip if the voice started early or overran the end.

I think the best way to work with **Voice Over** in the **Timeline** is to define an In and Out point as in Figure 4.52. If no points are defined, recording will begin at the point at which the playhead is parked and go until the end of the sequence, or until you run out of available memory, whichever comes first. You can also define an In point and go from there, or define an Out and go from the playhead until the Out is reached. Because the **Timeline** doesn't scroll as the sequence plays, it might be helpful to reduce the sequence to fit the **Timeline** window. **Shift-Z** will do this with a keystroke.

> **✎ Note**
> **Playback Levels:** Don't be fooled by FCP's vertical audio meters. These display the playback levels, and do not show the recording level.

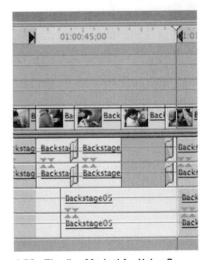

4.52 Timeline Marked for Voice Over

Recording is always done to a destination track that has free space. If there is no free space within the defined area of the recording, **Voice Over** will *always* create a new track. So if you record multiple takes, they will record onto the next lower track or onto a new track. The **Audio File** window, just above the meter, will give you the track information. If there is no free space, a new track will be created. You can name the recording in the **Audio File** window, and each take will be numbered incrementally.

After a discarded take, **Voice Over** will record to the previously assigned track with the previously assigned name. After a few takes, you may want to discard a previous take and reassign the targeted track so that **Voice Over** will work with the empty tracks you vacated.

If you're going to be doing multiple takes, make sure you use the **Mute** button to switch off tracks with previous takes so that they do not play back during recording. Once several takes are recorded, you may want to play back the various takes to see which is the best. Just use the **Solo** button to hear individual tracks to assess performance. You can also solo individual items, which may be as simple. Select the VO track you want to listen to, and choose **Sequence>Solo Item(s)** or use the keyboard shortcut **Control-S**. For some reason, this function has never been made available in the shortcut menus.

Tip
No Timecode in Voice Over: There is no timecode or other identifying information other than the assigned name with any **Voice Over** recording, if you need to reconstruct your project at a later date. It may be a good idea to keep this recording preserved on tape or other digital media like a DVD if you want to use it again.

After a recording session with **Voice Over**, it's a good idea to go into your hard drive and root out old unnecessary tracks that may be filling up your drive. It's probably simplest to do this from the application. Those takes you recorded that you no longer want can be deleted from your sequence, but they aren't automatically deleted from your hard drive. You can't make something offline from inside a sequence, but you can drag the unneeded takes into a bin in your **Browser** and from there make them offline, deleting them from the drive. Also remember, the recordings are only a part of your sequence and will not appear in your **Browser** at all, unless you put them there.

Summary

In this lesson we looked at working with sound in Final Cut. Performing split edits, overlapping sound, cutting with sound, overlapping and cross fading tracks, as well as FCP's new **Audio**

Double System Sound

When you shoot film, the sound is recorded on a separate audio recorder, what's called *double system sound*. More and more people working in video seem to be returning to double system sound, often using a DAT recorder to get better quality recordings than is possible recording directly to the camera. Handling this material has often been a problem for editors working in video. FCP4's **Merge** feature, which we saw earlier, makes this process simpler than ever.

4.53 Merge Clips Dialog

1. First capture your video and your separate sound track. If your video and audio have locked timecode tracks, FCP makes this merge a quick menu trip away.

2. Select the two pieces of material, video and audio, that you want to merge, and from the **Modify** menu choose **Merge Clips**. This will bring up the dialog box in Figure 4.53.

3. Select the **Timecode** button and click OK.

If your video and audio don't have shared timecode, it's still simple to do.

1. Open the video into the **Viewer** and find a common sync point that you can see and which is also audible. A clapperboard is, of course, the best way to do this, but a simple hand clap will suffice.

2. Mark the clap strike as your In point.

3. Open the audio file into the **Viewer** and find the audible clap strike there and mark that as your In point.

4. Now when you run **Merge Clips**, select **in points** in the **Merge** dialog box. Obviously if the clapperboards are end sticks marking the tail of the shot, you mark Outs on your media and use **out points** in the **Merge** dialog. When you merge the clips, a new clip is created in your **Browser**. The new clip takes its name from the video clip and adds *Merged* to the name.

Audio and video do not have to be the same duration or have the same start or end times. The application will create a merged clip long enough to cover the whole duration of the media, beginning with the one that starts first, video or audio, and ending with whichever ends last.

Mixer, its **Audio Peaks feature**, and its **Voice Over** tool. Sound is often overlooked, seeming insignificant or of minor importance, but it is crucial to making a sequence appear professionally edited.

When you want to smooth out cuts or to change between scenes, you might want to use transitions. That's what we're going to look at in the next lesson: how they work, and how to use them.

Lesson 5

Adding Transitions

Transitions can add life to a sequence, ease a difficult edit into something smoother, or give you a way to mark a change of time or place. The traditional grammar of film that audiences still accept is that dissolves denote small changes, while a fade to black followed by a fade from black mark a greater passage of time. With the introduction of digital effects, any imaginable movement or contortion of the images to replace one with another quickly became possible—and were quickly applied everywhere, seemingly randomly, to every possible edit. They can be hideously inappropriate, garish, and ugly. But to each his own taste. Transitions can be used effectively, or they can look terribly hackneyed. Final Cut Pro gives you the option to do either or anything in between.

Loading the Lesson

Let's begin by loading the material you will need for this lesson on the hard drive of your computer.

1. If you don't already have it on your media drive, drag the *Lesson 3 Media* folder from the DVD to it. We'll use this media again to demonstrate how transitions work.

2. You should also drag the folder called *Transitions* from the DVD onto your media drive. This contains samples of each of the 60 transitions available in FCP4.

3. Also make sure you have the *Projects* folder on your system drive.

4. Eject the DVD and look inside the *Projects* folder on your hard drive, where you'll find a folder called *Lesson 5*.

5. Inside that folder, double-click the project file *Lesson 5* to launch FCP4.

6. Once again, go through the reconnect process as in Lesson 5 on page 68.

Inside your copy of the project *Lesson 5* you'll find in the **Browser**:

- An empty sequence called *Sequence 1*
- The master clip *Food*
- A still image called *Gradient.pct*, which we'll use later
- The bin called *Clips*
- The bin called *Transitions*

We'll be working with the food clips again to see how transitions work and how to control them.

Applying Transitions

Next let's look at the transitions themselves. In the **Browser**, usually behind the project window, is a tab called **Effects**. If you open it, you see a window with a group of folders—sorry, bins—as in Figure 5.1. You'll notice more than transitions in this window. For the moment, we're going to concentrate on the *Video Transitions* bin.

The **Effects** window does not maintain strict interface standards: for some reason, the **Name** column does not force alphanumeric ordering. The order is created internally in FCP, and the first bin is *Favorites*. You can park your special transitions and effects here. It's probably empty now.

Note

As of this writing the wonderful FXScript DVE's created by Klaus Eiperle have not been included in FCP4 due to an oversight. I hope this will be rectified by the time you read this, and some of FCP's best transitions will be restored to the the application.

5.1   Effects Window

Double-click on **Video Transitions** to open the bin. It should look like Figure 5.2. The **Video Transitions** window shows yet more bins, and these bins contain a total of 60 video transitions. I'd be very surprised if any one has actually ever used them all in earnest on real projects, not just playing with them to try them out. The *Transitions* bin in your **Browser** contains previews of each of the transitions available in FCP4. We're going to try some of them out in this lesson, but first let's see how the *Favorites* bin works.

Favorite Transitions

Click on the disclosure triangle to twirl open **Dissolve**, which holds seven different types of dissolves. Notice that **Cross Dissolve**, which is the most commonly used transition in video or film, is probably in bold. Whenever a transition's name appears in bold in either the *Video Transitions* folder or in the **Effects>Video Transitions** menu, that indicates that the transition can be played back in real time. These transitions only appear like this if your system is capable of real-time playback.

5.2   Video Transitions Window

How many transitions appear as real time will also depend on your RT settings, which we saw in **Playback Control** in Lesson 1 on page 11. At **Safe RT** with the quality set to **High**, you'll get fewer transitions than with **Unlimited RT** set to **Low**.

Grab the **Cross Dissolve** and drag and drop the transition over to the *Favorites* bin. Twirl open the *Favorites* bin. You may notice that the transition in the *Favorites* bin is a duplicate. The usual behavior when moving items from one bin to another is that the item is relocated. But when moving an element to *Favorites*, a copy is created. You can put any transitions, video or audio; any effect; or even a generator into *Favorites*. Though multiple types of items can be placed into this bin, only the appropriate items will appear in the **Effects** menu below **Video Transitions** in *Favorites*, as in Figure 5.3. You can rename the transition or effect anything you want, so perhaps you'd like to keep handy an eight-frame dissolve. Just copy **Cross Dissolve** into *Favorites*. Change its name to something like **Frames**, and then change its duration to your favorite length. You may have to do this twice because the duration box sometimes sticks on one frame.

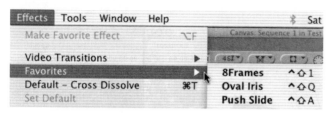

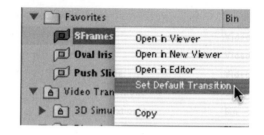

5.3   Video Transitions Favorites Menu (above)

5.4   Set Default Transition (right)

Notice in Figure 5.3 that below the *Favorites* menu item that's selected is the default effect, in this case, **Cross Dissolve**. It's simple to set the default transition. You can either:

• Set it with the menus by selecting the transition in the *Video Transitions* bin and choosing **Set Default** from the **Effects** menu, or

• **Control**-click on the transition in the *Video Transition* bin, and from the shortcut menu choose **Set Default Transition** as in Figure 5.4.

You can also create a favorite transition from one applied in the **Timeline**. This allows you set up a complex transition such as a page peel or a gradient wipe, which we'll see a bit later, and then save it into your *Favorites* bin.

1.   To do this, create the transition and set it up to taste in the **Transition Edit** window, which we'll look at a shortly.

2.   With the **Transition Edit** window active, choose from the **Effects** menu **Make Favorite Effect**, or use the keyboard shortcut **Option-F.** The effect will appear in the *Favorites* bin just as you set it up.

👉 *Tip*

Favorites: Your *Favorites* are saved as part of your *Preferences*. If you trash your *Preferences* file, your *Favorites* go with it. There is a simple solution to this. Drag the *Favorites* bin from the **Effects** panel and place it in your **Browser**. This is a copy of the *Favorites* bin in **Effects**, and it will remain with the project, even if the prefs are trashed. I keep a *Favorites* project containing a **Browser** with a constantly updated *Favorites* bin as well as a sequence to which I add color mattes or slugs to which whole effects or groups of effects applied. I save the project regularly as part of my backup routine to external drives and DVD disks.

After the default transition is set, it will appear underlined in the bin.

The default duration for all transitions is one second. You can set any duration you want in the **Transitions** bin, and that will be the default duration for that transition.

So what's all this about default transitions? In Lesson 3 we skipped two items in the **Canvas Edit Overlay**:

- **Insert with Transition**
- **Overwrite with Transition**

The default transition will appear in your sequence when you select **Insert with Transition** (**Shift-F9**) or **Overwrite with Transition** (**Shift-F10**), or use the keyboard or shortcut menu to enter a transition.

Checking the Media

1. Let's begin by opening up *Sequence 1*.

2. Next select the two clips from the *Clips* bin, *Food2* and *Food4*, and drag them directly to the sequence.

Remember these are all subclips, and so each shot you just placed in the timeline contains the full extent of the media for that clip on the hard drive. Or at least Final Cut Pro thinks so.

Let's try putting a transition onto the sequence we've laid out, the two *Food* shots.

3. Grab the **Cross Dissolve** transition from the *Dissolve* bin and drag it onto the edit point between *Food2* and *Food4*.

You see that this isn't possible because you get the transition drag icon with a small **X** as in Figure 5.5. Why is this happening? The answer is simple. There isn't enough media in either clip to perform the transition. The shots must overlap; frames from both shots must appear on the screen simultaneously. For a one-second transition, both shots have to have one second of media that overlaps with the other shot.

5.5 Transitition Error

1. Double-click *Food2* in the **Timeline** to open it into the **Viewer**.

2. Go to the end of the shot. Use **Shift-O** to take you to the Out point.

If **Overlays** are switched on in the **View** pop (Figure 5.6) as they normally are, you'll see the telltale film sprocket hole indicator on the right edge of the frame (Figure 5.7). This overlay tells you that you're right at the end of the available media for the shot. There needs to be extra media available to create the overlap for the transition, as shown in Figure 5.8.

The pale shot on the left has to overlap the dark shot on the right by half the length of the transition, and vice versa. If that media does not exist, you can't do the transition. FCP usually assumes as a default that the transition takes place centered around the marked edit point, not that it ends at the edit point. Therefore, to execute the default one-second transition, you need at least half a second, 15 frames, of available media after the Out point on the outgoing shot, and 15 frames in front of the In point of the incoming shot. In this case there is nothing, hence the **X**. Unless you think of it ahead of time, which many times you don't, you'll have to deal with it when you're fine tuning your edit. Often you'd rather not deal with transitions while you're laying out your sequence, leaving them until you've laid out the shot order.

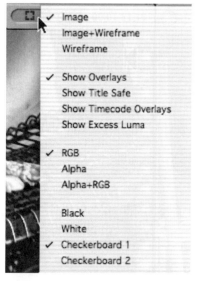

5.6 View Popup

5.7 Film Sprocket Overlay in the Viewer

🐎 Note _____

Positioning the Transition: The only time FCP does not presume to center the transition on the edit point is when there is overlapping media available on the incoming side of the transition and not on the outgoing shot. Then, if there is extra material on the incoming shot, FCP will end the transition at the edit point. However, if there is media available on the outgoing shot, but none on the incoming shot, FCP will not create a transition properly. If there isn't enough media to create a transition of the duration requested, it will make one for as much media as there is available, centering it on the edit point.

If you know you have extra media in the original clip, you can always go back to extend the media. If this option is available, it's easy to do in FCP. Select **Remove Subclip Limits** from the **Modify** menu.

5.8   Overlapping Video

However, in this case, extending the media will extend it into another shot, producing a flash frame during the transition, something to be avoided. To be able to put in transitions, we'll have to trim the Out point on *Food2* and the In point of *Food4*. Let's do that in the **Timeline**.

1. Select the **Ripple tool** from the **Tools** palette, or use the keyboard shortcut **RR**.

5.9   Ripple Tool in the Timeline

2. With the **Ripple** tool click just to the left of the edit point between *Food2* and *Food4* as in Figure 5.9.

3. With **Ripple** active, type in –15 for a 15-frame ripple. Notice the display that appears in the middle of the **Timeline** window (Figure 5.10). Press **Enter**.

This is the navigation shortcut for going back half a second. Because we're using the **Ripple** tool, we're rippling back half a second.

5.10   Ripple Value in the Timeline

4. Click on the right side of the edit point at the start of *Food4*.

5. This time type in *+15* and press **Enter** to ripple that side of the edit point by 15 frames.

We've now rippled *Food4's* In point by half a second, half a second off the end of the first shot, half a second off the beginning of the second.

6. Once you've rippled the two edits, go the edit point in the sequence between *Food2* and *Food4*.

7. From the menus, select **Effects>Video Transitions>Dissolve>Cross Dissolve**.

5.11 Clips Overlapping in the Transition Edit Window

Tip

Quick Transition: The quickest way to add a transition to an edit is to go to the edit point, park the playhead over it, and press **Command-T**. This will add the default transition with the default duration.

This adds a cross dissolve transition to the edit point. You can also go to the *Video Transitions* bin, either from the *Dissolves* bin or from *Favorites*, and drag and drop the transition onto the edit point. The transition does not need to be dragged only to the center line. It can also be dragged to the outgoing clip so that the transition ends at the edit point, or to the incoming clip so the transition begins at the start of the clip. This can only be done, of course, if there is sufficient material for this type of transition.

If you double-click on the transition itself in the **Timeline**, it will open into the **Viewer**. This is the **Transition Edit** window, which we'll look at in detail in a moment. Here you can see how the video overlaps and why extra material—handles—are needed on either end of the transition to create the effect (Figure 5.11).

Once it's in the **Timeline**, the transition displays in one of three ways, depending on how it was placed. Figure 5.12 shows the center position; the other two appear as in Figure 5.13, an end-on-edit transition, and Figure 5.14, a start-on-edit transition.

Notice the sloping line indicators showing the type of alignment in each case, and also note that the two latter transitions can only be half-second dissolves. When the sequence was rippled by 15 frames on each side of the edit point, only enough media was made available for a center-aligned transition. If the transition is

5.12 Center on Edit Transition

5.13 End on Edit Transition

5.14 Start on Edit Transition

to end on the edit point, the incoming shot has to be extended a whole second underneath the outgoing shot to accommodate it. Similarly, if you wanted to start the transition on the edit point, the outgoing shot has to extend one second into the incoming shot, one second beyond the start of the edit point. If we made these changes, then we could also easily change the type of transition alignment with a shortcut menu on the transition in the **Timeline** (Figure 5.15).

Using the Canvas Edit Overlay

Let's back up a bit to see another way to do this.

1. Delete everything in the **Timeline**.

2. Open up *Food2* from the **Browser** into the **Viewer**.

Because this will be the first shot in the timeline, I won't need to shorten the front of the clip.

3. Press the **End** key to take you to the end of the shot.

4. Type *–1.* (minus one period) and press **Enter.** This will move the playhead back one second.

5. Press **O** to enter the Out point and drag to the **CEO Overwrite** box, or press **F10** to overwrite it into the **Timeline**.

6. Open *Food4* in the **Viewer** from the **Browser.** This clip we will shorten front and end.

7. Go to the beginning of the clip and type *+1.* and enter an In point.

8. Then go to the end of the clip and enter an Out point one second before the end (type *–1.* and press **O**).

9. Drag *Food4* from the **Viewer** to **Overwrite with Transition**— not to **Overwrite.** Or enter **Shift-F10.**

The clip immediately drops into the **Timeline** after the first clip. The default transition has been added at the beginning of the clip, as well as a default audio cross fade (Figure 5.16). Adding the audio cross fade is a bonus that often enhances the edit and helps to smooth the transition.

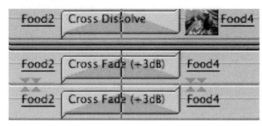

5.16   Transition with Cross Fade

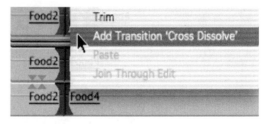

5.17   Transition Shortcut Menu

Contextual Menu Transition

A third method can be used to add the default transition.

1. **Control**-click (or right-click with a two-button mouse) on an edit point as in Figure 5.17.

2. Select **Add Transition**.

This procedure will evoke the defaults for transition type and duration, if sufficient media is available. If not, FCP will make a transition of whatever length is available. If no media is available, no transition will be created. If media is available only on one shot, the transition will be created offset on one side or the other. The shortcut menu transition will also add the audio cross fade.

Rendering

After you've entered a transition, you'll see that the narrow bar at the top of the **Timeline** has changed color from the normal mid-gray. It will have changed to red, green, yellow, or orange, depending on the type of transition you applied, your system capabilities, and your RT settings. If you are working with a system with no real-time capabilities, then a bright red line will appear over the transition, indicating that a portion of the sequence needs to be rendered.

Rendering means that the application has to create media for a portion of your timeline where none exists. Most of the two shots in your sequence are on your hard drive, but not for the 30 frames that make up this one-second cross dissolve, during which one shot is changing into the other. The material of one shot mixed together with another is not on your hard drive. All you've done is give the computer instructions to create that media. If you try to play across that part of the timeline with a non–real-time system, the **Canvas** will momentarily display the message in Figure 5.18.

5.18   Unrendered Warning

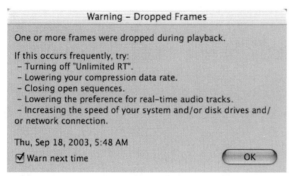

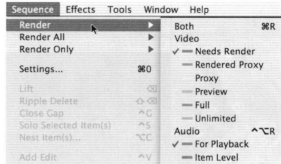

5.19 Unlimited RT Dropped Frame Warning   5.20 Sequence > Render

If you have a real-time capabilities, Final Cut can play through the timeline without prior rendering. It processes the transition on the fly in real time as it plays. If your system is capable of real-time transitions, this bar would appear green. Real-time transitions will be highlighted in bold in your bins and in the menu. If you have your RT settings, which we saw in Lesson 1 on page 12, on **Unlimited RT**, you may get a yellow or an orange bar. The yellow bar indicates that playback is a proxy only; that is, if you've created a complex setting for your transition, only the default will be visible in real time. Orange indicates that you will likely get dropped frames when playing through this area. If you do playback through you will normally get the dropped frame warning message in Figure 5.19. If you switch this warning off in the lower right corner, you can then work in **Unlimited RT** without hindrance, though with the occasional frame drop. To turn on the dropped frame warning, you'll have to go back to your **User Preferences** and switch it back on in the **General** panel.

Render Commands

FCP4 has made rendering extremely flexible. What gets rendered when is controlled by a complex combination of settings in the **Sequence** menu under **Render, Render All,** and **Render Only**.

The **Render** menu (Figure 5.20) controls rendering of a selection, either a clip, clips, or a segment of the **Timeline** marked with In and Out points. Normally only the red **Needs Render** bar is checked for both video and audio. If you want to force a render on any of the other available items, select it. It will remain checked in the menu. Whenever you give the **Render Selection**

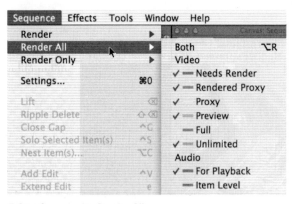

5.21 Sequence > Render All

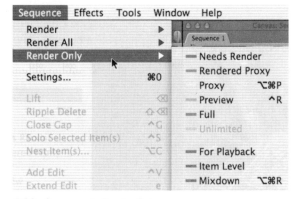

5.22 Sequence > Render Only

command (see Table 5.1), those checked items will be included in the render.

Table 5.1   Table Render Commands

Render All	**Option-R**
Render Selection	**Command-R**
Render Audio Selection	**Control-Option-R**
Render Proxy	**Command-Option-P**
Render Preview	**Control-R**
Mixdown Audio	**Command-Option-R**

In FCP4's render settings is the new ability to render audio at item level. This allows you to render a piece of audio such as an MP3 file or a piece of 44.1kHz CD music into the correct sampling rate as a separate item. Wherever you place that audio in your **Timeline,** it will be fully rendered to the correct settings. It will have a blue indicator bar on it to tell you it's been rendered as an item and will not need to be re-rendered.

The **Render All** menu (Figure 5.21) gives you same list except many more items are checked by default. The **Render Only** menu (Figure 5.22) is similar. It allows you to render selected items without changing the settings in **Render** and **Render All**. Note the inclusion in the **Render Only** menu of **Mixdown** for audio. This allows you to render out a mixed audio file of all your tracks, allowing easier playback. This is particularly important when outputting to tape.

Render Previewing

Should you want to look at your material without rendering it, in real-time, you have a couple of different options. One is **Quick-View**, in the **Tools** menu. The **QuickView** window (Figure 5.23) allows you to play through a section of video by building a cache file in RAM. The more RAM you have available, the more the application will able to store.

5.23 **QuickView Window**

There's only one button on the window, a **Play** button. Click to play; click to stop. Of course, you can also use the spacebar. No **J**, **K**, and **L** keys, however. There is only one direction and one speed: forward and looping. The **QuickView** window is like the Energizer bunny: it just keeps playing and playing, trying to cache as much as it can with any available RAM, until you press the spacebar to stop it. With the window set to **Auto** (in the **View** popup menu at the upper right), it will keep doing RAM previews of whatever is in the active window. Switch to the **Timeline,** and it will start previewing around the position of the playhead. Switch to the **Viewer,** and it will start playing that. The little popup also allows you to designate a screen to preview: **Canvas, Viewer,** or **None.** I don't know why there is a **None** option, to be honest.

The **Resolution** popup in the upper left does just that: sets the resolution of playback to **Full, Half,** or **Quarter** (Figure 5.24). The lower the resolution, the more you'll be able to preview, but the poorer the quality. The default duration for QuickView is two seconds, which is ideal for checking one-second transitions. To increase the amount of time previewed, use the **Range** slider at the bottom of the window. It goes up to 10 seconds. If you do increase the range to its maximum and you don't have enough RAM to hold 10 seconds of video as well as do the processing, **QuickView** will never be able to get the preview up to speed. It will always be dumping cached frames to pick up new ones. So either reduce the range or reduce the resolution.

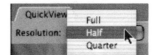

5.24 **Resolution Popup**

Another way that I like to play through a section that needs rendering is to use the keyboard shortcut **Option-P** or **Option-**. This is a good way to see if the transition will play smoothly, if there are any unforeseen flash frames or other unpleasant hiccups in the effect. The faster your system, the faster it will play through the transition. What's nice about this is that FCP caches the playback,

Render & Playback

☑ Filters
☑ Frame Blending For Speed
☑ Motion Blur

Render

Frame Rate: 33% ⇕ of Sequence Editing Timebase

Resolution: 100% ⬙ of Sequence Frame Size
50%
33%
25%

5.25 Render Control

so that the first time you play back using the shortcut, it might take quite a while, but the next playback using **Option-** will be considerably faster, even in real time on the slowest systems.

Render Control

Rendering settings were an important feature in earlier versions of FCP and were located close at hand in the upper left corner of the **Timeline** window, where the **RT** selection popup is now. If what is rendered has been made more complex in FCP4, the quality control of your renders has been greatly simplified. Normally FCP will render to full resolution, but it's still possible to adjust your render settings, though the process is a little more hidden than it used to be.

Render settings are now set in the **Render Control** panel (Figure 5.25) at the back of the **Sequence Settings**, which can be called up from the **Sequence** menu or with the keyboard shortcut **Command-zero**. Here you can set what you want to render, as well as control your render quality with the **Frame Rate** and **Resolution** popups. Setting these two popups to lower numbers will greatly speed up your rendering process.

In previous versions, changing from one render setting to another meant that you lost your renders, at least temporarily, and had to re-render. When you switched back to the original render setting, your renders would still be there. In FCP4 you no longer lose your render, not until you make an alteration to the material. This means that you can have material in various render resolutions throughout your sequence simultaneously.

Render Manager

The **Render Manager** is in the menus under **Tools>Render Manager**. This feature lets you selectively delete unwanted or old render files from your hard drive. What's nice about the **Render Manager** is that you can delete files not only from the project you're working on at the moment, but also from any other projects that are on your Scratch Disks. (Figure 5.26).

It's simple to delete files. Check in the **Remove** column the items you wanted deleted and press **OK** or the **Enter** key. It's good practice to go through the **Render Manager** periodically to weed out old render files. You might find some lingering items you'd long forgotten. It's probably a good idea to check through the **Render Manager** about every month or so.

Controlling Transitions

Once you've played back your transition a few times in **Quick-View,** you may discover that it doesn't look quite the way you'd want it to. You may want to shorten or lengthen it or shift the actual edit point. Assuming you have material available for this, it is easiest to do in the **Timeline** itself. To change the duration of the transition, grab one end of it and pull, as in Figure 5.27. It's a good idea to switch **Snapping** off before you do this, because it's easy to snap the transition down to nothing. As you pull the transition, a little window displays the amount of change as well as the new duration of the transition. If you have an audio cross fade as well as a transition, that will also change with your action. While you're dragging the transition end, you'll get the two-up display in the **Canvas** that shows you the frames at the ends of the transition (Figure 5.28). Notice the tell-tale film sprocket holes on the right edge of the frame. While extending the transition, I reached the limits of media available to one shot.

You can also change the edit point in the center of the transition. Move the **Selector** to the center of the edit, and it will immediately change to the **Roll** tool, allowing you to move the edit point and the transition along the timeline, left and right as desired (Figure 5.29). You can also ripple either shot, but to do that, you have to call up the **Ripple** tool (**RR**) and then pull either shot left or right, shortening or lengthening the sequence while not affecting the transition (Figure 5.30). Again, the two-up display in the **Canvas** will show you the frames you're working on.

Note

Exporting: Changing the Record to Tape settings in the RT popup will not affect export settings. If you export a sequence, it will export your material as it's currently rendered, regardless of the settings in the RT popup. So if some of your material has been rendered in low resolution, when you export there will be no warning that your material needs to be re-rendered at high resolution. There is also no way to force the application to do that.

Render Manager

Name	Type	Size	Remove	Last Modified
▼ 📁 Additional Render Files	Bin	918.3 MB		
▶ 📁 Animated Cutout	Bin	40.7 MB		
▼ 📁 FCP	Bin	577.2 MB	✓	
▶ 📁 Animated Comp	Bin	14.3 MB	✓	
▶ 📁 Drop Shadow	Bin	14.3 MB	✓	
▶ 📁 Sequence 1	Bin	265.6 MB	✓	
▶ 📁 Sequence 11	Bin	15.0 MB	✓	
▶ 📁 Sequence 11 1	Bin	207.1 MB	✓	
▶ 📁 threeLayers.p	Bin	34.3 MB	✓	
▶ 📁 Title 3D pan	Bin	26.4 MB	✓	
▶ 📁 FCP3	Bin	30.8 MB		
▶ 📁 Lesson 1 copy	Bin	146.7 MB		
▶ 📁 Lesson 2	Bin	3.4 MB		
▶ 📁 Lesson 5	Bin	15.1 MB		
▶ 📁 Sample Project	Bin	45.1 MB		
▶ 📁 Tips Project	Bin	59.3 MB		
▶ 📁 Lesson 5	Bin	3.4 MB		
▶ 📁 Lesson 5a	Bin	3.4 MB		
🖼 Render Files in Undo Queue	Render Files	23.3 MB		Unknown

Render Files Selected: 577.2 MB

Check in the Remove column to delete unwanted render files or free up disk space.

(Cancel)   (OK)

5.26 Render Manager Window

5.27 Lengthening Transition in the Timeline (above)

5.28   Two-Up Display in Canvas (right)

5.29 Rolling the Transition Edit Point

5.30 Rippling the Transition Edit Point

5.31 The Transition Edit Window

Transition Edit Window

Final Cut gives you another way to control the transition and fine tune it. This is done in the **Transition Edit window** (Figure 5.31).

Double-click on the transition itself in the **Timeline** window to bring up the window, which opens in place of the **Viewer**. The **Transition Edit** window displays the transition as a separate track between the two video tracks on which the clips sit.

Here you can control the transition. At the top is a small group of buttons (Figure 5.32) that let you position where the transition will occur. The transition will be placed in the default centered position between the two clips, shown by the middle button in Figure 5.32. Using the left button moves the transition so that it begins at the edit point. The right button in moves the transition so that it ends at the edit point.

The primary purpose of the **Transition Edit** window is to access the controls some transitions offer you. Here you can also fine tune the effect, to shorten or lengthen it as needed. As in the **Timeline**, you can do this by dragging either end of the transition. The **Canvas** displays the end and start frames for the two shots.

By grabbing the center of the transition, you evoke the **Roll** tool, which allows you to drag the transition forward and backward along the clips, provided there is available media.

You can also ripple edit either the end of either outgoing or incoming clip by pulling it. You don't have to call up the **Ripple** tool. Moving the cursor into position will change it to the appropriate tool. Different shades of blue indicate the limits of the media. As with all ripple edits, you are changing the duration of

5.32 Transition Alignment Buttons

➤ *Tip*

Alignment Shortcuts: You can switch between the three transition alignment types with keyboard shortcuts. **Option-1** sets to begin at the edit point, **Option-2** to center on the edit point, and **Option-3** to end on the edit point. These are the numbers on the keyboard, not the keypad numerics. Using the **Option** key with the keypad controls the **Autoselect** function for the audio tracks.

Transitions between Sequences

Because FCP allows you to place sequences within sequences, it sometimes becomes necessary to create transitions between them. This presents some problems. FCP treats each sequence as a complete piece of media. So as we've seen, if you have used the media to its limits, you can't create a transition.

If you want to create a transition between sequences, you have to either ripple the sequences in the **Timeline** or open the edit point into the **Trim Edit** window and ripple the outgoing sequence and the incoming sequence to allow room for the transition.

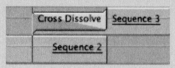

5.33 Sequences Overlapping for Transition

Another way (for many transitions, except those that don't require both clips to move) is to place the second sequence on **V2**, overlapping the first sequence, and place a start on edit transition at the head of the sequence on **V2** as in Figure 5.33. This will bring it in over the outgoing sequence without having to fuss with trimming.

Note
Navigating the Transition Editor:
The **Grab Handle** in the upper right corner lets you pull a transition from the **Transition Edit window** onto an edit point in the **Timeline**. This is useful if you've opened the editor directly from the *Video Transitions* bin. This is the only way you can grab it to drag the transition to the Timeline.

the tracks involved and may be pulling the alignment of clips on different tracks out of kilter.

Notice in the **Transition Edit** window the two sliders, one for **Start** and the other for **End**, each with adjacent percentage boxes. The transition starts at 0% completed and ends at 100% completion. You can adjust these sliders so that the **Cross Dissolve**, for instance, will pop in at more than zero to start or suddenly finish before the transition reaches completion. In **Cross Dissolve** this produces a rather ugly effect. There is also a small arrow button to the right of the **End** slider. This will swap the effect for you. Below that is a small circle with a red cross in it. This is the **Parameters Reset** button. Neither of these has value in **Cross Dissolve** but will be important later for more complex transitions, as we shall see in a moment. Also note that the **Reset** button does not reset the sliders nor the arrow, only the other parameters.

Using Transitions

Now that we know how to add and trim transitions, let's look at some of the transitions themselves. To change the transition from **Cross Dissolve**:

- Drag the new transition from *Video Transitions* bin in the **Effects** window and drop it on the existing transition in the **Timeline**, or

5.34 Cube Spin (above)

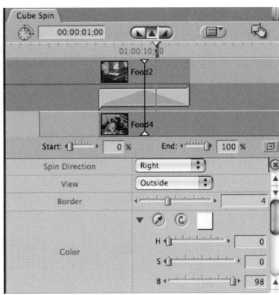

5.35 Cube Spin Control (right)

- Select the transition in the **Timeline** by clicking on it and then select a new choice from the **Effects>Video Transitions** menu.

I'm not going to go through each of the transitions, though I would like to highlight a few because they are representative and show you how the controls work in some of the other changeable transitions. To see what the transitions themselves look like, take a look at the *Transitions* bin in the **Browser**. This contains short clips that show how each of the transitions behave, with a couple of exceptions, all at their default settings. Many of the transitions have lots of variables, such as colored borders and the direction in which a motion transition occurs. Here are grouped samplings of the FCP's 60 available transitions. Most of the transitions under one heading, with the exception of the **QuickTime** group, will have similar controls and features.

Cube Spin

Cube Spin is a typical 3D simulation transition. It will roll your clips around as though they were stuck to either the outside or the inside of a cube (Figure 5.34).

The controls for the transition are fairly simple: a couple of pop-ups, sliders, and a color picker (Figure 5.35).

Spin Direction lets you change between right, left, up, or down.

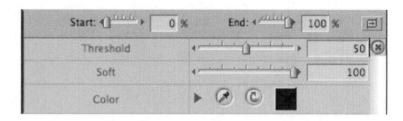

5.36 Dip to Color Controls

View can be either the default **Outside**, where you're looking at a cube turning in front of you, or **Inside**, with you inside the cube watching it turn around you.

The **Border** slider controls the width of the border, and **Color** lets you pick a color for the border either from the swatch, an eye-dropper, or opening the disclosure triangle for **Hue, Saturation,** and **Brightness** (**HSB**) controls.

The little arrow on the right edge of the controls will switch the direction of the motion from the currently set to the opposite. If it's set to right, it'll make it go left, for example, so it's not much use.

Dip to Color Dissolve

The default setting of the **Dip to Color Dissolve** using black as the color is the same as FCP's **Fade In Fade Out Dissolve,** but a couple of controls (Figure 5.36) make this unique.

One is **Threshold,** which determines when the fade will occur in the transition. The earlier the **Threshold,** the quicker the fade out will be, and the slower the fade in. The higher the **Threshold,** the slower the dip to color, but the faster the transition comes out of the color. Basically this allows you to create an asymmetrical fade out and fade in, which is often very useful.

Soft controls how long the color is held on the screen. Set at the default 100, the color (or the center of the fade) is no more than a couple of frames on either side of the edit point. By moving the slider into lower numbers, you can control how long the color remains on the screen. With the slider at zero, the color will pop on the screen and last the full length of the transition before popping off again. Combined with **Threshold,** you have full control to create an asymmetrical fade out and to specify how long the fade lasts on the screen before it comes back up again.

Another popular—perhaps overly popular—use of this effect is to specify a very pale color instead of black and then to make the

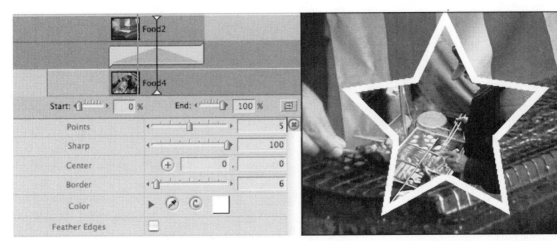

5.37 Star Iris and Controls

transition very short to produce a flash effect. It's commonly used for bridging two sections of an interview that would otherwise be a jump cut. There are other ways to do this, such as using a bright color for a **Luma Map** transition, which works well too.

Star Iris

Star Iris does exactly what its name says. It uses a star shape to wipe the image on or off the screen (Figure 5.37). The difference between an iris transition and a wipe transition is that an iris can have a variable center point. You can iris out from a person's head, for instance, while a wipe is always fixed around the center of the image.

The **Star Iris** controls include a **Points** slider, which varies the numbers of points in the star. The default is 5.

Sharp controls how pointy the star is. When set at the normal 100, the star is very angular. Bringing the value down toward zero, you can create an almost circular shape.

You can add a **Border** here, like in **Cube Spin**, or you can use **Feather Edges** of the iris. In this case, the **Border** slider controls the softness of the feathering.

Page Peel

Page Peel is often overused, but sometimes it really is the right effect, particularly for wedding videos (Figure 5.38). This transition has a number of controls that allow you to modify its look (Figure 5.39).

5.38 Page Peel

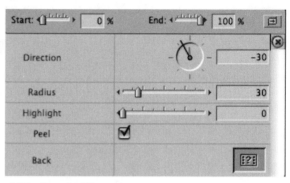

5.39 Page Peel Controls

1. The **Direction** dial sets the angle at which the pages turns back. The default is –30 and pulls the lower right corner toward the upper center of the image.

2. The **Radius** slider sets the arc of the page peel. A small number will make it peel very tightly, while a high number will make the turn of the page quite loose.

3. The **Highlight** slider puts a gleam of light on the back of the turning page. The farther to the left you move the slider, the more muted the shine becomes.

4. The **Peel** checkbox is defaulted on. With it unchecked, the page doesn't only peel back, it also curls under as it goes. The smaller the **Radius** value, the tighter the curl becomes.

5. The tiny arrow checkbox in the upper right corner toggles between peeling the page off, the default, and peeling the page on, an unusual variation.

Note

Static Well: Unfortunately, the Well won't track an image or change if a video clip is used. The Well uses the In point of the video clip as its map. In the case of **Page Peel**, there is no movement on the backside of the page. Sorry.

One of **Page Peel**'s interesting features is the **Well**, which lets you use another image as part of an effect. The **Well**, the indented filmstrip icon that controls the **Back** function, lets you map another image onto the back of the page peel. The default is to place the same image, flopped, on the back of the page, but you can use any image in your project.

To put a color on the back, as in Figure 5.38, use the **Generators** in the **Viewer** to create a color matte.

1. Open any clip into the **Viewer**. The **A** with the **filmstrip** icon in the lower left corner evokes the **Generators** (Figure 5.40).

2. Select **Matte>Color.**

3. Go to the **Control** tab (Figure 5.41) and click on the color swatch, the small gray box to choice a color for your backing.

4. Drag the matte from the **Video** tab of the **Viewer** into the **Browser.**

5. Reopen the **Page Peel** transition from the **Timeline,** and pull the **Color Matte** from the **Browser.**

6. Drop it into the **Well,** making it part of the transition.

👉 **Tip** _____

Selecting Color: Whenever you need to select a color from anywhere on your desktop, click on the color swatch to open the **Color Selector.** If you hold down the **Option** key, you will get an eyedropper that will let you select a color from anywhere on the computer desktop.

Push Slide

The **Push Slide** is often used when making still slide shows where one images pushes the other out of the frame and replaces it. The controls (Figure 5.42) are pretty straight forward, an **Angle** dial and controls for adding a **Border.**

Angle defaults to straight down, but you can set to any angle you want. At –90 the incoming image will slide in from the right and push the outgoing image off the left side of the screen.

The **Border** can be quite useful. It not only helps in separating the images more clearly, but it also covers the black band that appears on the edge of some digitized images. This is normally in the blanking area under the television mask and not seen by the viewer. However, if the image is moved, as it is here and in other digital video effects, the black edge becomes visible. The **Border** will help to disguise that, or at least make it a feature.

5.40   Generators Button

🐿 **Note** _____

Color Picker: The Color Picker offers a number of different color samplers. The RGB picker uses the Photoshop standard of 0–255 colors and is the best to work with for video. To keep colors NTSC safe, don't let the slider for any color exceed 235. This may produce color on the computer screen that looks muddy, but in video they'll be vivid without being oversaturated.

5.41   Color Matte Controls Tab

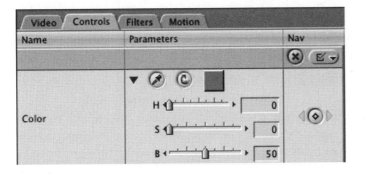

5.42 Push Slide and Controls

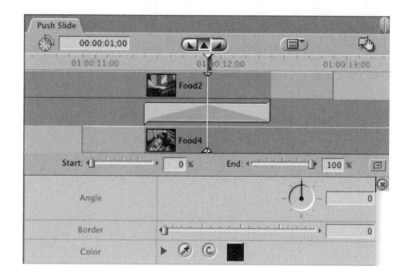

Gradient Wipe

The **Gradient Wipe** is a deceptively simple-looking filter with very few controls. Its real power lies in the **Gradient Well** (Figure 5.43). In its default condition, it's nothing more than a simple wipe from left to right.

In the **Browser** is an image called *Gradient.pct*. If you open it up and take a look at it in the **Viewer**, you'll see that it's a complex, grayscale checkerboard pattern. This is the basis of patterning in a gradient wipe. The image will be wiped on or off, based on the grayscale values of pattern image. The darkest parts of the pattern image will be where the incoming image will appear first, and the lightest parts will be where the image will appear last. In the gradient pattern we have, some of the outside boxes will appear first, as in Figure 5.44. The lower left to upper right diagonal of the image will still be from the outgoing shot. There is no end to the variety of patterns you can get to manipulate this control. If you don't like a pattern, replace it with another. To really see the power of transition effects, you should look at what Michael Feerer has created with his Video Spices. Check them out at http://www.pixelan.com. They add an important tool to Final Cut's transitions. His patterns can be used not only inside his own transitions, but inside **Gradient Wipe** as well.

Everybody has their favorites. **Gradient Wipe** is probably mine, after a simple cross dissolve. Klaus Eiperle has created an even more powerful version of **Gradient Wipe**, called **Softwipe**, which is well worth having. Find out about it at http://cgm-online.

Gradient		🔁
Softness	◁——┴——┴——┴——┴——▷	0
Invert	☐	

5.43   Gradient Wipe Controls (above)

5.44   Gradient Wipe Pattern (right)

com. I like it because it is so infinitely variable, and you can always find some way to make it look just a little different and just right for the effect. A trick I've used in the past is to use a grayscale frame of either the outgoing shot or the incoming shot as the image for the **Well**. It makes the transition like a slightly sharp-edged dissolve because the elements of the shot itself are affecting how the transition happens.

Conclusion

That's it for transitions. Everybody has their favorites, and there are probably many that you'll never use. Many should probably never be used. Next we'll look at the text and titling tools within Final Cut Pro itself.

Lesson 6

Adding Titles

Every program is enhanced with graphics, whether they are a simple opening title and closing credits or elaborate motion graphics sequences illuminating some obscure point that can best be expressed in animation. This could be a map with a path snaking across it or a full-scale 3D animation explaining the details of how an airplane is built. Obviously, the latter is beyond the scope of both this book and of Final Cut Pro alone. But many simpler graphics can be easily created within FCP. That said, I think all experienced users of this application will agree that the character generator included with the first version of Final Cut Pro was not as good as it could have been. With every full new version of the software, additional capabilities have added to the titler, functions such as built-in scripts for standard animations, scrolls (vertical movement), crawls (horizontal movement), and a typewriter effect, which is pretty neat. In version 2 Boris Script was added as an effect; in version 3 Boris Calligraphy was added as one of the **Generators**, providing more options for titling motion and 3D animation; and finally version 4 includes LiveType as a separate stand-alone application. LiveType warrants a book all of its own, which can't be included in this work. It is certainly a powerful special effects and motion graphics tool, a worthwhile investment of the time to learn its capabilities.

155

In this lesson, we will look at typical titling problems and how to deal with them. As always, we begin by loading the project.

Loading the Lesson

This should be familiar to you by now. Let's begin by loading the material you need onto your media drive.

1. First, drag over the *Lesson 6 Media* folder from the DVD onto the media drive of your computer. We'll be using some of this material as background media of our titles.

2. Make sure you have the *Projects* folder on your hard drive.

3. Make sure the DVD is ejected from your computer, and double-click the *Lesson 6* project file to launch the application.

4. Reconnect the media files as you have done in previous lessons.

Setting up the Project

Inside the project in the **Browser** you'll find a number of sequences that we shall explore in the course of this lesson. One of the sequences, *Sequence 1*, is empty, ready for you to use. There is also a master clip called *Kabuki* in the *Clips* bin.

1. Begin by opening *Sequence 1*.

2. Drag a clip—let's say, *Kabuki3*—from the *Clips* bin and drop it on **Overwrite** in the **CEO** (**Canvas Edit Overlay**).

Text Generator

6.1   Text Generator

Now let's look at Final Cut's **Text Generators**.

1. To get to the **Generators**, click the small **A** in the lower right corner of the **Viewer**.

2. Go into the popup menu, drop down to **Text**, slide across and pick **Text** again, as in Figure 6.1.

You'll notice that in addition to **Text**, there is also **Lower Third**, **Outline Text**, and the basic animations **Scrolling Text** and **Crawl**, as well as **Typewriter**. There are also the Boris Calligraphy title tools **Title 3D** and **Title Crawl**. We'll look at the Boris tools a bit later in the lesson, but let's start by looking at the way FCP's basic **Text** tool works.

Text

This is for very basic text graphics indeed, simple on-screen words. By selecting **Text** from the **Generator** popup, a generic text generator loads into the **Viewer** (Figure 6.2).

Notice that this generator has:

- A default duration of 10 seconds.
- A default length of two minutes.

6.2   Generic Sample Text in Viewer

You can assign any duration for a text file up to four hours. However, once the text file has been placed in a sequence, its duration can no longer be extended beyond the designated duration. So if you accept the default length and place the text file in a sequence, you can no longer make the duration go beyond two minutes. I don't know why it's limited this way. In the **Browser** you can designate any duration for a text file up to four hours. If you need to change to a long text file, you can drag it into the **Browser** and dial in a very long duration and then place it back in the sequence. You can always make it shorter, but not longer. It's a good way to create a video bug, that little graphic that's always in the bottom right of your TV screen—or your warning that a tape is only a check copy and not for distribution.

The first point to realize about this text generator is that at the moment it only exists in the **Viewer**. Usually the next step I take is to put it somewhere useful, either into the **Browser** or the **Timeline**. If you park the playhead anywhere over the shot in the **Timeline** and then drag the generic text generator from the **Viewer** to the **CEO** to **Superimpose**, the text will appear above the shot, with the same duration as the shot (Figure 6.3). It will create a new track above the set destination track.

You can also drag and drop the generator into the **Timeline** onto an empty track or the space above the tracks. Either way, you'll immediately see that the render line above the generator in the **Timeline** changes color. If your system has real-time capabilities, the line will be green. If not, it will be red, telling you that section of the sequence needs to be rendered.

Whether you drag the generic text generator to the **Timeline** or the **Browser**, remember that you are creating a copy of that generator. Be careful not to do anything to the generator in the **Viewer**. I've seen countless people do this. They lay the generator in the **Timeline**, work in the **Viewer**, and then wonder why the text in the sequence still says "Sample Text."

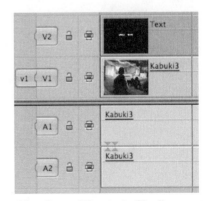

6.3   Supered Text in the Timeline

6.4 **Viewer: Text**

6.5 **Viewer: Text from Sequence 1**

6.6 **Plain Scrubber Bar on Clip Opened from Browser**

6.7 **Dotted Scrubber Bar on Clip Opened from Timeline**

First, you should open the new generator you created in the **Timeline**. Open it by double-clicking on the **Text Generator** in the **Timeline** window. The **Viewer** screen will look exactly the same, of course, except now you'll be working on the generator in the **Timeline**, which is what you want. The label area at the top of the **Viewer** will tell you where the text came from. Figure 6.4 shows the label for text generated in the **Viewer**. Figure 6.5 shows the label for text that's been opened from a sequence.

The other telltale sign that indicates whether a title or a clip has been opened from the **Browser** (or generated in the **Viewer**) rather than one that has been opened from a sequence is in the scrubber bar at the bottom of the **Viewer**. In Figure 6.6 the text has been generated in the **Viewer**. The scrubber bar is plain. In Figure 6.7 the text has been opened from the **Timeline**. The scrubber bar shows a double row of dots, like film sprocket holes.

☞ *Tip*_____
Viewing Nothing: If you place a clip in the **Timeline** over nothing, the blackness you see in the **Canvas** behind the clip is the emptiness of space. You can make it any color, or even a checkerboard, under the **View** menu, but this is only for viewing purposes. If you want an actual color layer, use the **Generators** to make a color matte. Make it any color you want and place it on the layer below all other material. For instance, if you're scaling down video clips and moving them about the screen, you may want to place an interesting color behind them. Or make something in Photoshop with a fancy design or gradient.
_____

Now we're ready to start making that graphic.

1. After you've opened the generator from the **Timeline** into the **Viewer**, click on the **Controls** tab at the top. You might also want to stretch down the **Viewer** to see all the controls (Figure 6.8).

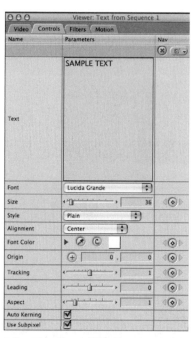

6.8 **Text Control Window**

These are the default settings. At the top is the text input window in which you type whatever you want to appear on the screen.

2. Click on **SAMPLE TEXT** and type in *Kabuki*, then do a return, and type *Performance*.

3. Click out of the window, or tab to the **Size** box. The default is 36 point, which is small even for these clips.

4. Type in a size of *72* and press **Enter**, which loads the size setting.

Above the **Size** slider is the **Font** popup, in which you can pick whatever TrueType fonts you have loaded in your system. If some fonts on your computer are not showing up, then they are probably PostScript fonts. Unfortunately FCP's **Text** tool does not work with PostScript, only TrueType. Boris Calligraphy—that is, **Title 3D** and **Title Crawl**—will work with both TrueType and Post-Script.

The **Style** popup lets you set text styles such as bold and italic.

Below **Style** is the **Alignment** popup. Alignment is usually called *justification*.

↘ Note

Font Limitations: the Font popup and all the settings in the text block will change all the letters for *everything* in the text block. You cannot control individual letters, words, or lines of text. This applies to all of Final Cut Pro's text generators except for Boris. Both Title 3D and Title Crawl have full text control, as we shall see. The one unintentional benefit of FCP's limitations is that it may prevent users from going wild with fonts, sizes, and colors.

Fonts and Size

Not all fonts are equally good for video. You can't just pick something you fancy and hope it will work for you. One of the main problems with video is its interlacing. Because video is made up of thin lines of information—the odd lines making up one field and the even lines the other field—each line is essentially switching on and off 30 times a second. If you happen to place a thin horizontal line on your video that falls on one of those lines but not the adjacent

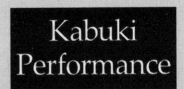

6.9   Serif Fonts

line, that thin, horizontal line will be switching on and off at a very rapid rate, appearing to flicker. The problem with text is that a lot of fonts have thin horizontal lines called serifs, the little footer that some letters sit on (Figure 6.9).

Unless you're going to make text of a fairly large size, it's generally best to avoid serif fonts. You're better off using a sans-serif font for most video work. You should probably avoid small fonts as well. Video resolution is not very high, the print equivalent of 72dpi. You can read this book in 10 point comfortably, but a 10-point line of text on television would be an illegible smear. I generally never use font sizes below 24, and prefer to use something larger if possible.

Safe Title Area and Safe Action Area

6.10 Safe Action and Safe Title Areas

Televisions have a mask on the edge that cuts off some of the displayed picture area. What you see in the **Viewer** and the **Canvas** is not what you get—far from WYSIWYG—and can vary substantially from television to television. That is why the **Canvas** and **Viewer** are thoughtfully marked with a *Safe Action Area* and a smaller area still that is defined as the *Safe Title Area* (Figure 6.10)

These are turned on with the **Image** popup at the top of the **Viewer** and **Canvas**. Make sure that both **Overlay** and **Title Safe** are checked to see the **Safe Action and Safe Title Areas**. What's within the **SAA** will appear on every television set. Because television tubes used to be curved, and many still are, a smaller area was defined as the **Safe Title Area** in which text could appear without distortion if viewed at an angle. Titles should remain, if possible, within the **Safe Title Area**. This is not important for graphics destined only for web or computer display, but for anything that might be shown on a television within the course of its life, it would be best to maintain these boundaries. That said, more often you're seeing titles that are well outside the **STA** and lying partially outside even the **SAA**.

Also note that FCP4 uses an **SAA** and **STA** that are slightly larger than previous versions and now conforms to the title areas used by other applications.

✎ Note

No Word Wrapping: FCP's titler is limited in many ways, and word wrapping is one of them. You have to put in the line breaks where appropriate, or your text is liable to run off the screen.

A word of caution: though the default setting is **Center**, the words in the text window are left justified. Ignore that. The popup rules; the text window just doesn't display intelligently.

The left and right alignment is not to the screen but to the origin point, the way it works in Illustrator and Photoshop. So if you want left alignment on the left side of the screen, you have to move the origin point about –300 or a little less to keep it in the **Safe Title Area**, depending on your format. This only applies in the **Text** tool. Other tools such as **Scrolling Text**, as we shall see, align to the screen as you might expect, with left as the left edge of the **STA**, and right as the right edge of **STA**.

Font Color is self-explanatory. It includes a color picker and a color swatch as well as a twirly triangle that opens up the **HSB** sliders and **Value** boxes.

The small icon between the eyedropper and the color swatch changes the direction in which the color moves if it's animated.

Hundreds of parameters can be animated in FCP4. Wherever you see a small diamond button like those on the left edge of the text control window, the parameter can have a keyframe defined and therefore be animated, just as we keyframed audio by placing a little diamond-shaped dot on our audio tracks in the **Timeline**. Animation is a complex subject and beyond the scope of this book.

Set the Origin of the text with a **Crosshair** button or with *x,y* values. You can use the crosshairs by clicking on the button and then clicking wherever in the **Canvas** you want the center point for the origin of the text to be. The value windows are more precise, of course. The first window is the horizontal, or *x* value; the second window is the vertical, or *y* value. The default is the center of the screen. This is centered on the baseline of the first line of text, in this case under the lower right edge of the *b* in *Kabuki*.

You can also position the text by moving it about the screen in the **Canvas**. If you change the **Image** popup at the top of the **Canvas** to **Image+Wireframe** (or use the **W** key to toggle through the wireframe functions), you can now grab the text block, or any other image for that matter, and move it about the screen and position it wherever you like. Make sure the text block in the **Timeline** is selected, and then a large cross will appear through the image with a blue border (Figure 6.11). This is the image with its wireframe outline. You can now move the text block about the screen. If you hold down the **Shift** key, you can constrain it to moving exactly vertically or horizonantally.

Tip

Positioning: When you set the Origin point of any image, you'll often find when positioning with the crosshairs that you land on a decimal integer. This will cause the image to soften and not be as clean as it should be. Always change the Origin point values to full value numbers, no decimals. This applies also to positioning text blocks with **Image + Wireframe**. Make sure the **Center** point values in the **Motion** tab of the **Viewer** are full integer values rather than decimals (Figure 6.12).

Tracking is the spacing distance between letters. The higher the tracking value, the farther apart the letters will get. Small increases in tracking will have a large impact on letter separation, and animated subtlety makes a pleasing enhancement to a title. As you move tracking down below zero, the letters will scrunch together. If you go low enough into negative values, the letters will actually squeeze into nothing and disappear.

Note

White: In previous versions of FCP, DV codec video was processed to what's called superwhite, beyond 100% luminance, which was the standard for digital video. Because of that, FCP's default titles exceeded broadcast specifications for video. In this version of FCP, DV material is no longer processed as superwhite, but only to white levels, that is, 100% luminance. So even a pure white graphic will not exceed 100%.

Note

Tracking: The **Auto Kerning** checkbox near the bottom of the controls as to be checked on or **Tracking** will not function.

6.11 Image+Wireframe in the Canvas

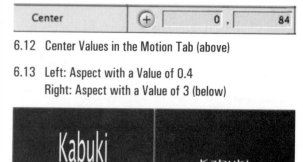

6.12 Center Values in the Motion Tab (above)

6.13 Left: Aspect with a Value of 0.4
Right: Aspect with a Value of 3 (below)

Leading (pronounced *ledding*, as in little bits of lead spacing used in hot metal typesetting) is the spacing between lines. The default is zero. A setting of –100 moves the text up so that it's all on one line. A value of 100 moves the text down a whole line.

Aspect adjusts the vertical shape of the text. Low numbers stretch text, and higher numbers squeeze the text (Figure 6.13). Be careful with the **Aspect** control. Very little movement from the default of 1 will cause ugly antialiasing (stair-stepped edges) to appear around the text.

Auto Kerning adjusts the letter spacing based on the letters' shape rather than absolute values and should be left on. It looks much better than it was in previous versions of the applications and not as tight as it used to be.

Check the **Use Subpixel** box for better quality.

Tip

Flickering Text: Interlace flickering caused by serifs and other fine lines can be alleviated somewhat by smearing the image across the interlace lines. It is easiest to do this with text created in Photoshop, where you can applying a one-pixel vertical motion blur. You don't have to soften the whole image like this. If there are particular portions that appear to flicker, you can select them with a marquee or lasso, slightly feathered, and then apply the vertical motion blur to just that portion of the image.

Or in FCP you can duplicate the **Text Generator** in the sequence and stack one on top of the other. Apply a slight **Blur** or **Antialias** filter to the bottom copy. Only the slightly blurred edge that sticks out from underneath the unblurred copy will be visible, smearing the edge. You can also darken the lower copy to give the text a slightly harder edge.

6.14 Drop Shadowed Text

6.15 Drop Shadow Controls

Drop Shadow

Drop shadows are important to give the image some depth and separation. It would be quite useful for our text where the white of the letters is over the bright highlights on the image below (Figure 6.14). You can add a drop shadow to your text in the **Motion** tab of the **Viewer.** The control panel has all the expected features: **Offset, Angle** of offset, **Shadow Color, Softness,** and **Opacity** (Figure 6.15).

You have to activate the **Drop Shadow** with the checkbox in the upper left corner.

Offset controls how far from the image the shadow appears. What might be puzzling about the **Offset** slider is that it goes into negative numbers. You'd think this would just change the direction of the shadow. Doesn't the angle do that already? Yes, it does. But when you animate them they behave differently. When you animate **Offset,** the shadow slides underneath the image from one side to the other, while if you animate **Angle,** the shadow seems to circle the image.

The default **Offset** works well for stills, video clips, or other large images, but not so well for text. When using **Drop Shadow** with the basic **Text** tool, you'll want to bring the value down, probably into the 2–5 range.

The **Angle** dial will point your shadow in whatever direction you want. The default direction, falling off to the lower right, is the most commonly used drop shadow angle.

Softness lets you control the amount of blurring on the edges of the shadow. Though the slider goes up to 100, the shadow isn't as soft as it might be. Other softening sliders, such as those we'll see in **Outline Text,** will make very dissipated shadow areas.

6.16 Opacity Slider

The **Opacity** slider defaults to 50%, which is probably too low for use with text. You might want to push up **Drop Shadow's Opacity** to 100 and use the **Softness** slider to take the edge off it.

Opacity

Opacity is the transparency of an image or text. There are two ways to control it:

- With the slider the **Motion** tab of the **Viewer** (Figure 6.16)
- Directly in the **Timeline**

Adjusting opacity in the **Timeline** is exactly like adjusting audio levels.

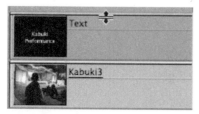

6.17 Opacity Level on Clip

1. Make sure **Clip Overlays** is turned on with the button in the lower left corner of the **Timeline,** or use the keyboard shortcut **Option-W.**

2. With the black **Opacity** level line visible in the **Timeline** (Figure 6.17), pull down on the line with the resizing cursor to make the image semitransparent.

Rather than pulling down the overall opacity of the image, let's undo that and animate the opacity to add a fade in and a fade out to our text.

3. Make sure that nothing is selected in the **Timeline** (**Command-Shift-A** to **Deselect All**) and that the playhead is at the very beginning.

4. Type in **+1.** and press **Enter** to move the playhead forward one second.

5. Take the **Pen** tool and click on the **Opacity** line at the playhead to add a keyframe.

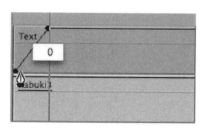

6.18 Fading In Opacity

6. Grab the line at the very beginning of the clip with the **Pen** and pull it all the way down, as in Figure 6.18.

7. To add the fade out at the end, go to the end of the clip. Use **Shift-O** to take you to the Out point, which is on the last frame of video.

8. Type in **–1.** and press **Enter** to move the playhead back one second.

9. With the **Pen** tool add a keyframe at the playhead.

10. Finally, grab the end of the **Opacity** line with the **Pen** tool and pull it down to complete your fade out, which should look like Figure 6.19.

Another way to add a fade in and fade out on text is to select the start or end of the clip and use **Command-T** to add the default cross dissolve. This will create either a start on edit or an end on edit to fade in or fade out the text as in Figure 6.20.

Reducing the opacity of a text block down to 90% will help to soften it and blend it better into the underlying image.

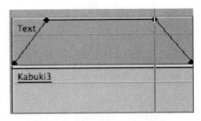

6.19   Opacity Fade In and Fade Out

6.20   Transition Fade In and Fade Out

Subtitles

Subtitling is a laborious, time-consuming business. The first problem is always the translation, especially making it match brisk dialog or narration. The best advice I can offer is to keep it simple and easy to read. The important thing is not to translate the text literally but to convey the sense. The text needs to follow the spoken words closely, which is why subtitles often need to be shortened and condensed.

Technically, the easiest way to generate subtitles in FCP is to make a couple of templates in your *Favorites* bin or in the **Browser** and keep bringing those into the sequence. Because the text is generally smaller than you would normally work with in video, you should always use a sans serif font. I prefer good old Helvetica. The size should be about 28. I prefer to use yellow with a saturation of about 85% for the text color, with a slight black drop shadow. Yellow shows against a white or pale shirt better than white with a drop shadow, I think. The text should sit on the edge of the Safe Title Area. Set the text at the bottom of the screen with the origin point of a 720 image with a *y* value of about 160. Try to keep to one line of text. Only go to a second line if you have to, but never go to three lines; it encroaches too much into the picture area. For two lines of text, set the *y* axis a little higher. A value of about 135 should do it.

Another trick is to use a black color matte behind the text. Keep it to just the size of the text and reduce the **Opacity** down to 10% or 20%, creating a translucent shadow area behind the text, making it more legible and reducing flickering in the text.

The **Superimpose** function can be useful in subtitling because it creates text clips that are exactly the length of a particular clip.

Basic Animation

Though complex animation is beyond basic editing in Final Cut, understanding simple animation is important, and it's easy to do. Animation is based on the concept of keyframes. When you change the properties of an image—in text, for instance—you define how it looks. When you apply a keyframe, you define how it looks at a particular moment in time, at a specific frame of your video. If you then go to another point in time, some other frame of video, say five seconds further into your video and change the values for the image, you will automatically create another keyframe which defines how it looks at that point in time. The computer will then figure out—it will *tween*—what each of the intervening frames of video has to look like over that five seconds. We've already done some animations, when we animated audio levels and when you animated the opacity of the text to fade it in and out. Let's do a simple motion animation.

1. With *Sequence 1* open, which should have *Kabuki3* and a *Text* clip on **V2**, make sure the playhead is at the beginning of the **Timeline**.

Let's animate the **Tracking**.

2. If you have transitions applied to the beginning or end of the *Text* clip, or an opacity fade in or fade out, remove them.

3. Open the *Text* clip in **Viewer** and go to the **Controls** tab. Either grab the **Tracking** slider and pull it down to **–4** or dial in **–4** in the value box. The text should look scrunched together as in Figure 6.21.

6.21 Text Tracking at –4

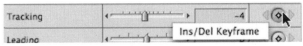

6.22 Tracking Keyframe Button (above)

6.23   Text Tracking at 8 (right)

4. Now click on the empty diamond keyframe button next to the **Tracking** value (Figure 6.22). The little button will go green to indicate that you've added a keyframe.

5. Scroll down to the timeline to the last frame of the clip and change the tracking value to **8**. The **Canvas** will show the text spread out as in Figure 6.23.

6. Scrub the timeline to see the animation in the **Canvas**.

7. If you have a system with real-time capabilities, you're done. If not, you'll have to render out the animation to see it, or use **QuickView** from the **Tools** menu.

If you like, add the transitions back onto the *Text* clip to make a smooth effect. That's it. You've created your first Final Cut Pro motion graphics animation. The finished sequence is in the **Browser** called *Tracking Animation*.

Note

Navigating with Keyframes: Be careful when using the **Down** arrow key to go to the end of a clip. When FCP takes you to the next edit, it takes you to first frame of the next clip. So to get to the last frame of the clip, you need to use the **Down** arrow and then the **Left** arrow to take you back one frame. Where you want to go is not the next edit, but rather to the Out point, the last frame of the clip.

Visibility

It's sometimes helpful to see a single track of video in a multiple-track stack of clips. This can be done two ways, either with the **Visibility** button at the head of the track or with soloing. The **Visibility** button will switch off the visibility for the entire track. **Option**-clicking on the **Visibility** button will make all others tracks invisible. This can be handy, but it also means that if you have anything rendered out, everything that you've rendered will be lost. In **User Preferences** there is a checkbox for a warning if visibility changes will delete rendered files.

An option that avoids switching off a whole track is to use soloing. Select the clip you want to see, even if it's on **V1** underneath layers of other video, and choose **Solo Item(s)** from the **Sequence** menu, or use the keyboard shortcut **Control-S**. This will toggle off the visibility of all but the selected items.

Be warned that the **Preferences** warning does not apply to soloing. It only applies to switching off visibility of whole tracks. Switching off visibility of items using soloing *will* delete your render files and will do so without warning, but it will only be for the area that's affected by the soloing; it will not be for the whole track.

Lower Thirds

A lower third is the graphic you often see near the bottom of the screen identifying a speaker or location. They're simple to create in Final Cut, though they are fairly limited. If you want to create something more exciting or stylish, you'll probably find it easier to accomplish in Photoshop or in **Title 3D**, which we'll look at later on page 181. **Lower Third's** very limitations make it to easy to use.

Click on the **Generators** button, and in the menu drop down to **Lower 3rd**. Figure 6.24 shows the simple lower third Final Cut generates. It's set down in the lower left corner of the **Safe Title Area** for you.

You can create the graphic in the **Viewer** before you move it to the **Timeline**, but remember, what you move to the **Timeline** is a copy. I always find there is less chance of a mistake if I move the graphic to the **Timeline** first and then open it from there. Also, once it's in the **Timeline**, you can put the playhead over it and quickly see what you're doing in the **Canvas**.

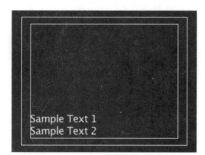

6.24 Lower Third

Open the **Controls** tab in the **Viewer** (Figure 6.25), and you'll see that the **Controls** are quite different for lower thirds. You have some new parameters, and you are missing a property as well. There is, for instance, no alignment popup.

You have two lines of text for which you can set any font, size, or color. You can make a line as long as you want—of course, if you make it too long, it will run off the screen. Unlike the regular text window, each text box here can only hold one line of text.

At the bottom of the controls is the **Background** popup. It lets you choose between the default **None; Bar,** which is a thin line between the two lines of text; and **Solid,** which is a block of color that appears behind the two text lines. You can apply one or the other, but not both. You could however add another lower third beneath it, with no text, just the background, as shown in Figure 6.26.

6.25 Lower Third Controls

Scrolling Text

FCP's **Scrolling Text** is called up the same way as the other text elements in the **Text Generators** menu. It looks startling at first because it opens in the **Viewer** with a blank screen, checkerboard or black. Don't panic.

6.26 Lower Third with Bar and Background (above)

6.27   Scrolling Text Controls (right)

Drag it to the **Timeline** or **Browser** and then double-click the new version to open it back into the **Viewer**. Go straight to the **Controls** tab (Figure 6.27), which looks pretty familiar, especially the top few items.

As in other text blocks, all the text has to be the same size, color, and font. For more elaborate rolling or scrolling text, use Boris Calligraphy's **Title Crawl**.

The control called **Spacing** is actually tracking. I have no idea why it's still called **Spacing**. It does not mean vertical spacing. For that you use **Leading**. I'm not sure either why **Leading** is represented as a percentage rather than value, as in other **Generators**.

Indent only works with left- or right-justified text. With left justification (or alignment), the text indents about 10%, about the Safe Title Area. To move the text block farther to the right, use the **Indent** slider.

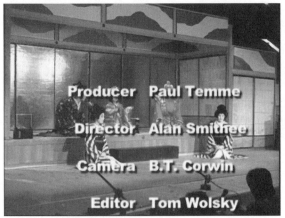

6.28 Gap Width Default 5%

6.29 Fade Set to 25%

Gap Width lets you set the spacing between vertical columns of text. This space is often called the *gutter*. It defaults to 5%, which is rather small. **Gap Width** only works with center alignment. You activate it by typing an asterisk in your text at the point where you want the column to separate, as in "Producer*Paul Temme" (Figure 6.28).

You can't make your font size too large because the text will quickly run off the screen. Entering returns to make two lines will not honor the gutter, unfortunately.

Fade Size is an interesting control. It allows the scroll to fade in as it comes in off the bottom of the screen and fade out as it disappears off the top (Figure 6.29).

Direction is set in a popup and can be the conventional upward movement, or it can be changed to downward.

How fast the scroll moves is determined by the length of the scroll in the sequence. The longer the scroll, the slower the movement. This is one of the places where **QuickView** is a godsend. It's the easiest way to check your scroll speed. Set the playhead in your sequence somewhere in the scroll and activate **QuickView**. The two-second default or a bit more should be enough to tell you if your scroll is moving at the speed you want. If it's too slow, make the scroll shorter. If it's too fast, make the scroll longer. Change the duration either by typing in a new duration in the **Viewer** or by dragging the end of scroll in the **Timeline**.

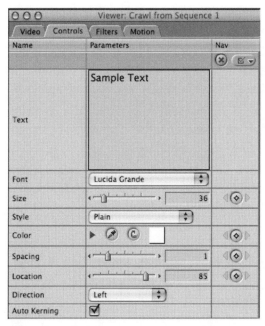

6.30   Crawl Controls (above)

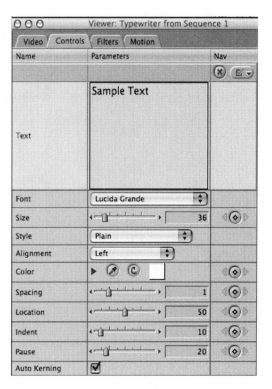

6.31   Typewriter Controls (right)

Crawl Text

Crawl is the horizontal version of a scroll. The controls should be pretty familiar by now, but they have a couple of different features (Figure 6.30).

Spacing again is **Tracking**. The **Location** slider defaults to **85**, which is the bottom of the **Safe Title Area**. Reducing the number will move the crawl higher up in the screen. A value of about **20**, depending on the font and size, puts the crawl at the top of the **Safe Title Area**.

Typewriter

Let's look at **Typewriter** next, which works especially well if you use a typewriter monospace font such as Courier.

The controls give you a small degree of flexibility (Figure 6.31).

Alignment defaults to **Left** so that the typing begins on the left edge of the **Safe Title Area** and works its way across. Be careful with the line layout, because it's easy to type right off the screen.

Because the text doesn't wrap, you have to put in a return wherever you need a line break.

Location sets the vertical height of the typing. The default is 50, the center line of the screen. A setting of about 20 moves the text block to the top of the **Safe Title Area**, which is probably where you should start if you have more than a few of lines to type on.

Indent sets how far in from the edge the text is set if it is either left or right aligned.

Center alignment has an odd effect. The typing happens in the center of the screen, and the line of text spreads out from the center. It's unusual and may be worth playing with.

The default **Pause** value of 20 produces the action of a brisk typist, depending on how much text there is to type. The way it works is that the higher the **Pause** value, the longer the text is held on the screen before the end of the clip. So the three variables are:

- The length of the clip
- How long the text holds after the typing is completed (that's the **Pause** value)
- How much you have to type

If you have a lot to type, set the **Pause** value fairly low. If you set it high—for instance, 100—no typing will occur; the text will just be there and spend 100% of the time paused on the screen.

Outline Text

I saved **Outline Text** for last because it's the most complex of FCP's **Text Generators**, with the greatest number of controls. Figure 6.32 shows only part of the controls. We'll look at the rest of them in a moment.

Because **Outline** is meant to be a big bold text, perhaps with video in it, the default font size is 64. It defaults to white text with a broad black outline.

In the **Outline Text** controls, **Tracking** returns instead of spacing, and **Aspect** returns as well. This is useful if you want an image to fill the letters. It lets you make the lettering taller or shorter. Again, be careful of antialiasing if you pull it around too much.

Line Width is more conventionally called *stroke*. It's the edging around the letter. You can make it disappear to nothing, or you can make quite large, up to 200 (Figure 6.33).

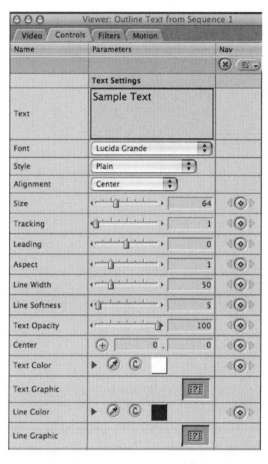

6.32 Default Outline Text Controls (left)

6.33 Line Width Value of 200 (below)

The **Softness** setting is for the stroke. It defaults to 5. I wouldn't put it any lower; the edges would start to look quite blocky. If you push the values up near 100 with a very large stroke, you get a kind of wispy background.

The **Text Opacity** control is self-explanatory, though I'm not quite sure why it's here. Note that this controls the opacity for all the text as well as the stroke. You cannot, unfortunately, use this tool to create an outline with a transparent interior.

Center is what's called **Origin** in the standard **Text** tool, 0,0 being the middle of the screen.

Now we come to **Text Graphic** and **Line Graphic**. These allow you to insert still images into the outline using the **Well**. We saw the **Well** on page 150 in the previous lesson on transitions, and it works the same way here: drag the image or clip from the **Browser** and drop it in. It would be nice if video played inside the

	Background Settings		
Horizontal Size		0	
Vertical Size		0	
Horizontal Offset		0	
Vertical Offset		0	
Back Soft		0	
Back Opacity		50	
Back Color			
Back Graphic			
Crop			
Auto Kerning			

6.34   Background Settings Panel (left)

6.35   Both with Background Set to Horizontal Size 150 Vertical Size 20 (below)

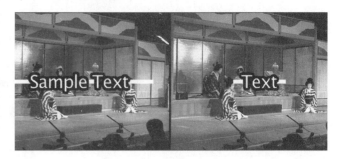

Outline Text; it doesn't, unfortunately, neither in the text nor in the **Line Width**. It only displays the In point of the video.

Let's look at the rest of **Outline Text**'s text control panel, the **Background Settings** (Figure 6.34).

The default is for the background to be off. You turn it on by increasing the horizontal and vertical size. The horizontal size acts in relationship to the amount of text you have—the less text, the less effect the horizontal value has; the more text, the farther the background extends (Figure 6.35).

Horizontal and **Vertical Offsets** set the screen position relative to the text, so it's not strictly an origin point. If the text is set high in the screen, so will the background. On the other hand, with the text high in the screen and the **Vertical Offset** set to negative numbers, the background will be pulled down in the screen (Figure 6.36). Remember these are all animatable properties, so the background can move in relation to the text, while the text position can also be animated.

A little bit of **Softness** will go a long way. Small amounts of softness will have a big impact on the blurring of the background. You'll probably need to make the background size quite large so that the softening doesn't dissipate it too much. **Softness** and **Opacity** add great tools to background and can be used for other elements besides **Outline Text**. The problem is that the background seems to be tied to the text. That's easy to overcome. In the **Text** window, use a bunch of spaces, even blocks of spaces with returns to make shapes that the background will work behind.

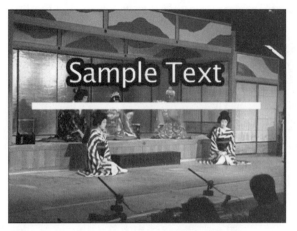

6.36 Outline Text with Vertical Offset Set to −100

6.37 Title and Background

Nesting

In the **Browser** is a sequence called *Title and Background*, which is made up of a number of FCP titling tools. The output appears in Figure 6.37, but if you open it in FCP, you'll see it in color. I'll show you how it was built up.

If you open the sequence *Title and Background*, you'll see that it is made up of two layers. On **V1** is the video clip *Kabuki1*, and on **V2** is a text block called *Title Composite* and another called *Title Composite Japan*. These are nests. Nesting is an important concept to understand in Final Cut. Because you can have sequences within sequences in FCP, you can also group layers together into nests to form a sequence of their own. You'll notice in the **Browser** there are sequences called *Title Composite* and *Title Composite Japan*. These are the elements that appear on **V2** in *Title and Background*. Let's build these nests together.

Text

1. Start by duplicating *Title and Background* in the **Browser**. Select the sequence and use **Edit>Duplicate (Option-D)**.

2. Open the duplicate *Title and Background copy* by double-clicking on it, or select it and press **Enter** or **Return**.

3. Use **Command-A** to select everything in the **Timeline** and then **Delete** to empty the sequence.

4. Next drag the clip *Kabuki1* from the *Clips* bin into the beginning of the **Timeline** on **V1**, and then move the playhead so that it is parked somewhere above the clip.

5. From the **Text Generator** popup in the **Viewer**, select **Outline Text**. .

6. Drag the **Sample Text** block to the **Canvas** to **Superimpose**. This will edit it into the timeline to **V2** above the video clip.

7. Double-click on the **Outline Text** block in the **Timeline** to bring it back into the **Viewer**.

8. Go to the **Controls** tab. First change the text to *DAMINE*, the name of the village where this video was shot.

9. You can, of course, use whatever text, color, or settings you want, but this is how I built this image:

Font	Arial
Style	Bold
Point Size	98
Tracking	4
Line Width	23
Color	muted red: **Red 201, Green 69, Blue 69**

Tip
Renaming: It's helpful to rename the **Outline Text** before we create a new one. **Control**-click on the **Outline Text** on the top track, and select **Item Properties** > **Format** from the menu. In the **Format** dialog you might want to change the name to something like *DAMINE*.

Because the letters looked too jammed together, I set the **Tracking** to 4.

That's it. You have the basic text block. Now let's set the background white glow.

Background

1. First, pull the **Outline Text** block upward, holding down the **Shift** key to constrain movement to the vertical. Drop the text block on the empty space above.

This will create a new track and leave **V2** empty for the background.

2. In the **Viewer** create a new **Outline Text** block from the **Generators**.

3. Drag the new text block to **Superimpose**, and open it on **V2** from the **Timeline** back into the **Viewer**.

Your **Timeline** should now look like Figure 6.38. This is going to be the background white glow.

6.38 Timeline with Video Clip and Two Outline Text Blocks (above)

6.39   Text and Background over Video Clip (right)

4. In the text block, hit the spacebar 13 or 14 times; that is, type in 13 or 14 empty spaces. Use the default font size, which is fine.

We've now made "text" for the background to work with.

5. Scroll to the **Background** controls and set the following:

Horizontal	200
Vertical	200
Back Soft	50 (blurs the background considerably)
Opacity	100

Your **Canvas** should like something like Figure 6.39.

6. Place the cursor on the patch panel at the head of **V2**, hold down the **Control** key, and from the shortcut menu, select **Add Track** (Figure 6.40).

7. Do this three times so that you have three empty tracks between the two layers with the **Outline Text** blocks.

8. In the **Viewer** from the **Generators** button, select **Matte> Color,** as we did to make the color backing for the page peel transition in the previous lesson. Again, this will fill the screen with midtone gray.

9. Set **V2** as the destination track by clicking on the **V2** button at the head of the **Timeline**.

10. Drag the color matte to **Superimpose** to edit it into the empty **V3** track.

6.40 Adding Tracks

11. Double-click the **Color** in the sequence to open it back into the **Viewer.**

12. Go to the **Controls** tab and set the color to the same dark rose as the *DAMINE* title. Use the color picker if the title is visible in the **Canvas.** It should be, if the playhead is sitting over the clips.

13. After setting the color, go to the **Motion** tab and twirl open the **Crop** and **Opacity** controls (Figure 6.41). I used these settings:

Top Crop	64
Bottom Crop	32
Opacity	75

14. Open another color matte, and place it in the sequence above the red bar you just created. Or you can **Option-Shift-** drag to duplicate the color and place it on the track above.

15. Make the color of this matte green (**Red 20, Green 97, Blue 19**), and in the **Motion** tab set:

Top Crop	64
Bottom Crop	38

16. One more color matte to make. Generate the matte and bring it to the sequence below the top **Outline Text** block.

17. Set the same green color and these **Crop** values:

Top Crop	70
Bottom Crop	32

Your sequence should have six layers in it (Figure 6.42):

- The video clip on **V1**
- **Outline Text** block on **V2**, which creates the soft glow area
- Three color mattes on the layers above
- At the top, another **Outline Text** block, the one that holds the actual text DAMINE.

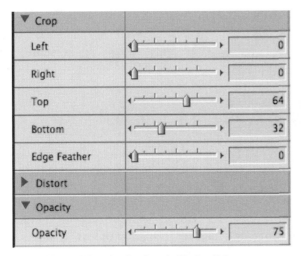

6.41 Crop and Opacity Settings in Motion Tab

6.42 Timeline after Making Text and Matte Layers

Putting It All Together

1. Make a marquee selection in the **Timeline** window, or **Shift**-click all the layers, *except* the video layer on **V1**. Leave that unselected.

2. From the **Sequence** menu, select **Nest Item(s)**, or use the keyboard shortcut **Option-C**.

This will bring up a dialog box that lets you name the new sequence you're creating.

3. Call it *Title Composite 2*, to distinguish it from the sequence in your **Browser** already called *Title Composite* (Figure 6.43).

This nest appears in the **Timeline** as a block called *Title Composite 2*. It will also appear in your **Browser** as a sequence. That block of text in your sequence can be moved around wherever you like and used again and again.

6.43 Nesting Dialog

Drop Shadow

You thought I forgot the drop shadow on DAMINE. Here is the beauty of nested sequences.

1. Double-click the nest. It opens as a whole separate sequence in a new tab in the **Timeline** window.

2. Double-click on the **Outline Text** block called *Damine* at the top to open it in the **Viewer.**

3. Go to the **Motion** tab, and check the box for **Drop Shadow**. Enter these settings:

Offset	4
Angle	135
Shadow color	Green: **Red 62, Green 139, Blue 54**
Softness	15
Opacity	80

The drop shadow is done. This change will now appear in every iteration of that sequence wherever it appears anywhere in your project.

Here's what else makes this beautiful: suppose I've built this complex text block, and I want to change the actual text, but nothing else.

1. Duplicate *Title Composite 2* in your **Browser**.

2. Change the name of the duplicate to *Title Composite Japan 2*.

3. Double-click to open the duplicate into the **Timeline**.

4. Double-click on the top Outline Text block to open it into the **Viewer**, and in the **Controls** tab replace the word *DAMINE* with the word *JAPAN*.

Nothing else changes, just the text block and its drop shadow. Easy, isn't it?

Boris Calligraphy

Boris Calligraphy includes **Title 3D** and **Title Crawl**. These really supersede FCP's text tools in many ways, giving the user great control and flexibility with titling. It is a feature-packed tool, an application within itself, really. I'm going to show you some of its principal tools, but for a thorough look at its capabilities, consult the excellent PDF in the *Boris Calligraphy Docs* folder inside the *Extras* folder on the Final Cut installation DVD. Boris Calligraphy tools are installed by default when you install FCP4.

6.44 Title 3D Interface

Title 3D

You call up **Title 3D** from the **Generators,** which will launch a separate titling window, a part of the Boris interface (Figure 6.44). This text window is the first of five tabbed windows that allow you access to **Title 3D's** powerful and complex tools.

Unlike the FCP text box, this text window is truly WYSIWYG. Most importantly, each control can be applied to each letter or group of letters separately. So now, with little trouble, you can make a garish combination of colors and fonts, a regular ransom note.

Before you do anything in this window, you may want to click on the second tab and change the default **No Wrap** to **Wrap** (Figure 6.45). I don't know why it defaults to **No Wrap.** You can leave the wrap default at 512, which will fit inside a standard 720 video image's Safe Title Area.

The **Top-down Text** and **Right-to-left reading** checkboxes at the bottom of the window are great for vertical, Hebrew, or Arabic text.

📎 Tip
Starting up Title 3D: Title 3D and Title Crawl can be quite slow starting up sometimes. If you're going to be doing a lot of text work—for instance, if you're creating subtitles—try this little trick to speed up the window opening. Go into your system *Library/Fonts* and move out the fonts you don't actually need to work with. Leave the basic fonts and those you need for your subtitles. If you have many fonts in your library, you'll notice a substantial difference in the time it takes to load up Title 3D and Title Crawl or any of the other text tools in FCP.

6.45 Text Wrap

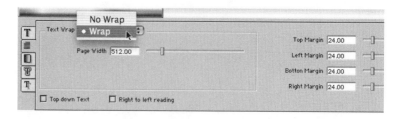

After you've set text wrapping, go back to the text window to enter your text. The main window allows you to enter and select text, which you can then adjust with the controls at the bottom part of the window.

The text window works much like most text applications, such as Word. The ruler at the top of the text window allows you to set tabs for precise positioning of text elements (Figure 6.46). Use the **Tab** key to navigate from one tab indent to the next. After you've set a tab, you can double-click on it to toggle from left justified to right justified to center justified. This tool is especially useful when making long scrolls like movie credits that often use columns and indents for different sections.

The white area in the ruler is the active text part of the screen, while the gray area beyond is the word wrapping.

Let's look at some of the phenomenal text control in Calligraphy. In the bottom portion of the screen, the first popup obviously sets the font. The two buttons to the right will move you up and down through your font list. Below the **Font** popup is a **Point Size Value** box. The two buttons to the right of that will incrementally raise and lower your point. To the right of the font controls are six buttons that let you set:

- Normal
- Bold
- Italic
- Underline

6.46 Title 3D Text Window Ruler

6.47 Style Skew Y 45°

- Superscript
- Subscript

Below that, three **Paragraph** buttons let you set justification:

- Left
- Center
- Right

The **Tracking** slider adjusts the letter spacing globally.

Kerning adjusts the spacing between individual pairs or groups of letters without affecting the overall spacing. It allows you to control individual letter spacing. It's important for many fonts, especially when you are writing words like *AVE*, where you need to slide the *A* and *V* closer together than fonts normally place them.

Leading controls the line gap between all the lines in the window.

The **Style** controls allow you a truly astonishing degree of control over text and begin to show why this text tool is called **Title 3D**. Individual letters or groups of letters can be skewed left and right on the baseline with **Style Skew X**. They can be swung like doors with **Style Skew Y** as in Figure 6.47. The value boxes in these controls let you set the degrees of skew (the lower box) and numbers of rotations (the upper box), which can be used in conjunction with the animation controls for keyframing.

Style Baseline will allow you to raise and lower letters separately, while **Style Scale X** and **Style Scale Y** will let you scale individual characters on the *x* and/or *y* axis independently from each other.

The **All Styles** popup at the bottom lets you change to **Basic Style**. You see basic limits in the text window. It does speed up preview, which can get quite slow with long text windows with complex styles.

> **Tip**
>
> **Text Control Shortcuts:** If any value box is active, you can make the values go up or down by holding down the **Option** key and tapping the **Up** and **Down** arrow keys to raise and lower the values. **Shift-Up** and **Down** will move in 10-unit increments. The **Tab** key will take you to the next value box, and **Shift-Tab** will take you to the previous value box.

Bitmap or Vector

How is this enormous flexibility of text possible? When you scale up text created with the FCP text tools, the image quickly becomes jagged around the edges, yet here you can separately scale individual letters to very large sizes, twisting and skewing them, and yet you'll see no apparent antialiasing or stair-stepping on the edges of the letters. This is possible because Calligraphy works with vector graphics, while FCP text creates bitmapped graphics.

When a bitmapped graphic is created, the color and position of each pixel in the image is defined. If you then scale that image, you have to scale the pixels and try to create pixels where none previously existed. When a vector graphic is created, no pixels are actually defined; only the shape, based on lines and curves, is defined. So if you scale a vector graphic, you're redefining the shape; no actual pixels need be created until the image is displayed on the screen.

The scaling for the vector graphic has to be done within **Title 3D** and should not be done using the **Scale** slider in the **Motion** tab.

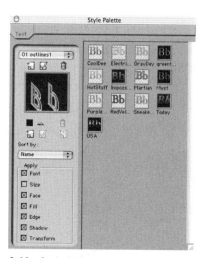

6.48 Style Palette

The **Percentage** popup lets you change the display size of the text window, a useful feature if you have a lot of text and want to quickly move around in it.

Boris FX Support will connect you to Boris's online web support system.

The **Reset Style** button will reset all the parameters for the words in the text window. It will not, however, reset fonts or font sizes, wrapping, tabs, justification, or margins.

The **Style Palette** is a great tool (Figure 6.48). It allows you to create your own text style and to name and save it. This way you can replicate styles from file to file and even project to project and efficiently. You can download many **Style** presets from the BorisFX website http://www.borisfx.com.

The **Import File** button allows you to bring into the **text** window a previously created plain text file or RTF (Rich Text Format) file. All the justification and styles applied there will be honored in **Title 3D**.

Cancel and **Apply** are self-explanatory.

This is only the first couple of tabs in **Title 3D**.

The third tabbed panel, **Text Color**, lets you set the text fill and opacity (Figure 6.49). The little checkbox in the upper left corner lets you turn off the fill, so that you have only the text outline.

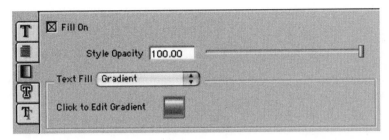

6.49 Text Color

The **Text Fill** popup lets you choose to fill the text with a color or with a gradient. If you choose **Color**, the **Style Color** swatch allows access to the system color picker that we saw earlier. If you choose **Gradient**, you will get access to an incredibly powerful gradient editor (Figure 6.50), which allows multiple color points as well as transparency. To add color points, click below the gradient bar display.

The fourth tabbed window lets you set the width and opacity for the **Text Edge**, and not just a single edge, but up five separate edges for each letter (Figure 6.51). Each edge can be **Plain, Bevel,** or **Glow**, and can be **Center, Inside,** or **Outside**. The slider on the right controls the softening blur for each edge. The variations possible with five edges are nearing infinite. More than anyone could need. To apply an edge make sure you activate it with the checkbox. Each of the five edges can be activated or switched off separately, which helps in trying out different looks.

The fifth panel sets the five separate **Drop Shadows** (Figure 6.52). These can be either a standard **Drop**; a **Cast** shadow, which slopes away from the text; or a **Solid** shadow with sides. Drop and cast shadows don't have **Highlight** or **Shade** color, but they have a **Softness** control that appears when the shadow popup is changed. Each shadow also has controls for color, distance, opacity, and

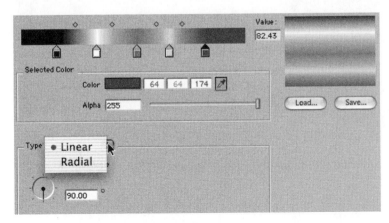

6.50 Gradient Editor

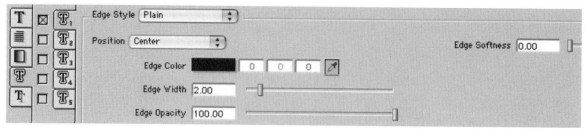

6.51 Text Edge

Note

Interlace Flickering: If you're doing text animation on interlaced video, check the 1:2:1 **Deflicker** box to reduce interlace flickering.

angle. Again, the drop shadow isn't activated until you click on the appropriate checkbox for one or more of the shadows.

Unfortunately, while you're working in **Title 3D**, you cannot see the text composited on top of the image, but once you've created your text, drag it to the **Timeline** or **Superimpose** it over a clip that's already there.

If you need to change or adjust the text, double-click the **Title 3D** file in the **Timeline** to open it into the **Viewer.** Then click on the **Controls** tab to open all the controls for **Title 3D** (Figure 6.53).

To access the text window to change the letters or styles or any of the other controls, click on the **Title 3D** logo at the top of the controls panel. Notice that all of the items that have the little diamond keyframe button on the right. Each of these parameters is keyframable, though there are some that you probably don't want to animate.

The **Geometry** section controls the text overall, changing:

- **Position**
- **Distance**
- **Scale**
- **Tumble**
- **Spin**
- **Rotate**

6.52 Drop Shadow

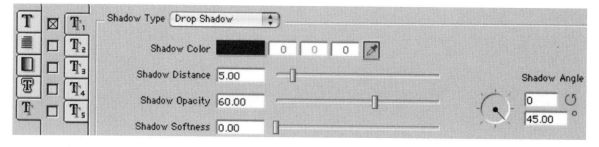

🐾 *Note*

Position sets the center point for the text. Boris uses a center point based on the upper left corner of the image. In the DV format the center point is 360,240. This is a common positioning scheme in many graphics and compositing applications. FCP is one of the few to use a 0,0 center-positioning system. With Calligraphy you just have to make different calculations or use the crosshairs to click a position in the **Canvas**.

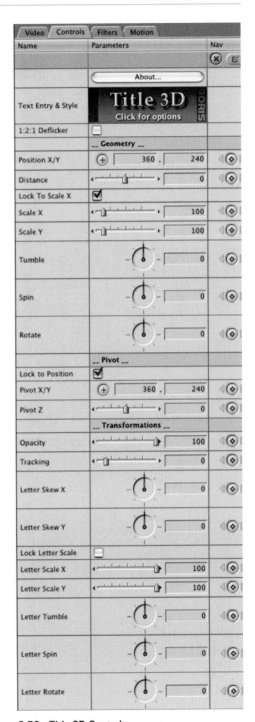

While **Position** places the text in the screen, **Distance** makes the text appear nearer or farther away. If you want to make the text seem as though it's coming from the distance to the camera, animate the **Distance** parameter, not the **Scale**. The movement of **Scale** will get slower and slower as it gets bigger. This does not happen when animating **Distance**. Unfortunately, the smallest distance, moving the slider to the right, is 5, which may not be enough to make the text disappear into infinity. Nor can the largest scale value 800 make the text seem to fly from the horizon toward the camera and past it. To do that, you'll need to use a combination, primarily animating **Distance** and adding a bit of **Scale** animation to make the text start from zero. This is the **Scale** value you want to adjust to get clean, large fonts, not the **Scale** in the **Motion** tab.

Tumble, **Spin**, and **Rotate** will turn the entire text block around on the *x, y,* and *z* axes, respectively.

Pivot controls the point around which the text tumbles, spins, and rotates. If the **Lock to Position** box is checked, the controls have no effect. With the box checked, the text will rotate around the selected pivot point, which can be set with numeric values or with the crosshairs button.

Neither **Tumble** nor **Spin** controls function with the **X/Y** controls, but their movement is affected when the **Z** slider is activated.

Transformation affects all the letters in the text block, but it affects them individually. In Figure 6.54 the image on the left has its **Geometry** tumbled –50° and spun 60° while the image on the right has its **Transformation** tumbled –50° and spun 60°.

6.53 Title 3D Controls

6.54 Geometry vs. Transformation

Notice that on the right each letter is moving, while on the left they are moving together. Also notice that on the right the **Tumble** factor appears quite limited when **Spin** is applied. You'll get more displacement of the text using **Letter Skew** rather than **Letter Tumble** if **Spin** is added.

Title Crawl

Title Crawl is accessed from the bottom of the **Generators** popup and shares many of the same controls as **Title 3D**. The text window that's evoked when **Title Crawl** is called up functions identically in both Calligraphy title tools. The real difference is seen in the **Controls** tab of the **Viewer** (Figure 6.55). Here there are far fewer keyframable options: no geometry, no transformation.

The **Animation** popup lets you set:

- **None**, the default
- **Roll (Scroll)**
- **Crawl**

Mask Start and End and **Blend Start and End** are the same as FCP's **Fade Size** tool, only with more control. Here you can fade the start and end separately, as well as control the amount of fade, here called *blend*. The **Reverse Direction** checkbox does just

6.55 Title Crawl Controls

Text Entry & Style	Title Crawl Click for options		
1:2:1 Deflicker	☑		
Animation Style	None Roll Crawl		
Mask Start		0	◁◈▷
Mask End		0	◁◈▷
Blend Start		0	◁◈▷
Blend End		0	◁◈▷
Reverse Direction	☐		
Position X/Y	⊕ 320 ,	240	◁◈▷
Opacity		100	◁◈▷

that, makes a roll reverse from the default bottom-to-top direction to top-to-bottom, and reverses direction of the standard right-to-left crawl to left-to-right.

To do a crawl, make sure **Word Wrap** is switched off.

The speed of the roll or crawl is determined by the amount of text in the text window and the duration of the text block in the timeline. The longer the block, the slower the motion. **QuickView** is especially useful here, to determine whether the text speed is appropriate, a couple of seconds will be enough to give you an idea if the scroll is moving too fast or too slow.

Photoshop Titles

Because the titler was so weak in earlier versions of Final Cut, many people took to using Photoshop as the FCP titler. What a great titler it is, infinitely malleable, with many additional elements, like banners and bars and gradients, which are more difficult to construct in FCP than in this great graphics application. Anything you can imagine is possible.

What you should first know about working in PS is that you should use only RGB color space—no CMYK, no grayscale, no indexed color. They don't translate well to video.

One problem with using PS is the issue of square versus rectangular or non-square pixels. Because PS is a computer program, until recently it worked in square pixels exclusively, while most video other than High Definition uses the CCIR601 or rectangular pixel. This presents a minor problem. If you are using the latest version of the Adobe product, Photoshop CS, the problem has been solved for you because CS lets you choose either pixel aspect ratio that you want to work in. For multilayer work, use the non-square pixel presets for your work and import that material directly into FCP. The important point is to understand how FCP handles still-image files. It handles different-sized images in different ways. Single-layer files are treated one way; multilayer Photoshop files or PS files with transparency are treated another way. For single-layer images, use the following square pixel sizes. Use them also if you are working in earlier versions of Photoshop.

1. If you're working in the DV format using CCIR601 pixels at 720×480, create your PS files at 720×540.
   If you're working in standard CCIR601 format, 720×486, then create your PS files at 720×547.

Pulling Photoshop Effects

Many users encounter problems with Photoshop images with text layers or with layer effects applied in PS, such as drop shadows or any of the other vector-based layer effects or adjustments the application can do. None of these translate to FCP; the layer effects and adjustment layers do not appear at all. The problem is that the layer effects are not applied to the image but remain with PS so that they can be changed at any time without having to recreate the layer. It's like nondestructive editing in Final Cut Pro. There is a way around this, however. The effects have to be rasterized. To do this, just merge the layer with the effect into an empty PS layer.

6.56 Merge Down

1. Make a new blank layer beneath the layer you want to rasterize.

2. From the **Wing** menu of **Layers** palette, choose **Merge Down** (Figure 6.56).

This fixes the effect with the image onto the empty layer. Of course, now the layer effects are no longer editable.

Another method, if you only have a few layers that you don't mind merging together, is to use **Merge Visible or** a variation of it.

1. Create a blank layer at the bottom of the layer stack.

2. Select the blank layer use **Command-Option-Shift-E.**

Unlike the normal **Merge Visible** from the Photoshop Layer menu, this keyboard command will not collapse the layers into a single layer but will copy the content of all the visible layers and merge them into the single blank layer. With this method you still have the editable layers in the PS document. If you switch off the visibility for the upper layers in PS, when the file is imported into FCP, the merge layer will be visible, and the other layers will be present as well, only with their track visibility switched off as they were in Photoshop.

This is something you should do at the very end: merge the layers as needed, and squish the file to its CCIR601 format, while still keeping an original PS file copy in its original format with the original images, text layers, and effects, separated and still editable.

Use these sizes for single-layer PS files with the square pixel aspect ratio. If you are creating a multilayer document or a document using Photoshop transparency, and you are working square pixels, such as earlier versions of Photoshop, create your graphic and then move on to step 2.

2. After you've made your graphic, go to **Image Size** and, making sure **Constrain Proportions** is deselected and **Bicubic** is selected, change the height of the image to 480 or 486, as appropriate (480 for DV material, 486 for full-format digital video).

This squashes the image down, distorting it, changing it to a file that FCP recognizes as using CCIR601 rectangular pixels.

3. Save your file. I save out a separate PS file that has been converted to CCIR601 format and keep the original so I can correct the typos I usually make.

When you bring a 720×480 PS file into FCP, the editing software assumes it's been prepared to use in a DV sequence. When placed in a DV sequence, the image will work perfectly and be treated as a rectangular pixel image.

There are templates for the common formats in the *Extras* folder of the book's DVD. The images are black with white Safe Action and Safe Title Areas markers. Guides have also been set up for SAA and STA. Table 6.1 gives a list of these formats, their rectangular pixel size, and the square pixel equivalent that should be used in Photoshop with square pixels.

Note
Important Preset Update: Be aware that the DV and CCIR601 presets used by FCP4—720x540 and 720x547, respectively—are not the preset sizes that were used in earlier versions of FCP. These are also not the preset values that Adobe uses in Photoshop 7 or CS.

Table 6.1   Photoshop Specifications

Format	Rectangular pixel size	Square pixel size
DV NTSC	720×480	720×540
NTSC CCIR601	720×486	720×547
DV NTSC 16:9 (Anamorphic)	720×480	853×480
NTSC CCIR601 16:9 (Anamorphic)	720×486	853×486
PAL	720×576	768×576
PAL 16:9 (Anamorphic)	720×576	1,024×576

You're not always making a graphic that needs to fit in the video format. Sometimes you're making a graphic that is much larger, one you want to move around on to make it seem as though you're panning across or zooming in or out. To do this, you need to make the image much greater than your video format, perhaps 2,000×2,000 pixels or more.

If you are working with a layered image in Photoshop CS, you should create it using non-square pixels. If you're using an older version of Photoshop you still should squeeze the image down to rectangular pixels before you bring it into FCP. To do this, rather than using pixel values, use percentages and reduce the height of the image to 90% or, if you want to be anally precise about it, 89.886%. Again, you should not resize these images if they are single-layer images without Photoshop transparency. FCP understands these are square pixel images brought into a CCIR601 world and will handle them appropriately. If they are PS layered files with transparency, FCP treats them as separate sequences and does not adjust for CCIR601 pixels. The rules of the road may be unnecessarily complex, but the bottom line is if it's a single-layer file, let FCP do the resizing; if it's a PS7 or older file, squeeze it before you import it.

The easiest way to work with Photoshop files that you want to lay over video is to create your PS files over transparency, PS's checkerboard background. This transparency will be honored when you import the file into FCP. It's important to understand that PS files come into Final Cut as separate sequences. This means that when you bring a PS file with multiple layers, all its layers remain intact as separate layers in a FCP sequence. There each layer can be animated and affected separately, just as we recently saw with nested sequences.

The only time Photoshop files do not import as a sequence is when they are made up of a single background layer or are saved as flattened images or in some other file format, such as PICT.

Resolution

For people who come from a print background, it's important to note that video doesn't have a changeable resolution. It's not like print where you can jam more and more pixels into an inch of space and make your print cleaner, clearer, and crisper. Pixels in video occupy a fixed space and have a fixed size, the equivalent of 72dpi in the print world, which happens to be the Macintosh

Transitions with Still Images

If you want to put together a group of still images with transitions between them, you can simplify the process in a couple of ways. When you import the files, make sure you leave enough room in your **Still/Freeze Duration** preference to accommodate the transitions. Sequentially number the stills you want to import and place them into a separate folder on your hard drive. Next, import all your stills as a single folder using **Import > Folder** so that they come in as a bin. Set a default transition that you want to use for the effect. If it's something unusual like a special page peel, put it in *Favorites* before you make it the default. Then drag the bin from the **Browser** straight to the **Canvas Edit Overlay** and drop on **Overwrite (or Insert) with Transition**. All the stills will miraculously dump from the bin and appear in the **Timeline** with the page peel between them. The technique works beautifully with flattened PS files or other image formats.

It's a little quirky when used with a regular PS file that comes in as a sequence. The first transition will come as a start-on-edit transition and be the correct duration. The others will be end-on-edit transitions and half the duration because they can't overlap the material between sequences by extending them. So if you want a one-second transition, set your default effect to two seconds. Then all the stills will come in as one-second end-on-edit transitions, except for the first one. It will be start on edit and the full two seconds, but that's easier to fix than fixing every transition between every still image.

screen resolution. Dots per inch are a printing concern. Forget about resolution. Think in terms of size: the more pixels, the bigger the picture. Do not think that you can make an image 720×480 at a high resolution like 300dpi or 600dpi and be able to move it around in FCP. Certainly you'll be able to scale it up, but it will look soft, and if you scale it far enough—to 300%, for instance—the image will start to show pixelization. FCP is good at hiding the defects by blurring and softening, but the results are not really as good as they should be. FCP is a video application and only deals with pixel numbers, not with dpi.

Scanners, on the other hand, are designed for the print world where dpi is an issue. Because scanners generate lots and lots of pixels, this is very handy for the person working in video. You can scan even a quite small image at, let's say, 300 or 600dpi, and your scanner will produce thousands of pixels, which will translate into video as a very large image. You now have an image that's much larger than your video format of 720×486 pixels. If your scanner can generate an image that's 2,880 pixels across, it's making an image four times bigger than your CCIR601 video frame. You can now move that very large graphic around on the screen and make it seem as though a camera is panning across the image. Or you can scale it back, and it will look as though the camera is zooming back from a point in the image. Reverse the process, and it looks as though the camera is zooming into the image.

Summary

In this lesson we've gone through FCP's title tools, Boris Calligraphy, and the task of bringing Photoshop title files into Final Cut.

In the next lesson we'll look at the different forms of editing—documentary, music, action, and dialog—and how to work in them using Final Cut Pro 4.

Importing Image Sequences

At some time you might want to import an entire folder of still images as a sequence, one frame for each picture. There are a couple of simple ways to do this. Start off by making sure that the stills are properly numbered sequentially, such as PICT001, PICT002, PICT003, and so on. One way to bring this material into FCP is to use the QuickTime Pro Player. With the player open, select from its **File** menu **Select Open Image Sequence**. Navigate to the folder and select the first image in the list.

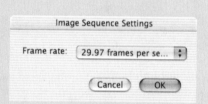

6.57 Image Sequence Import Dialog

When you click **Open**, you'll get the dialog box in Figure 6.57, which allows you to set the frame rate for the still images. The sequence will open as a QuickTime movie. Now export from the QT Player to whatever file format you're working in setting the compressor, frame size, and frame rate.

The second way is to import the image sequence directly into FCP. Before you import the correctly sequentially numbered still images, go to your FCP **Preferences** and set the **Still/Freeze Duration** to one frame or whatever frame rate you want to use. Two frames for every still is common in animation. Now import the whole folder containing the still images. This will bring the folder in as a bin. Create a new sequence. Open the bin of one or two frame still images, select all, copy, and paste into the new sequence, or just drag the bin into **Overwrite** or **Insert** in the CEO. You can now use that sequence as a nest that acts like any other clip in FCP.

The important advantage of doing this in the QT player is that once the sequence is exported, it's a clip like any other. It no longer needs to go through the render process in FCP every time you make a change.

Lesson 7

Editing Forms

The moment of the edit, where one shot changes into another, is dictated by rhythm—sometimes by an internal rhythm the visuals present, sometimes by a musical track, more often than not by the rhythm of language. All language, dialog or narration, has a rhythm, a cadence or pattern, dictated by the words and based on grammar. Grammar marks language with punctuation: commas are short pauses; semicolons are slightly longer pauses; periods are the end of an idea. The new sentence begins a new idea, a new thought, and it is natural that as the new thought begins, a new image is introduced to illustrate that idea. The shot comes, not on the end of the sentence, not in the pause, but on the beginning of the new thought. This is the natural place to cut, and it's this rhythm of language that drives the rhythm of film and video, particularly so in documentary production. Dialog presents different problems. Cutting on speech from one speaker to the next, though apparently mandatory in sitcoms, is usually monotonous to watch. Action and music may not have language to guide their rhythm. Music, of course, will have its own, while action has the internal rhythm of movement within the frame that will drive the pace of the cuts. In this lesson we'll look at cutting these various forms.

Each of the many common editing forms requires a different approach to the material. The forms I'd like to look are:

- Documentary
- Music
- Action
- Dialog

Obviously these will all overlap to some extent or other. Each has its own variations, and techniques that apply to one will get used in others, but these four offer the principal challenges an editor might face. Though narrative film, the Hollywood and independent feature film, is the most visible film and video production, it makes up only a very small fraction of production in America and around the world. On any single weekend day in June, probably more wedding videos are produced in America than all the feature films made in Hollywood in a year, and some of those wedding videos are longer than feature films. Or maybe they just seem that way. Final Cut Pro is being used on a vast range of projects— by three-time Academy Award–winning editor Walter Murch on *Cold Mountain* for Anthony Minghella all the way down through television networks like CNN, to commercials, corporate videos, wedding videographers, and even serious hobbyists—and in every format from film resolution and High Definition down to DV and even web video. The extensibility of Final Cut is a significant factor in its popularity.

One of the first points to consider in any production is the form in which it will be delivered. This should not be happening when you are in postproduction, but rather when you are writing, and congruent to that, when you are planning production, when you are shooting, and then finally when you are editing. If your end product is a film to be seen on a large screen, it's shot in a certain way and edited in a certain way. Shots can be held longer because there is so much to see and so much space for the eye to cover and travel around. The same movie seen on the small screen of a television set will appear to be cut too slowly, because you take in the whole image without your eye moving, so you take it in more quickly. Of course, you also see less detail.

If your project is intended for delivery on television, it should be shot for television's limitations of luma and chroma values. If it's shot for delivery on a computer screen, you aren't bound by those limits, but perhaps by greater limits dictated by compression. If you're going to squeeze your video down for web delivery, you need to shoot it with as few moves as possible, use few transitions (which don't compress well), and shoot plainer, less busy backgrounds. Delivery should be the first consideration in a production, not the last, and every step of the process, from scripting through final editing, should bear the delivery mechanism in mind.

Film and video production starts with an idea and expands outward. It grows fuller and more detailed, but everything refers back to the original idea. What determines how the production is edited is in that original idea. It goes from the script which governs:

- What and how the video is shot
- Where the emphasis is placed
- What is looked at in the scene and from what angle
- What elements are created for juxtaposition

The elements are the shots. Often a scene will be shot all the way through repeatedly from a number of different camera angles to give the editor the greatest variety of selection material. This is conventional in all types of production, even sometimes in documentaries. It's certainly common in commercials, in corporate videos, and of course in narrative film.

On the other hand, a director who knows in his mind how the shots will be cut together will probably be more effective than one who shoots lots of cover material without a clear idea of how it will come together. Without having an idea how the material will be put together, it's difficult for the director to judge the pacing within each shot. If the action is slow within the shot, then the shots will have to be cut together slowly. If the action is fast paced, it will force the editing to be fast. The key to good editing is in timing, and that timing starts in the camera. For instance, if camera moves are not well timed, it becomes difficult to pace the material well when it's being cut. Whether zooming or panning, the camera movement itself should last no more than a few seconds. In well-shot material there are no random movements. The camera movements are deliberate and precise; the pan goes from object A to object B and stops. There is a tendency for camerapeople, particularly novices, to use moves to make static material more interesting. Pans and tilts and zooms appear to enliven what might otherwise be dull or static material.

Shots are generally on the screen no more than 5–10 seconds. For faster paced editing—in commercials, for instance—shots often last a second or even less. That isn't to say that the camera shoots shots that are that short, but the editor cuts them down to just the few frames that best serve the material.

Every editor comes out of a movie saying he could take 10 minutes out of it. Maybe the picture would be improved by the trims, but often enough it would be ruined. There is a danger in chipping away too much, in too finely honing a piece, eventually cutting into the core and damaging the material. As the editor you get used to seeing the pictures again and again. You see the content more quickly. You understand the flow of the shots more quickly, and then the danger is that you mistake your understanding and comprehension of the material for that of the audience, an audience who has never seen the film before. This happens less often when a director has a clear vision of the picture and has been able to convey that vision. The greater danger comes when the director's concept is unclear both to him and to you. Then the risk of overcutting increases. Directors confident in their ideas, who know clearly what they want, tend to shoot less, with little extra cover. Sometimes this will get them and you as the editor into trouble in the cutting room. But when it works, when the director's vision is clear and well executed, the outcome can be very, very good, but when it doesn't, the results tend to be very, very mediocre. Uncertain directors tend to overshoot, giving the editor a vast range of choices and angles, more than he probably wants, certainly more than he needs. This is where the greatest danger comes in overcutting, putting in too many angles to fit in every vision—a bit of this, a bit of that, and in the end, not much of anything.

I am often asked how long it takes to edit something. The only answer I can usually find is that it takes as much time as you have. The constraints of time can have two causes: deadline, as in broadcast airtime, or cost, because of limitations of budget, or a combination of the two. I have worked on news pieces that should have taken an hour to edit that have been cut for air in less than 10 minutes. And I have worked on pieces that could have been cut in an hour that took weeks. An edit can go on endlessly. It never really finishes; it stops. Painters often talk about painting in this way, that you just reach a point where the work stops and you say that is it. Eventually you reach a point at which all your additional effort isn't making it better, just making it different, rearranging the shots, making adjustments so subtle that they can be seen only on the 20th viewing. It's often better to stop earlier rather than later.

As I wrote in the beginning of this book, editing is about selection, arrangement, and timing. The classic example is the three shots of the burning building:

A.   The building on fire

B.   The building exploding

C.   Three men running away

In this order the audience sees it as three men escaping the exploding building. If you see A, then C, followed by B, you might think the men are trying to escape the fire and are caught by the explosion. If you see C, then B, then A, you will probably suspect the men caused the explosion that left the building burning.

The editor's first decisions are:

1.   Which shot to use

2.   In which order the shots should appear

3.   For how long each shot should be on the screen

Whether the editing takes place when the writer scripts one shot and then another, or the director stages a scene to be shot with a certain continuity, or in some moment of serendipity in the cutting room when one shot is placed next to another, that is where movies are made.

Editing creates the visual and aural juxtaposition between shots, but this process does not begin in the cutting room. If it did, the picture would be doomed. The process must begin in the head of the writer or producer or director. It must then carry forward to all aspects of script writing, production design, and on to the shooting process with all camera crew and the production team. Only after all those steps does it arrive in the editing room to be put together and shaped into its final form. If the process of editing was not begun earlier, the editor is fighting an uphill and inevitably losing battle.

Editors like to think they can make or break a project. They most certainly can break one, and they can certainly rescue one, but for a project to be really good requires not only that it be edited well but that it be shot in such a way that it *can* be edited well. This doesn't only mean that it is beautifully photographed; the most beautiful shots that can't be edited together effectively are pointless. That long, slow lingering zoom out becomes an anchor that drags down the video. That perfectly smooth pan along the treeline down to the shore brings the video to grinding halt. Do you know what the viewer looks at when he or she watches this type of pan? They're staring at the leading edge of the screen, watching for what's coming around the corner. It isn't only slow movement that will destroy a sequence, but the very camera angles chosen to show the scene. Poorly placed cameras, poorly composed shots and ineffective staging will do more to kill a video beyond what even the finest editor can resurrect.

Loading the Lesson

Before we begin looking at the various editing forms, let's load the material you'll need for the lesson onto the media hard drive of your computer.

1. Drag the *Lesson 7 Media* folder from the DVD to your media drive.

2. If you don't already have it, bring the *Projects* folder from the DVD onto your system drive.

3. Eject the DVD, open the *Projects* folder on your system drive, and double-click the project file *Lesson 7* to launch the application.

4. Once again, choose the **Reconnect** option to relink the media files when the **Offline Files** dialog appears.

Setting up the Project

Inside the project, you'll find these sequences in the **Browser**:

- An empty sequence called *Sequence 1*
- A bin called *Music*, which contains a four clips.
- A bin called *Action Cut*, which contains a master clip, two subclips and a sequence, which we'll look at later.
- Another bin called *Heartwood*, which contains the another master clip as well as some subclips and a few sequences.

Documentary

Documentary is a loosely used term for factual film or video production. Generally these are productions that usually present facts and have a narration, either a disembodied voice or one made up from those appearing in the video. Documentaries are the type of shows you might see on the Discovery Channel or National Geographic. Documentary, news, reportage, informational, and even instructional are all variations of the same type of video. Even wedding videos are forms of documentary production in the purest sense: they document an event but often include other material that records the couple's background. Wedding videos come in a great many styles and use a variety of techniques.

Documentaries fall into two large groups:

- Programs that are tightly scripted to start, shot to a pre-written narration, and edited from that, with few changes along the way

- Programs that are wholly made up in the editing room, with a structure and a narration that is crafted to fit the material.

Many documentaries fall somewhere in between. Again, wedding videos provide the classic example, the ceremony is the tightly scripted portion of the production, while the reception might be largely unscripted. In its unscripted form, the documentary is created by the producer, director, and cameraperson on location. Good, experienced camerapersons, whether they realize it or not, are actually scripting the story as they shoot it. Certainly every good news cameraperson is shooting with the correspondent's voice reading the lines in his head. Chances are that if it isn't shot for any particular purpose, it will probably not find any use at all. Once the material has been shot, it's the director's and editor's responsibility to bring from that material all that it has to offer.

Documentary can be a factual, accurate representation of events, or it can be an imaginative, poetical, loose interpretation of reality. Either way, documentary can start fully scripted, wholly unscripted, or something in between. One feature that all forms have in common is the tendency to shoot vastly more material than necessary, sometimes with shooting ratios as high as 25:1, even 100:1.

Many documentary scripts aren't written so much as found, or so says my friend Loren Miller. There's much truth to that. The mass of material in a documentary is often best sorted out on paper before the picture is attacked. The paper edit is crucial, and the paper edit is the mining for the script that's in the material,

Music and Narration

A common dilemma that's often posed is whether it is better to cut to the rhythm of the music or to the rhythm of the narration in a sequence. I don't think you have to choose between the two. If you have to make that choice, then there is probably something more fundamentally wrong with the sequence. There should either be music to which you're cutting or there should be narration. I dislike productions that slather music under everything. You should bring the music up for a purpose, and while it's up full, you should be cutting to the music. Then when you bring in the narration, you should fade out the music under the narration. Just keeping it there as a bed, I think, is almost always wrong (unless it's integral to the scene that's being narrated).

If you're having to choose between cutting to one or the other, the music or the narration, then the music doesn't belong there: either it's the wrong music, or it's the wrong narration. Even in a sequence where music is a key element—a video about dance, for instance—you are cutting to the rhythm of the music while the music is up and then to the narration when it's up, even if the music continues underneath. Often with this kind of production, it's better to make the narration quite sparse and punctuated more frequently than you normally would with sections of music. So you get a phrase or a sentence or two at most, then go back to the music and dance briefly, before returning to another short piece of narration. What should be avoided is the tendency to have a blanket of narration lying on top of a blanket of music.

Michelangelo finding the statue that's in the stone. The paper edit can be done from transcripts, from log notes, on an Excel spreadsheet, or on 3×5 cards. The idea is always the same: move the information around, find the links, find what flows together, find the conflicts, the drama, and visual strength in the material and put it together into a coherent plan that can be taken into the cutting room.

The unscripted documentary benefits greatly from the advent of nonlinear editing systems, because not only does it give the editor very powerful search tools, but it also allows quickly trying many combinations of images. You can try different sequences and archive them, but avoid taking this to extremes. Don't start a new version of a sequence every few edits. You'll probably find yourself getting confused, or at least undecided about which to use. Better would be to keep substantially different versions of a sequence or a show. As a documentary develops a idea for a structure of the material may come up, seem like a good idea at the time, but then lead to a muddle later on, forcing you to backtrack to an earlier version which flowed better and worked better as a whole. Because the structure of a documentary can change often and radically before it's completed (probably more so than most narrative films), it's important to keep these major changes as separate sequences. On large projects it's better to archive them as entirely separate project files for simplicity's sake.

In loosely scripted documentary material, after you work through various shot orders, the frames themselves can seem to impose a continuity by being adjacent to each other. Certain shots will seem to want to go together, as will others. Then groups of images coalesce into clusters, and the clusters form logical strings, until the whole is built out of the parts and a structure has imposed itself on the material.

Organizing your material is crucial to working efficiently in the documentary form. Well-organized bins with many notes throughout are more than beneficial, they're mandatory. We looked at organization earlier in Lesson 2 on page 33. You may want to review that.

Documentary generally uses a narration track to carry the information, whether it's a disembodied voice of God speaking truths or an ever-present narrator who wanders through the scene, or even if it's pieced together from interviews. The narration becomes the bed for the video.

What many editors like to do is build a bed of the primary audio track and its synchronous video. So if the video starts with a short piece of music, lay down the music on a lower audio track, leaving the primary tracks open for the video. Then the narration comes in. Lay down the narration on a separate track. Then when a piece of an interview comes in, lay in the sound bites in their entirety with the sync picture, jump cuts and all. The picture can always be covered later. Then perhaps more narration, and then another musical break. You can go on and on, building the entire sound track like this until it looks something like Figure 7.1. FCP's **Voice Over** feature comes in handy here, for recording the kind of scratch recording, a rough narration, to lay down as the basis for the bed.

At this stage, the laid-out video might have a distinctly blocky look to it, but as the material is worked, more and more overlapping of sound and picture will begin to appear.

7.1   Documentary Sound Bed

☆ *Tip*
Notes: Another handy use for the
Voice Over tool is to make notes
while you're watching the video.
Use headphones to hear your track.
Clip on a lavaliere mic as close to
your mouth as you can get it, and
set off to play your sequence. This is
kind of like recording dictation,
except that it records right in your
Timeline in line with what you're
commenting. Your comment, "That
shot's too dark" appears right
underneath the shot that's too dark.
Another use for **Voice Over** is to
record rough translations in foreign
locations. It's often cheaper, and
easier to get a translation done right
on the spot, recording it to your
PowerBook with its built-in micro-
phone. If it's good enough you can
use your location recording, or get it
re-recorded later. But having the foreign language content translated on
the spot can be a great time saver
when you get into the cutting room.

Some people like to work in a very linear fashion, tightly editing the material as they go. It's quite natural to build a sequence this way, this is the natural way a story progresses, linearly. On the other hand, I think the benefit of laying out the bed is that you get to see what the whole structure is like, where emphasis needs to be placed, where more graphical explanation is needed perhaps, where there are parts that may need to be cut because they're tak- ing too much time, or a minor point is being dwelt on too long. Without the whole, it's hard to get that sense of how the material is paced and stands up as a structure.

Once the bed is laid out, the sound track flowing smoothly, the content making sense, progressing sensibly from point to point to conclusion like a well-crafted essay, then the pictures are put in to fill the gaps in the track. Having laid down your bed, you're ready to put in the B Roll material. The pacing of the editing is now dic- tated by language, the rhythm and cadence of speech, which can vary greatly from speaker to speaker, from language to language. Usually I add the B Roll material to V2 over interview portions if needed. This makes it easier to go back to the interview at a later stage without having to edit it back into the **Timeline**, which may, in its early stages while the first B Roll material is being added, look something like Figure 7.2.

The bed, of course, is just a starting block and is not inviable by any means. It's often ripped open to insert natural sound breaks. The multiple track tool to select everything after a certain point in the timeline is very useful for this. You can call it up from the **Tools** or with the **T** tool. By tapping **T** four times, you'll bring up the **Select All Tracks Forward** tool (Figure 7.3). Or if you press **T**, the single track tool, and then hold down the **Shift** key, you'll tog- gle to **Select All Tracks Forward**.

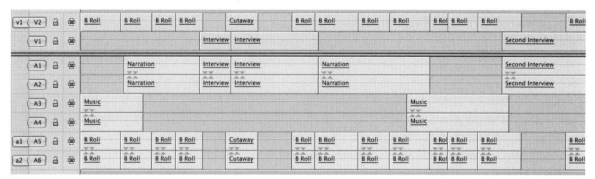

7.2   Documentary Bed with B Roll

7.3   Select All Tracks Forward Tool

What is a B Roll?

You may have noticed that one of the FCP default **Labels** is called **B Roll**. In the old days that were not so long ago, a television anchorman or reporter would lay down a commentary track or do an entire on-camera narration, originally as film and later as videotape. Called the A Roll, it would be loaded on a machine, either telecine or VTR. Then shots illustrating the narration would be cut together and loaded on a second machine. This would be the B Roll. Both would be fed into a control room and gang-synced together so that the director could either cut back and forth or use effects to switch between the two. B Roll became the generic term for any cover video, regardless of how it was assembled into the production. B Roll is material that shows what someone is talking about, the shots of the car accident as the police officer describes it, or they can be contrapuntal shots, pictures of wealthy homes while the narration describes poverty in the country. All of these shots serve to illustrate, refine, or comment on the narration, interview, or other voice over.

B Roll can also be cutaways. Any editor will tell you that cutaways are the most useful shots. You can never have too many, and you never seem to have enough. No editor will ever complain that you have shot too many cutaways. A cutaway shot shows a subsidiary action or reaction that you can use to bridge an edit. It's usually used to contract time, as we'll see a bit later. It's the shot of the onlookers watching. It's that overly used shot of a person's hands. The shot of the interviewer nodding in response to an answer is called in England a *noddie*. The noddie allows you to bridge a portion of the interviewee's answer where the person has stumbled over the words or has digressed into something pointless. A wide shot that shows the whole scene can often be used as a cutaway. Make note of these useful shots as you log your material.

➤ **Note**

Misused Montage: Montage in its weakest form is used as a quick way to convey information. The travel sequence is the most clichéd: character leaves, plane takes off, plane lands, character walks out of terminal and gets in a cab, cab pulls up at curb, character walks into a building. This is superficial montage to convey minimal information.

In practice, of course, an hour-long documentary is usually not laid out as a single bed, but rather broken into sequences that are edited separately and then brought together into a final sequence. Opens are often built separately, often by entirely separate companies specializing in motion graphics, 3D, and compositing with tools such as After Effects. Even while staying in-house, specialist sequences can be laid down separately.

Editing documentaries is not often about continuity of action, but rather about continuity of ideas, putting together images that separately have one meaning, but together have a different meaning and present a new idea. This is the concept of *montage*. The term has come to be used in a few of different ways, but the original form established by Russian filmmakers in the 1920s was based on this idea.

In this powerful concept, you can put together two shots that have no direct relationship with each other and thereby create in the audience's mind a quite different idea, separate from the meaning of its parts. This juxtaposition of unrelated images to make the audience draw a continuity of ideas is often done with a sequence of usually quick, impressionistic shots, often with motion. Montage can mean a collection of shots that serve to contract or expand time by being cut together. It can be used to create the sense of location or process—for instance, shots of various aspects of car production build up to create an impression of the process. A variety of shots of the Damine festival produce an effect that gives the flavor of the town and the event. The common trick to make montage effective is fast pacing, using speed to quickly build block on block, shot on shot, to construct the whole. Because of time limitations, montage is often used in commercials. It's a quick and concise way to convey a variety of impressions that make up a single whole.

The juxtaposition of shots with very different audio may preclude the use of natural sound because of the harshness of the edit. It often becomes necessary to use unnatural sound or music or to use a split edit to reinforce the point of the intellectual edit. By splitting the sound, the edit happens twice, multiplying its effect. When intercutting material to create tension, what's commonly done is not to cut the sound with the picture, but to keep a constant sound or music to which the editing and the action paces itself.

Another commonly used form of montage is a complex compositing effect to overlay multiple changing images on the screen. This type of montage was popularized by the great filmmaker, theoretician, and teacher Slavko Vorkapich and is now most commonly seen in program openings and main title sequences, where it incorporates graphical elements as well as photographic ones. A classic example is the opening for the Super Bowl. A few years ago CBS created a wonderful montage in which we see small boys playing football on a lawn, then NFL stars repeating their motions in a stadium while the narration talks about a uniquely American sport, the spectacle, the fun, the camaraderie in play and performance, and the celebration as fans, as participants, both as children and as professionals, as Americans. It is deeply complex, emotional, full of evocative ideas and concepts, and brought together through images, music, and special effects. It creates a powerful, persuasive impact, even with something as simple as two shots, a football player and lightning. The shots have no direct relationship, but together they form a continuity of ideas.

Music videos are often montages, metaphors repeated often enough to become clichés, such as the suitcase in the Country & Western video. One good thing about cliché is that the repetition can be honed ever finer. A shot of a guy flirting with a girl, shot of another girl's hand picking up the suitcase tells the whole tale of any number of C&W songs.

Montage isn't confined to documentary or music videos. It is occasionally seen in feature films such as the climatic baptism scene in *The Godfather*. Here, with Bach's music and the Roman Catholic liturgy as a background, Michael Corleone literally becomes a godfather while eliminating his principal enemies, the two ideas intercut and built up together into a classic piece of cinema editing.

Music

Music videos are the staple of MTV, VH1, and CMT. All popular music recording artists have videos made to accompany their music. It's an essential ingredient in artist and record promotion. The key point to remember about editing music videos is that it's about the music. Everything is dictated by the rhythm, the tone, and texture of the music—whether you're working on a project that will be created entirely from computer-generated animation

---

Foreign Language Versions

French and Spanish are often spoken very quickly, yet seem to take many more words to say the same thing as English, so despite the rapid speech, the editing often seems contrapuntal because it is paced so slowly. Re-editing for different languages can be a frustrating experience. Extending material to fit a sentence or shot may not always be best. Because of the rapid speech, new material might have to be introduced. So more shots are used to match the cadence while maintaining the coverage of a single scene. If the material was originally shot for English, finding extra clips to fit foreign language versions can be an exercise in futility.

7.4   Music Markers

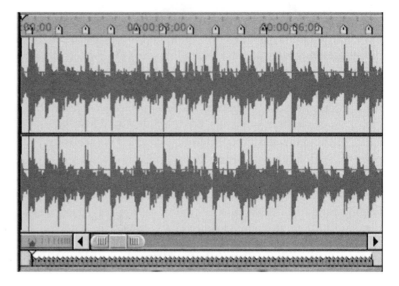

or from a multicamera shoot of a performance—where the edit point comes on each shot is driven by the beat of the music.

Marking the Beat on the Track

Finding the beat is the first step you'll have to take. The simplest way is to mark it up. You probably have an excellent piece of music to try this out on; if not, use the *Jumptown* music that comes with FCP4's tutorial material. It's on the FCP installation DVD inside the folder *Extras/Final Cut Pro Tutorial/NTSC Tutorial (or PAL Tutorial)/DanceShots*. Drag this file from the DVD onto the media drive of your system.

1. Open your project and import the music track called *Jumptown* from the media drive. It will appear in the **Browser** as *Jumptown.aif* and have the speaker icon.

2. Once the file is imported, open it into the **Viewer** and play it.

3. Once you've got the rhythm, start again. As it plays, tap out the beat on the **M** key. You'll quickly fill it up with little green markers (Figure 7.4).

You'll probably notice how not all the markers line up exactly with the spikes in the beat. The visual display of the waveform is really helpful here.

4. Step through the markers (**Shift-down** arrow takes you to the next marker; **Shift-Up** arrow takes you to the previous marker), repositioning them as you go.

5. If the marker is late (after the beat), just add a new marker on the beat. Then go to the incorrectly positioned marker and delete it (**Command-`**).

6. If the marker is early (before the spike in the waveform), reposition the marker with **Shift-`**, which will pull the marker up to the playhead.

Once you get into the groove of it, you can quickly clean up your markers until they're exactly placed.

Now that you've marked up, you're ready to start laying in picture. First drag the track into the **Timeline** and then lock those music tracks with the handy little locks on left end of the **Timeline** (Figure 7.5). That music track shouldn't be going anywhere, and you don't want to accidentally overwrite it when you put in some video. You can also use the keyboard shortcut **F5** followed by the track number, so in this case you'd press **F5** followed by **1**, and then **F5** followed by **2** to lock **A1** and **A2**. You are now ready cut up your shots and edit them into the **Timeline** based on the markers attached to the music clip.

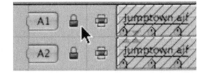

7.5   Track Locks

Marking the Beat on the Timeline

Another way to work with markers, rather than putting them on the clip itself, is to lay your music into your sequence first. Then rather than placing the markers on the audio track, you can tap out the markers in the **Timeline**. FCP has a way to work with markers that's handy for music videos: **Mark to Markers**.

1. Place *Jumptown.aif* in the **Timeline**.

2. Lock the audio tracks so that nothing can move them or overwrite them.

3. Make sure nothing is selected in the **Timeline** (**Command-Shift-A**). With the playhead at the start of the sequence, begin playing the track, tapping **M** to the beat as the music plays. This will add markers to the **Timeline** itself.

4. After you've placed the markers in the **Timeline**, move the playhead to a point anywhere between the first pair of markers, and select from the **Mark** menu **Mark to Markers**. Or press the keyboard shortcut **Control-A**.

Now all you have to do is find the shot to place between those markers and the In and Out points you've created.

7.6 Mark to Markers in the Timeline

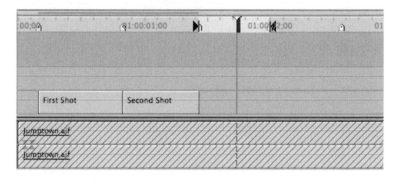

5. Open a clip from the **Browser** into the **Viewer** by double-clicking on it.

6. Find where you want the clip to begin, and mark an In point.

7. Press **F10** to **Overwrite**. The shot will be cut into the **Timeline** in the marked position.

8. Move the playhead between the next pair of markers, and press **Control-A**.

By repeating the process a couple of times, your timeline will soon look like Figure 7.6. It's a very efficient way for quickly roughing out your shots for a music video.

If you to want to use any natural or sync sound with your music video, you might want to add a couple of tracks and move the music down, leaving the primary tracks, **A1** and **A2**, free for the video.

It's no coincidence that many editors are musicians at heart and often play musical instruments. Editing is so much about rhythm and cadence, both of which are usually dictated by sound. Edit to the beat: either the cut is on the beat, or the event in the shot is on the beat. When you cut on the beat, the edit appears on the moment of the beat, on the spike in the waveform. If you are cutting a drummer pounding the skins, if you cut on the beat, you are cutting on the moment he is striking the drum. The strike on the drumhead explodes the edit into the next shot. However, to see the drummer beat the drum, you really need to cut off the beat so that the edit occurs in the gaps between strikes. This way the action is placed on the moment of the beat, on the spike in the waveform.

For most music you can cut either on the beat or off the beat. I'd guess most music is cut on the beat, as in the tip about slugs. This

☆ Tip

Slugs: Some people like to lay a slug from the **Generators** into the video track and go along, with **Snapping** turned on, cutting the slug at each of the markers (Figure 7.7). Each of these slugs becomes the basis for a shot that's cut on the beat of the music. With **Replace** you can quickly drop shots onto each slug. Place the playhead over the slug you want to replace, and drag the clip to **Replace** in the CEO. You just have to make sure there is enough media for the length of the slug you're replacing.

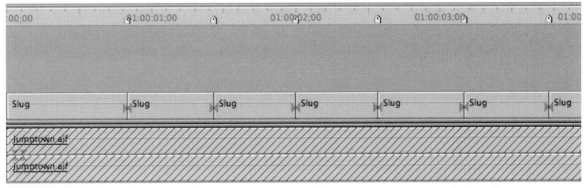

7.7   Bladed Slug

works pretty well and will always produce acceptable results. Placing the cut on the beat works especially well for stills or other images without much action. However, if there is strong action in the shot, it's often better to cut off the beat.

Take the obvious example of a shot of a drummer striking his drum. If you're cutting on the beat, you're cutting to or away from the drum on the very frame on which it's struck. Here you might want to set up a rhythm that has you cutting off the beat and placing the action on the beat:

- The fist strikes the table.
- The door slams.
- The drum is pounded.
- The guitar chord is struck.
- The couple kisses.

All of these moments need to be seen. The impact event should happen on the beat; the edit, hidden between the beats. No video will have just one or the other, which would make it horribly monotonous, but a mixture of the two, changing back and forth through the rhythm of the music and of the images.

Tip

Sequence Chorus: Music is about repetition: passages and choruses that often repeat. Using FCP you can create a sequence that repeats for each chorus. You may not want each chorus to be exactly the same, but have small variations, though the structure and rhythm and many of the shots may repeat. The simplest way to do this is to duplicate copies of the first chorus sequence, as many as you need, and make the variations in them. The various chorus sequences can then be dropped into the final sequence as needed.

Multicamera Editing

Multicamera performance recordings are edited somewhat differently from straight linear sequences. There are many ways to work, but FCP4 has introduced some great new tools to facilitate this. Though it does not have true multicamera play back, the application has features which will allow you to simulate this.

One of the trickiest parts of working with multicamera material is to sync up the video. Ideally, the material is shot with cameras that can have their timecodes slaved to each other. One camera becomes the master camera, and all the other cameras run timecode that is jam-synced to the master, so that the timecode on each camera is identical. This means that at any single moment in a performance, you can see what each camera is doing.

Let's see how to do this with using the source clips in the *Music* bin.

1. Begin by creating a new sequence. Call it *Multicam*.

2. Edit the shot called *Camera 1* onto V1 on the sequence.

3. Because all the other shots have the same audio, deselect the audio tracks so that you'll bring into the sequence only the video portion.

4. Stack *Camera 2*, *Camera 3*, and *Camera 4* on the tracks above **V1**.

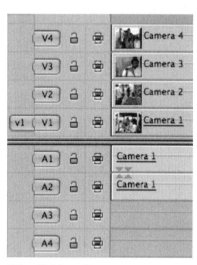

7.8 Multicam Sequence

With all four cameras stacked and synced together on **V1** though **V4**, they should look like Figure 7.8. We'll come back to this in a moment. There is only one stereo pair of audio associated with *Camera 1*, which is the master shot. The other cameras are all synced to the master audio from the main camera recording.

FCP provides a way to slip each camera into sync and to make sure they are in sync. It will display the timecode for each of the shots stacked up in the **Timeline** (Figure 7.9). The figure shows the original timecode of the clips, which isn't available to you, where all the clips *Camera 1* to *Camera 4* all begin with zero timecode. The **Timecode Overlays** can be called up from the **View** menu (**Option-Z**). They can also be called up with the **Image** popup at the top of the **Canvas** or the **Viewer.** Notice in the graphic that a couple of the tracks are slightly out of sync by a few frames. It's easy enough to nudge them back into sync. Simply select the clip and tap the left or right bracket (< or >) to move the clip along the timeline.

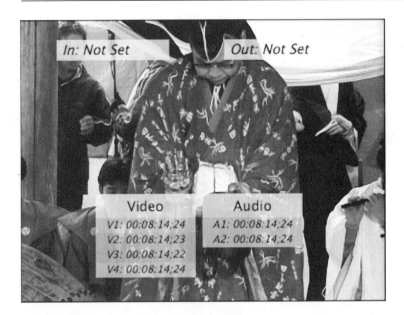

7.9   Timecode Overlay

Often it isn't possible to shoot the material with cameras with synced timecode. Then it becomes necessary to sync the clips manually. Sometimes the waveforms of the various clips can be used to help do this; sometimes it's just a matter of fiddling with the clips. It really helps, however, to shoot it properly in the first place. As the shoot begins, all cameras should point to a common place and record a syncable event like a clapperboard strike, or a handclap, or a camera flash—anything that all the cameras can see at the same time. Once the clapperboard is taped, the cameras shouldn't stop rolling until the performance is over or their tape runs out.

Let's go back to our *Multicam* sequence. Once you've created your stack of camera shots, we'll use that sequence to create a multicamera display of your material.

1. With all your tracks laid out in sync in the *Multicam* sequence, select everything in the sequence and copy it.

2. Create a new sequence and call it the *Edit* sequence.

3. Add a **V2** track to the new sequence and set it as the destination track.

4. Now paste all the clips into the sequence so that they're stacked as they were in *Multicam*, except beginning on **V2**. The audio will by default be edited onto **A3/A4**.

5. Go back to the *Multicam* sequence and resize each of the layers down to 50%.

6. Position each of the layers in a different quadrant of the **Canvas**. To do this precisely for DV material, use the Center point settings in Table 7.1.

Table 7.1   Center Point Settings

	X value	Y value
Upper Left	−180	−120
Upper Right	180	−120
Lower Left	−180	120
Lower Right	180	120

Place the *Multicam* sequence inside the *Edit* sequence on the empty **V1**.

7.10 Gang > Follow

7. **Option**-double-click the nested *Multicam* sequence to open it into the **Viewer**.

8. From the **Gang** popup at the top of either the **Canvas** or the **Viewer**, choose the **Follow** function (Figure 7.10).

Tip

Autoselect Shortcuts: Command-1 on the keypad toggles **Autoselect** on and off for **V1**. **Command-2** for **V2**, **Command-3** for **V3**, and so on up to **V8**. **Option-1** toggles Autoselect on **A1**, **Option-2** on **A2**, **Option-3** on **A3**, and so on up to **A8**. **Command-zero** on the keypad toggles **Autoselect** on and off for all video tracks, while **Option-zero** does the same for the audio tracks. **Option**-clicking the **Autoselect** button on a track will toggle **Autoselect** for that video or audio track, that is, switch all other video or audio tracks on and off.

As you move through the **Timeline**, through your stack of camera angles, the display in the **Viewer** will show you exactly what shot is available to you from each of your cameras as the playhead in the **Viewer** is ganged to follow the playheads in the **Canvas** and the **Timeline** (Figure 7.11).

One good thing about this technique is that on the fastest computers, with **Unlimited RT** you should be able to do all this in real time. On slower machines it might be advisable to export your *Multicam* Sequence and then reimport it as a single video clip rather than a nested sequence.

You can look through your *Multicam* sequence in the **Viewer**, adding markers with notes to which camera to take at any point. To edit your video, just use the **Blade** tool, or better yet, FCP4's new **Autoselect** feature together with the **Control-V** keyboard shortcut. Lock **V1** with the *Multicam* nest so you don't cut it by accident. You could also lock **V2** with *Camera 1*, because that camera is either visible or is covered with another shot. Use the

7.11 Viewer and Canvas Ganged

Autoselect function to choose which tracks you want to cut. Autoselected tracks will be cut with **Control-V**, while unselected tracks will be left untouched. As you cut your material away, revealing just the shot you want to see at any one time, your timeline will start to look something like Figure 7.12. Notice tracks **V3** and **V4** have the **Autoselect** function turned on. The selected destination track, **V2**, has no effect on which tracks are edited.

When working with multiple tracks like this, it's generally best to get most of your editing done before you begin to put in transitions or do effects that require rendering.

The easiest way to maintain sync across all the cameras—which may not have matched timecode, unless they were all slaved to a single generator during recording—is to use **Auxiliary Timecode**.

7.12 Cut Timeline

7.13   Modifying Timecode

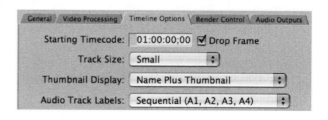

Tip

Multicamera: For multicamera editing, some people like to work with wide tracks with the **Timeline** switched to filmstrip mode. This way you can actually see the pictures in the sequence to help while you're cutting the shots.

Another use for the **Voice Over** tool: play through your material and call out the shots just like a studio director. Press the **M** key to add a marker as well as you play through your material.

Select the clip in the **Browser**—or with the clip in the **Viewer**—choose **Timecode** from the **Modify** menu. This will bring up the dialog box in Figure 7.13. In addition to setting the **Auxiliary Timecode**, you can also set an **Auxiliary Reel Number**, which might be useful to you. Notice in this box that you can change not only the **Auxiliary Timecode**, but also the **Source Timecode**. Use this with great care. This is one of the few functions within FCP that will actually affect the media on your hard drive. If you change the **Source Timecode** in this window, you will permanently change the timecode of your source media on your hard drive.

Now when the clips are laid out in the **Timeline** and opened in the **Viewer** you can switch to **Aux TC** by control clicking in the current time window in the upper right of the **Viewer** and select **Aux 1**.

You can help this further by changing the **Timeline** start time to match the timecode of the clips, so everything, each clip and the **Timeline** itself are all running to matching timecode references. You can change the **Timeline** start time in **Sequence** Settings (**Command-Zero**) under the **Timeline Options** tab by dialing a new **Starting Timecode** number (Figure 7.14).

7.14   Setting Starting Timecode for Timeline

Action

By action I don't mean only the movies of Governor Schwarzenegger or *Charlie's Angels*. Action might be in any feature or short narrative film. All forms of video might use elements and techniques of action, where what occurs in one shot continues smoothly into the next. While documentary is often based on noncontinuous shots and the juxtaposition of apparently unrelated images, action films are based, within each scene, almost exclusively on continuity, a smoothness that makes the film appear almost seamless. The director has to shoot the scene so that the elements match as precisely as possible, that movements repeat as exactly as possible, that the appearance of people and things (and the content of objects like beer glasses) change as little as possible from shot to shot. Editing action is often about finding that precise moment to match two events together as closely as possible.

The Line

The first lesson they teach budding directors in film schools is the Rule of the Line, sometimes called the 180° rule. It's a simple rule, and because it's simple, it always works. The rule is basically that through every scene the director stages, there runs a line, an axis, which his camera cannot cross. In the case of a couple speaking to each other—let's say the man on the left and the woman on the right—then the Line runs through their heads (Figure 7.15).

The director must keep his camera on the one side of his chosen line. He can move the camera anywhere he wants within that 180° arc. As long as he does, the man (A) will always remain on the left side of the screen and the woman (B) on the right. As long as the scene is shot from any position in that 180° arc, such as camera positions 1, 2, or 3, A will always be looking from the left side of the screen toward the right, and B will always be looking from the right side of the screen toward the left. As soon as the camera crosses the Line, such as in position 4, the relationship between the two will suddenly change. A will now be looking from right to left, B from left to right. The audience will become disoriented, thinking that one has turned his or her back on the other.

The convention is that the Line isn't crossed and that someone looking camera left is placed on the right of the screen, and vice

7.15 The Line

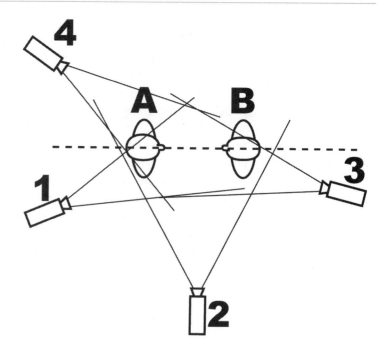

versa. This means that the viewer's eyes are sweeping back and forth across the screen, like a voyeur eavesdropping on a conversation.

More and more, the directorial convention seems to be to place characters on the same side of the screen, so that someone looking camera left may be on the right side of the screen, but in the next shot the character facing them will be looking camera right, but will also be on the right edge of the screen. The viewer's eyes now never have to move. The same effect is achieved by crossing the line. Two characters are sitting at angles to each other, and the camera repeatedly crosses the line. They seem to swap places with each cut, but the audience keeps looking at the same point on the screen. This is both destabilizing, creating tension, yet evoking intimacy because the audience is (the director hopes) riveted, perhaps even mesmerized, by a point on the screen.

The principles of the Line apply to objects or people in motion. If a direction of movement is established, such as left to right across the screen, movement must continue in that direction, or the audience will think that the objects or people have turned around and are going back where they came from.

To get over the problem of getting to the other side of the Line, directors use simple tricks like tracking around the subject, which visually defines for the audience that the line is being crossed. For objects in motion, the common trick is to place the camera directly on the line itself, so the car, for instance, is either going directly away from you or coming straight at you. After that shot, the director can then place the camera on either side of the line, because again the audience has received a visual clue that the line is being violated.

To achieve this continuity of action and avoid a lot of jump cuts, the director should vary the shot by changing the size/angle of the shot. As we saw, a small change will create a jump cut. Shots should change a full size greater: close shot to medium shot to long shot, not close-up to close shot, nor medium shot to medium long shot. The angle change should be 40° or more to make it effective.

These are the most basic rules of action direction, but they do work and work effectively. And like most rules, not only are they often broken, but they're really made to be broken. If you do break them, though, you should know why, and break them on purpose to good effect.

These ground rules, of course, carry over to editing, so that the directions established on the stage or location are maintained in the cutting room.

The basis of this type of editing is cutting on action. An action can be any movement:

- The moment when someone walks in the door
- When someone sits in the chair
- When the hero pulls the heroine into his arms

It's the moment the editor uses to draw the audience into the action or back them out of it.

There are three possible places to cut an action:

- Just before the action takes place
- During the action
- After the action is completed

Each of these has a different contextual meaning for the audience. In the *Action Cut* bin in your **Browser** is a sequence called *Action Cut Sequence*. In this sequence, five separate edits are shown:

- In the first, the cut to the closer shot of the priest takes place before the priest rises. Placing the cut before the action occurs emphasizes the action.

- In the next edit, the cut occurs after the action is completed. This emphasizes not the action but the object or person you're cutting to. Cutting before the action begins or after the action is completed makes the edit more pointed, more apparent to the audience.

- The third edit shows the cut during the movement itself. Cutting during movement has the tendency to conceal the edit, probably the preferred edit in many circumstances.

- The fourth edit cuts away before the action takes place, but unlike the others, it moves from a close shot to wider shot.

- In the final edit, shot again changes from close to wide, but this time the edit takes place during the movement.

Sometimes it is important to mark the event before it occurs. Sometimes it is necessary not to disrupt the action but to let it complete before we move on. Sometimes it's best to make the action flow as smoothly as possible, to conceal the edit within the movement. In the first three edits in *Action Cut Sequence,* the edit goes from a medium shot to a closer shot. If the cut is going the other way, as in the fourth and fifth edits (close shot to wider shot), it generally works better to place the edit before the action takes place rather than during the action. None of these rules are by any means hard and fast. Every situation will vary; every cut will be different and require a different decision. These are the decisions you have to make, and you have to make them somewhere in one of those 29.97ths of a second.

Dialog

Dialog is the other key ingredient in feature and short-form narrative film and video. Action editing and dialog together form the main techniques used in narrative film. In dialog films, the order of shots often goes all the way back to the writer, whose choice of words, the sequence of imparting information within the dialog, will be the first steps in determining the order of shots. Eventually we arrive at the editor, who has a selection of material and an order of shots to some degree determined by the content, be it dialog, narration, or intellectual logic.

If your production is intended for theatrical release, be aware that the screen you're editing on is considerably smaller than the screen it will be projected on. It will take longer for the audience to read the image because there is so much of it and so much

➥ Tip

Two-Thirds: As a rule of thumb, cutting on action generally works best when the cut comes about two-thirds of the way through the movement, rather than right after the movement starts or at the midpoint. That way the movement really just finishes in the second shot.

detail. It's important to try to visualize your monitor as a theatre screen and not a television set. You need to be looking inside the picture that will be much larger than your audience, rather than simply at the image, which is what you do when you are watching TV, where you can see and absorb the whole image without your eye have to track or travel around the screen.

Modern editing is based on the idea of seamlessness; the narrative film especially stresses the hidden edit, both in action and in dialog. The editor in these types of film is often looking for the most natural place to cut. Editing is the decision of the moment, the one frame that precisely defines the moment of change from one image to another, the moment the great Walter Murch calls "the blink of an eye." This is the moment the viewer blinks, the moment he has enough of one image and is ready for the next. In a carefully edited sequence, that moment is predicated by the edits that came before it and by the sound that links them together.

Emotion is the key to storytelling and is perhaps even more important than the story itself. Though some may say this is twice as important as the story, if the story is not there or not sustained, no level of emotional development will be believable or sustainable. The two are more intrinsically entwined, and simple numerical divisions are not real measures of a shot's importance. Similarly, mechanical devices such as the Line that allow the audience to suspend belief and help draw them into the reality of the story should not be dismissed as mere props. If the audience withdraws because it's abruptly jarred by poor direction and staging, the story and its emotional drive will suffer.

As so often in editing, sound is the principal driving force behind the timing of edits, probably none more so than in dialog sequences. This does not mean the edits come with the sound; they may in fact come against the sound, and most often do. You almost never slavishly cut with the person speaking; you often cut to a person after they begin speaking or perhaps more commonly before they begin to speak. It's often unnatural to cut on the gap; either you cut after the response begins, as though you're an observer reacting, or you cut while the first person is still speaking, anticipating the response.

Think of how you watch a conversation. You generally look at the speaker, perhaps occasionally glancing at the listener. When the listener interjects, you hear the voice and then turn to the source of the sound. The audio precedes the video; you hear the sound and then you see the source of the sound. Sometimes this is overt, such as the famous Hitchcock transition from seeing a woman's mouth opening to scream, hearing a train whistle, and then seeing the rushing train. More usually, the transition is considerably more subtle. In narrative film the editor often works on the assumption that the viewer grasps the situation and anticipates the response. One person speaks, and while they're talking, you cut to the other, to see the reaction and anticipate the response before it begins. The second person responds, and during the response, after the subject and verb establishes the sense, you cut back to the first person to await another response. Murch contends that you blink as you change your point of view, and this blink is the edit. You hear the door open; you turn to see who is entering the room. When we turn our heads, we often blink. When we're looking at the door to see who has entered, the door is already open. It is unnatural to see the door before it begins to open, though it's often used to create anticipation and suspense.

Sometimes you hold longer on the listener, especially when they're being told some piece of news that you already know. When your wife is telling a story that you've heard many times, usually you don't watch her retelling the tale; you watch her audience to see their reactions. This is especially true when someone is being told terrible news like a death in the family. If you know the news, you watch the reaction; but if you don't know the news, if it is being revealed to you for the first time, you usually watch the messenger, at least at first.

How long you hold an image on the screen is dictated by how long you want the viewer to look at it. Sometimes this is very brief. You look left and right to cross a street, and you see the two images of the street for only the briefest of moments, probably less a second each. Often you hold on an image much longer to give the viewer a chance to look around it, to study the image. The more complex the image the longer it needs to be on the screen. The word STOP in white letters in a black ground can on seen in a few frames; an Ansel Adams photograph of Yosemite's Half Dome needs to be lingered over.

Because editing dialog is such a unique, yet common, problem, let's look at a short, simple scene and see how to put it together. There is no right way to edit any scene of dialog; no two editors will pick exactly the same frames, or perhaps even the same takes, or the same pacing, to assemble a scene.

There is a conventional pattern to structure scenes, still followed so much of the time that the audience notices when it's not. The convention is to begin with a wide, establishing shot, then move from there to medium shots, move in to close-ups as the scene intensifies, and perhaps return to the wide shot after the climax of the scene.

Another convention is to follow your character:

1. We see the character.
2. We see what the character sees.
3. We see the character react.

The shot progression quickly goes from wide shot to a series of *singles*; these singles being simple close-ups and their respective *reverse angles*. It is important in this structure that the characters are consistently sized on screen. It would be unsettling for the audience if the sizes of the close-ups varied greatly while we're switching from one character's point of view to the other. It's important to establish the frame size for the scene so that the actors maintain their relative size in the frame.

In your **Browser** is a bin called *Heartwood*, which contains the clip *Heartwood*. This is a master clip made up from the slightly edited rushes of a movie called *Heartwood*, an independent production, directed by Lanny Cotler and produced by Steve Cotler, starring Hilary Swank, Eddie Mills, and the late Jason Robards. This is a short scene between Sylvia (Hilary Swank) and Frank (Eddie Mills) in which he's trying to persuade her to run away with him. The scene was shot, as is common in film production, with a single camera. Editing the scene shot with multiple cameras is somewhat easier, as in a multicamera musical performance, but the techniques and the end result are very similar.

This scene opens as the couple comes out from an old trailer. The camera tracks slightly with them to their marks, and then becomes the master wide shot for the scene. The wide shot is followed by singles of Frank and Sylvia, close-ups of each of the actors' performances. There are a couple of flubs at the beginning, but the singles are only one take of many. By giving you only one real take, I've simplified your editing choices considerably. In reality, you could choose lines from a number of takes, as long as you maintained the integrity of the performance.

1. Look through the material. It's only about four and one-half minutes long.

In the *Heartwood* bin I have already made up the subclips for you—*Frank*, *Sylvia*, and *Master*, which is the wide, two-shot of the argument. You can use the empty *Sequence 1* in the **Browser** to do your edit.

In this scene, let's begin with the wide shot because that's the only cover until the actors reach their marks.

2. Drag the subclip *Master* directly into the **Timeline** or to the **Canvas** to **Overwrite** to edit it into the sequence. Leave it stretched out for the whole length of the scene.

3. Play the master shot until the first line of dialog, "Look, we can make it."

4. Mark an In point in the **Timeline**. This is where we're going to edit in the first close-up. The timing can be trimmed and adjusted later, but this is your staring point.

5. Switch off the audio for the master shot tracks **A1** and **A2**.

6. Create a new video track by **Control**-clicking in the head of track and choosing **Add Track** from the shortcut menu.

7. Set the new **V2** as the destination track, and set **A3** and **A4** as the destination audio tracks (Figure 7.16).

8. Open up Frank's and Sylvia's subclips into separate viewers. **Control**-click on each of the clips and select **Open in New Viewer.**

7.16 Master Shot in Timeline

Though you can't gang-sync the two **Viewers** in FCP—both windows playing at the same time—it's nice to have them open at the same time (Figure 7.17).

9. Cut the dialog up in the subclips line by line starting with Frank, and Overwrite each piece of video and audio into the destination tracks, back and forth between the couple.

Sometimes it's easier to find the edit point in the **Audio** tab of the **Viewer**, such as when Frank says, "I'll do anything for you." (Figure 7.18).

After you've worked through the lines, you'll have the basic structure of the scene in close-ups, cut in its most boring, conventional manner. The audience sees who's speaking, each in turn. By covering up the master shot but leaving it on **V1**, you have it available when you want to cut back to it (Figure 7.19).

At any point when you want to pull back to the master shot—for instance, where Sylvia shoves Frank —just cut out the close-ups on **V2** to reveal the master clip. Unfortunately, Sylvia's shove

7.17 Two Viewers, Canvas, and Timeline

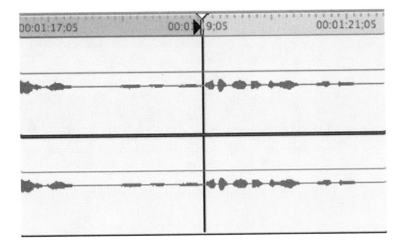

7.18 In Point Marked in the Audio Tab

7.19 Close-ups Laid in Timeline

doesn't come in the same place in the dialog in the master shot as it does in the close-ups. You might need to slide the master clip up the timeline a bit. Generally good, professional actors will keep the pacing of a scene and the timing of each take remarkably consistent so that shots can match easily. Because Frank's performance varies a bit, you'll probably need to cut off some of the close-up so the lines don't repeat in the wide shot, but if you pull up the master shot and overlap the audio on the close-up tracks, **A3/A4**, it'll match pretty closely. Delete what you don't need from the close-ups, and then cut back to them on **V2**. Use the **Track** tool (**T**) to select **V2** and **A3/A4** when you need to pull up the close-ups. You might want to return to the wide shot for the end after Sylvia turns away (Figure 7.20).

Despite the inconsistent dialog, the performances here are paced carefully. There is nothing worse than trying to cut together a scene in which the actors rush the performance for the takes on which they are off camera.

After you've cut through the dialog like this, you'll immediately see how arid it is, the beginning rushed as the lines trade back and forth quickly, the middle section slower where they're longer

7.20 Final Cut

pieces of dialog. Where you adjust the shots is up to you and the director and the weight you want to give the scene. The basic question is usually, whose scene is it? Though *Heartwood* is really Frank's movie, a coming of age story complicated by timber and environmental issues, the scene is more Sylvia's, I think, and Hilary Swank gives a lovely performance. If you accept the premise that it is Sylvia's scene, you should cut it so it weighs more heavily in her favor; if it's Frank's scene, it'll weigh more on his performance and on his reaction to what she says.

I find it best to leave the sound mostly untouched, except to tweak it for any extraneous dialog. I work primarily by **Option**-clicking the video edits and using either the **Roll** tool in the **Timeline** or **E** to **Extend Edit** to alter the cut point while leaving the sound track as the bed.

At the end of the first close-up of Sylvia, I let her remain on screen over the beginning of Frank's line, "I'll do anything." Letting the dialog start first motivates the cut as though you are a bystander following it. You hear the voice, and then you turn to see Frank. Because Frank's line is short, I again waited for Sylvia's responding question "Anything?" before turning to her.

One problem is the type of lengthy speech like Sylvia's where you might want to drop in a cutaway of Frank to see his reaction to her words. I look through Frank's takes in the **Viewer** and found a reaction I liked to use. The truth is the reaction I used doesn't come quite at the moment Sylvia says her dialog, but it seems to fit nicely as a reaction to her simile about her father. After deselecting the audio destination tracks (because we only want Frank's picture and not the sound that goes with it), I dragged it into the empty space above **V2** to create a new **V3**. The nice thing about stacking the cutaway vertically rather than editing into *Sylvia* is that it's much easier to move up or down the timeline or stretch it or shorten it as I like.

I also added a couple of other cutaways, one of Sylvia when Frank says, "This is what people do." Again, the moment Sylvia's shoulders sag didn't quite come on the line, but I think it works nicely here. I like using cutaways because it gives the audience a chance to see the other person's response without losing the intimacy of the scene by backing out to the wide shot.

In the *Heartwood* bin there is a sequence called *Heartwood Sequence*, which is my version of the scene. There are endless possible variations. In the film the scene was played largely in the master shot with one close-up of Sylvia and one of Frank. The movie edit is in *Movie Sequence*. It was probably right for the movie, but for this little exercise, I went for the intensity of the close-ups rather than standoffish look of the wider shot.

You might not have the opportunity to edit material shot by an excellent director and cameraperson, with an Academy Award winning actor and outstanding performances. If the direction, camerawork, and acting isn't there, it's much harder to edit the scenes. There is only so much you can do, and sometimes no amounting of stitching will be able to make a silk purse out of a sow's ear.

Summary

There are many film and video forms, and the lines between them are sometimes blurred, sometimes to the detriment of the content and of the medium. Sometimes though the blurring of documentary and narrative film, music, and dialog, which is basis of the American musical, can give a richness and texture to a film that would be missed if the story were told conventionally.

We've only looked at some of the most common editing forms, but there are others that have conventions of their own—corporate videos, informational, weddings, special interest videos, and on and on.

In the final lesson, we'll look at outputting your material from Final Cut Pro.

Lesson 8

Outputting from Final Cut Pro

This is the easiest part of working with Final Cut Pro, I think, the part where you output your material to tape or for export for the web, DVD, or myriad other uses.

The two basic ways of outputting are:

- Exporting, if you're going to another computer application or CD or DVD or web delivery, or

- Recording to tape, if you're going to traditional broadcast or analog tape delivery

Because it's probably the most common requirement for Final Cut Pro users, let's look at outputting to tape first. We'll see exporting later on page 235.

There are basically three ways to get material from your computer to tape:

- **Record to Tape**
- **Print to Video**
- **Edit to Tape**

229

Record to Tape

You can get your edited material back out to tape in several different ways. The simplest one, and probably the most commonly used way, is to record to tape. Put the playhead at the beginning of the timeline, put your deck into record mode, and hit the spacebar. This is a fast, effective, and simple-to-use method.

Before you record to tape, you should always mixdown your audio. Use **Sequence>Render Only>Mixdown** or the keyboard shortcut **Command-Option-R**. Do this even if you only have a single stereo pair of audio. It's much easier for your computer and your drives to play back a mixdown file than it is to mix your audio on the fly. Also, the default audio quality playback is set to **Low**. If you just record to tape, you will get low-quality playback. However, whenever you mixdown your audio, it's always done to high quality, and that's what you'll get when you record to tape.

The **RT** button setting in the upper right corner of the **Timeline** lets you switch between **Use Playback Settings** or **Full Quality**. This actually has no effect on recording to tape manually. It only affects the other record functions that we'll see in a moment.

There is one other trap in recording to tape, either manually or with **Print to Video** or **Edit to Tape**. If you have set your **Render Controls** in **Sequence Settings** down to low values to speed up rendering, that's the playback quality you'll get. Unlike previous versions of FCP, you cannot now switch to high quality and automatically force a re-render. You have to switch to high quality and then reset each effect that was rendered at low resolution to force it to re-render at high quality. There is no force re-render function, unfortunately. This is also true of exporting to tape and is a significant issue in Final Cut Pro 4.

Playing back from the **Timeline** has the advantage of speed and convenience. It is useful also for make quick test recording. In addition to the traps we've have already seen, some other disadvantages are that you don't get to put in bars and tone and neat countdowns, slates, black leaders, and trailers, unless you physically add them to your sequence. If you want these features, you can use **Print to Video** or **Edit to Tape**.

Print to Video

Print to Video and **Edit to Tape** are both found under the **File** menu. If you have a sequence selected in the **Browser** or an active **Timeline**, you can call up **Print to Video** from the menu or use **Control-M**. This brings up the dialog box in Figure 8.1.

In this dialog you can set any number of options for program starts and ends. You can add bars and tone and set the tone level, depending on the system you're using. A number of different digital audio standards are used, if you can call anything that has variables as being a standard. Different systems use –12, –14, –16, or –20dB as digital audio standards. Analog uses a variety of other standards around 0dB. Check with your final destination before selecting a tone level.

The **Slate** popup lets you use the:

- **Clip Name**
- **Text**, which you can add in the text window
- **File**, which is any still image, video, or audio file

So if you have an audio slate recorded, selecting the file and navigating to it with the little **Load** button will play the sound during your mastering session.

> **✎ Note**
> **PtV Limits:** Though you can loop FCP's **Print to Video** as many times as you want, the sequence had better be fairly short. The duration of any **Print to Video** recording is limited. It can't be longer than four hours, which is probably more than enough for most people.

You can use FCP's built-in countdown, using a form of Academy leader. Or you can use a countdown of your own by selecting **File** in the **Countdown** popup.

One of the hardest tasks for a hard drive to do in digital video is finding, seeking, and playing back multiple tracks of audio simultaneously. As in recording to tape, it is important to always mixdown your audio first. FCP will render out a single audio file that mixes down all your tracks. Your system will run more easily, and you're less likely to have dropped frames during that crucial playback to tape. I suggest mixing down every time you output to tape, whatever method you use. I also suggest always switching off **Mirror on Desktop** to conserve system resources for outputting.

When you start **Print to Video**, FCP will write a video and, if necessary, an audio file of any material that needs to be rendered. It will go through this routine for every **Print to Video**.

Again, be aware of the render issues mentioned previously on page 230. Material rendered in low resolution will still be maintained in your final output unless you manually find it and force it to be re-rendered at full quality. If you have rendered with low resolution, mixed resolution, or think you may have done so, the only safe and sure method around this problem is to use **Render Manager** from the **Tools** menu and to delete the render files associated with that the sequence you want to export. Make sure your **Render Control** settings are at full quality and re-render everything.

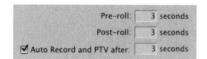

8.2   Auto Record Preference

After it's finished writing the video and audio files, FCP may prompt you to put your deck into record. Press **OK** for playback to start. It may also be set to **Auto Record**, to automatically put your deck in record mode and set it off after a specified number of seconds. This function is set in the lower right corner of the **Device Control** panel in **Audio/Video Settings** (Figure 8.2).

Edit to Tape

Print to Video is an excellent tool, but if you're working in DV with a camera or deck that allows assemble editing, which is pretty much all of them, or if you have a professional deck that allows insert editing to tape, then **Edit to Tape** is the tool for you. It's also called up from the **File** menu.

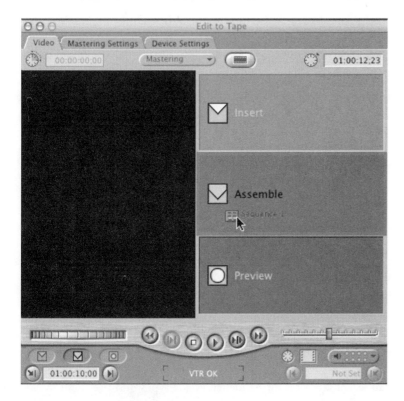

8.3 Edit to Tape Window

Edit to Tape uses the same type of window as Log and Capture, only with an edit overlay (Figure 8.3). To perform an Assemble edit or Insert edit, you have to enter at least an In point. Simply dragging a sequence from the Browser into the Edit to Tape window will activate the Edit Overlay. It offers you the choices of Assemble, Insert, or Preview, assuming your deck is capable of those functions. Most DV camcorders and decks can do an Assemble edit. If so, you can select your edit mode here, or with one of the buttons in the lower left corner.

The controls will operate your deck with the usual buttons or the J, K, L keys. You can assign In and Out points on the deck for Assemble or Insert edits, either with the usual buttons as in the Log and Capture window or with the I and O keys.

On the lower right side of the Edit to Tape window are selector buttons that let you choose the tracks you want to enable for insert editing, any combination of video or two audio tracks (Figure 8.4). New in this version of FCP is the little stopwatch button that allows you to insert timecode onto a tape.

8.4 Insert Selector Buttons in Edit to Tape Window

8.5   Top of the Edit to Tape Window

At the top of the **Edit to Tape** window, in addition to the duration on the left and the current time on the right, are two buttons (Figure 8.5). The one on the left is a popup that lets you select between **Mastering** and **Editing**.

In the **Mastering** panel you have access to **Bars and Tone, Leaders and Trailers,** and **Looping**, just as you do in **Print to Video**. You select them in the **Mastering Settings** tab in the **Edit to Tape** window. In the **Mastering** panel, you can set whether you record whole or part of a sequence by selecting from a popup **Entire Media** or **In to Out**.

With the **Editing** option, you can do an Insert edit, assigning both In and Out points on the tape or In and Out points in your sequence in any combination to define a three-point edit. In the **Editing** option, you don't have access to leaders and trailers and the other extras you get with **Mastering**.

The button on the right will black a tape for you. This lays down on your tape a video black signal with continuous timecode. You need this for an **Insert** edit, and you'd certainly want to black at least the first minute of a tape before you do an Assemble edit. Clicking the **Black and Code** button brings up a dialog where you can select any of your **Sequence Preset** types and use them as the type of Black and Code to be laid down. Or you can use the **Current Settings** or make up a new one with the **Custom** selection. After you click **OK**, you'll get a warning dialog before you can proceed. Clicking **OK** will take the tape in the record deck back to the head and begin the process of recording Black and Code to your tape. During the recording you'll see on your computer monitor the video output, poorly displayed as during capture. If you have **Mirror on Desktop During Recording** switched off in your **External Video** preferences, instead of the picture you'll see a large black box the size of your output with the words "**Output of Video in Progress.**" You can quit the Black and Code process at any time by hitting the **Escape** key.

⟍ Note_____
Preedit Calibration: Before doing either an Assemble and certainly an Insert edit, you should calibrate your deck in **Device Control** preferences, making adjustments in **Playback Offset**.

When you're ready to begin the edit, drag the sequence into the **Edit Overlay**, and the process will be initiated. As in **Print to Video**, FCP will first render out what's necessary before beginning the **Edit to Tape**. As soon as that is completed, FCP will take control of your deck, queue it to the correct point, pre-roll it, and put it into Record mode as frame accurately as your system can manage. Again, during the **Edit to Tape** process, you'll see the video or the **Output of Video in Progress** window. The **Escape** key again will allow you to abort the edit at any time.

If you only want to insert a portion of the timeline into a portion of the tape, you'll have to do an Insert edit. If your deck is accurate enough, it's easy to do. What you'll really be doing is a linear, tape-to-tape, three-point edit, only in this case, one of the tape decks (the player deck) is your computer. Set the In and Out points on your record machine, and mark the In point in the timeline to create the three-point edit. Drag the sequence to **Insert** to execute the edit.

Export

You can access the different formats and ways of exporting from FCP from the **File** menu (Figure 8.6). From here you can export to **QuickTime Movie**. In earlier versions of FCP, this was called **Final Cut Pro Movie**; but whatever it's called, it offers a number of options. You can also export:

- **Using QuickTime Conversion**, what used to be exporting to QuickTime
- **Using Compressor**

Matching Timecodes:

A common request is to lay off to tape a sequence in which the timecode on the tape matches the TC in the timeline. To do this, you need a deck that's at least assemble-edit capable, preferably one that's frame accurately controlled through RS-422. If your deck can address the timecode—that is, allows you to start at whatever TC number you enter—you have an added advantage. The traditional linear tape-editing method is to start the timecode on the deck at 58:00:00 or 59:00:00. This gives you a minute or two with a little fudge factor to begin the tape. That time can be used to lay in bars and tone, slates, countdown, black, whatever you want. Do this with the **Mastering Settings** tab on the back of the **Edit to Tape** window. This allows you access to all the options you had in **Print to Video**. Then at 1:00:00:00 straight up, your program begins. If your timeline begins at the default time of one hour, the TC on your deck will match the TC in the timeline, frame for frame.

If you can't address the TC on your deck, it's still possible to do, though not as neatly. Start by recording a chunk of black at the beginning of your tape. Put a 10-second slug of black at the head of your sequence in the timeline so that your program begins 10 seconds into the timeline. Next, using the **Timeline Options** tab in **Sequence Settings** (Command-zero), set the **Sequence Start Time** to zero. Mark an In point in the sequence at the beginning of the program, where the 10-second slug ends. Now enter an In point on the tape for the Assemble edit at 10:00 exactly. Assemble to that point, and the TC on your tape will match the TC in the timeline. If you want the bars and tone as well, you'll have to add them to the timeline to keep sync with the TC on the tape.

8.6 File > Export (above)

8.7 QuickTime Movie Export Dialog (right)

- To FCP's companion applications, LiveType and Soundtrack
- As well as **Audio to AIFF(s)**
- **Audio to OMF**, an Avid standard audio file format for digital audio applications such as Pro Tools.

Other export options include:

- **Batch List**
- **Edit Decision List (EDL)**

QuickTime Movie

Let's start with **QuickTime Movie,** the first in the **Export** list. Though you are exporting a QuickTime movie, FCP is still listed as its creator type. So if you launch the resulting movie, it will launch Final Cut Pro.

You can export a sequence as a digital file into a **QuickTime Movie** in several ways:

- From the active **Timeline** window directly from the sequence you're working in
- From an active **Viewer**
- From the **Browser** by exporting a sequence or clip

Click on the item and go to **Export>QuickTime Movie**. Any way of navigation will bring up the dialog box in Figure 8.7.

Here you can rename your sequence, if you wish, and you can set standard FCP settings from the **Settings** popup.

Settings can either be current or selected for anything in your **Sequence Presets Audio/Video Settings** panel. Or you can select

Custom, which will actually call up the **Sequence Presets** window and let you create a custom preset right there.

The **Audio/Video** popup allows you to export just audio, just video, or both.

The two checkboxes at the bottom of the dialog box are the crucial: **Recompress All Frames** and **Make Movie Self-Contained**. Normally you do not want to recompress the frames; they've probably been compressed already into DV or Motion-JPEG. You want to use the compression that's already there.

You would want to use **Recompress All Frames** only if you have material from different codecs or with different data rates in a single sequence and you want them to use a uniform, fixed codec and data rate. In such cases, you have to use **Make Movie Self-Contained** to create a single video file for your sequence.

But you have another choice. If you uncheck **Make Movie Self-Contained**, FCP will generate a reference movie. This is a relatively small file that points back to the original media source files. It will play the contents of the sequence as you laid them out. The reference movie will play back from the QT player, and it can also be imported into other applications such as After Effects. The real advantages to making reference movies are the speed in generating the file and the comparatively small file size. If anything in the FCP sequence needs to be rendered, it will still have to be rendered for the reference movie, and the audio files will also be duplicated as a mixdown of your tracks. No other application can call up FCP's effects and motion to do rendering within it. The reference movie is treated just like any other QT clip inside After Effects or the QuickTime player. FCP and the importing application do not need to be open at the same time for this to work. You do, of course, need to have access to all the source media included in the sequence, because a reference movie only points to existing media source files on your hard drives. It's not a complete video clip in itself. Be warned: If you delete any of the media needed for the reference movie, it will not play. It will be a broken QuickTime file.

Export to QuickTime Movie is an important tool because it is the only way to export a sequence from FCP without recompressing the video. All other exports, including export to **QuickTime Conversion**, will recompress the frames.

Creating a reference movie is probably the best way to get your material from FCP to iDVD. If you've set chapter markers in your timeline, these can be exported to iDVD by setting the **Markers** popup to **Chapter Markers** or **DVD Studio Pro Markers**. Either will work.

For Soundtrack and LiveType

Both of these export functions use the **QuickTime Movie** module, but they provide different presets.

For Soundtrack defaults to exporting a reference movie. That is, **Make Self-Contained Movie** is switched off. Also, the **Markers** popup is set to export **Audio Scoring Markers**. Scoring markers are useful for setting hit points in your score in Soundtrack.

For LiveType is similar. It also exports a reference movie that's not self-contained, only here the **Markers** are set to export **All Markers**.

Using Compressor

Export **Using Compressor** is a unique function. It doesn't actually export anything. Again, it's only available when the **Canvas** or **Timeline** are active. What it does is launch the Compressor application directly.

Because of its great flexibility and power, this should be the preferred method of export when you are doing a video or audio file conversion. Activating the function immediately brings up the **Compressor Batch** window. Click on the **Presets** button in the upper left corner to open the available presets and to create your own (Figure 8.10).

Most of the presets are for MPEG-2 and MPEG-4, but you can create your own preset for whatever you want, as we saw in Lesson 1 on page 31 when we looked at creating a Droplet to convert audio CD files to digital video sampling rates.

Export **Using Compressor** allows you to export to MPEG-2 with great precision and control for use in DVD Studio Pro, especially if you create your own presets to add in filters which allow noise reduction, gamma correction, and others.

✎ Note_____
Soundtrack and LiveType: Note that these two functions will not export from the **Browser** or from the **Viewer**. They will only export a sequence if the **Timeline** or the **Canvas** is the active window.

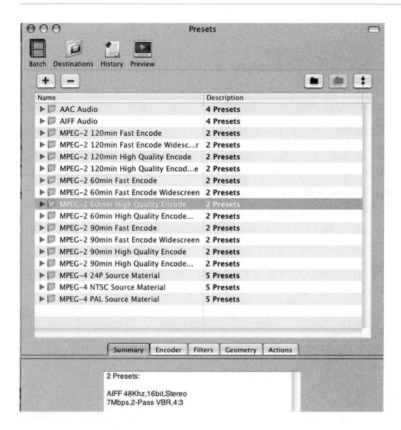

8.8 Compressor Presets

QuickTime Conversion

QuickTime Conversion is the catch-all for every form of file conversion and still export from FCP. I would have liked for **Still** export to be separated, but it's hidden in here as well (Figure 8.9).

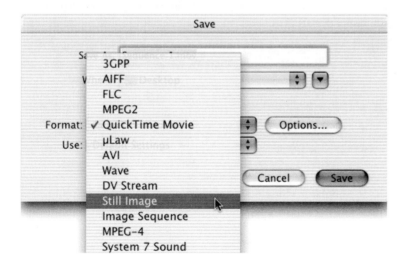

8.9 QuickTime Export

Video Export

Final Cut Pro has a number of video export choices. They include:

- FLC, an 8-bit format used for computer animations
- AVI, a PC video format
- DV Stream, DV audio and video encoded on a single track

These are video formats. Some, such as AVI and QuickTime, allow you to use a number of different codecs. DV Stream is used by iMovie, not by FCP. Do not export to DV Stream if you're going to a video-editing application other than iMovie.

In **Quicktime Conversion,** the **User** popup offers a stack of common Internet or CD settings.

To export to a movie file, use the **Options** button and select the correct video and audio settings (Figure 8.10).

The default compressor is **Video,** but if you click on the **Settings** button, you get exactly the same **Settings** dialog box as you get when you press the **Advanced** button in **A/V Settings** for **Sequence Presets** and **Capture Presets.** You can set the compressor, quality, and frame rate just as before. Be sure to set DV's **Quality** slider to **Best** for final output. The **Quality** slider will affect the recompression quality. Only use **Low** or **Medium** for a test output or some other intermediary use.

The **Audio** dialog box is also the same as you've seen in **Sequence Presets** and **Capture Presets.**

One setting that's slightly different in the QT export is the **Size,** which offers you either the current frame size or a custom size you can dial in.

Exporting with QuickTime allows you to use a variety of different codecs for compression, such as, among others:

- Animation
- Cinepak
- DV-NTSC
- Motion-JPEG A
- Photo-JPEG
- Sorenson Video 3

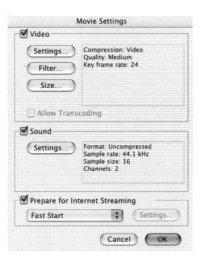

8.10 QuickTime Video and Audio Options

Sorenson Video 3 is an excellent codec for web compression. Photo-JPEG is used to reduce file size. It works with FCP's **OfflineRT** capability. An important codec is Animation, a high data rate, lossless compression codec often used to transfer material between various applications such as After Effects and Live-Type. One advantage that the Animation codec has that others don't is that it can carry alpha channel information with the video. This allows you to create a composition in LiveType, for instance, and bring it into FCP without loss. LiveType always renders into the Animation codec, though you can export from it to another codec if you which. With an alpha channel, your Live-Type composition can be overlaid on other images. When you export from FCP using **QuickTime Conversion** with the Animation codec with an alpha channel, make sure that for **Colors** you select **Millions+.** The plus is the alpha channel.

To create good quality web video, you should have separate compression application, such as Compressor or Sorenson Squeeze. To create video CDs, you'll need an application, such as Cleaner or Toast, that allows compression to the MPEG-1 codec. This is a heavily compressed codec, but a remarkable one in that it can actually play back off the very low output of a CD and still produce a full-screen, full-motion image. Cleaner will also allow you to create Real media as well as Windows Video Media.

To create a DVD, you need an authoring application such as iDVD or DVD Studio Pro. If you're using DVD Studio Pro, one of the options available in the **QuickTime Conversion export** window will be MPEG2, the DVD compression format. This is a much improved MPEG2 export module and includes 2-pass Variable Bit Rate compression (Figure 8.12).

Exporting to **QuickTime Conversion** allows you to add filters to your clips or sequences. Most QuickTime filters are available directly within FCP, with a notable exception, **Film Noise** (Figure 8.13).

This filter adds an old-time film look to your video, as though it were scratched and dirty. A small QT movie runs in the bottom left corner showing you how much schmutz you've added to the picture. Here you can set amounts of **Hair and Scratches** that appear on your video, from very low to fairly well-destroyed. You can't control the grain, however, but you can add that in FCP before you export. In addition to **Hair and Scratches**, the popup at the top will take you to another panel where you can set the

> ✎ *Tip*
>
> **Rendering**: If you create a composition in FCP and you want to export it with an alpha channel, make sure you do not render it first. If you do render it, FCP will export the render file regardless of the codec requested in **QuickTime Conversion** and regardless of whether you want to export the alpha channel. If you leave the material unrendered you will see an **Unrendered** warning in the export module (Figure 8.11), but the alpha channel will export correctly if you use **Animation** and **Millions +** .

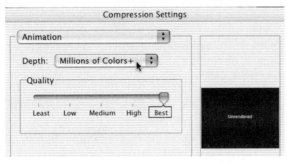

8.11 Exporting Alpha Channel (above)

8.12 QuickTime Conversion Editor (right)

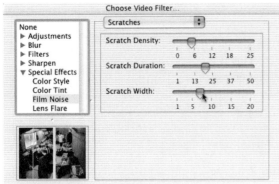

8.13 Film Scratches Panel

8.14 Dust and Film Fading Panel

amount of dust on your video as well as tinting the film (Figure 8.14). The sepia is quite subtle, and the 1930's color film is suitably garish.

Image Sequence Export

Two other types of **QuickTime Conversion** export are often used: **Image Sequence** and **Still Image**. Image sequences are useful for rotoscoping and animation work. They provide high-quality output without loss. Select **Image Sequence** from the **Format** popup and click on the **Options** button to set the file type (Figure 8.15). You can set any frame rate, and exporting will create one frame of uncompressed video for every frame you specify. This can easily generate a huge number of files, so be sure to first create a folder in which to put your image sequence.

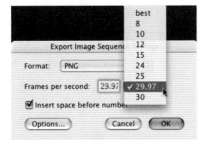

8.15 Image Sequence Export

Still Image Export

Quicktime Conversion export allows you to change the **Format** popup to export still images. This is how you get frames of video out to your computer for web or print use. Your stills will only be 72dpi, probably not good enough for fine printing. Photoshop plugins such as Genuine Fractals can help improve the image's appearance.

The **Options** button for **Still Image** export uses the same dialog box as **Image Sequence**, including frame rate. Don't be confused; leave the frame rate blank.

The still you're exporting may very well be in CCIR601 rectangular pixels. This is not a problem if you're going back to a video application, but in print or on a computer display, the stills will look squashed. Photoshop will fix this problem for you. If the still image comes from DV, in PS go to **Image Size**. Switch off the **Constrain Proportions** checkbox, and either upsample the image by changing the size to 720×540 or, for better quality, downsample to 640×480. Either way, you'll end up with a 4:3 image in the correct pixel aspect ratio. If you're working with a 720×486 image, then downsample to 648×486. Check **Resampling** and select **Bicubic** whenever you resize in PS.

If you're going to export stills for web or print work from video, especially video with a lot of motion in it, you'll probably want to de-interlace it. You can do this either in FCP before you export the frame by using **Effects>Video Filters>Video>De-interlace**. Or you can de-interlace in PS as well. It's in the **Filters** menu under **Video>De-Interlace**. I normally do it in Photoshop because I think its **De-interlace** feature works better than FCP's built-in one, which simply drops one of the fields.

Audio Export

FCP can export to a number of different audio formats including:

- AIFF
- μLaw
- Wave
- System 7

Below the **Format** popup is a contextually sensitive **Use** popup. So if you select **AIFF**, for instance, in the **Use** popup you'll get common audio file settings (Figure 8.16).

8.16 AIFF Export Use Popup

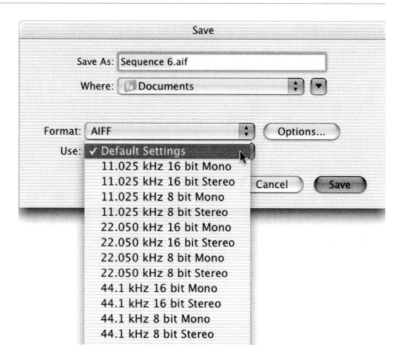

Notice that the selection does not include any of the DV sampling rates, although AIFF is the most commonly used format for audio files with Final Cut. Use the **Default Settings** option to give you the same sampling rate as that of your sequence.

Export Audio to AIFF(s)

This export module is new to Final Cut Pro 4. It allows you to export your sequences tracks as pairs of audio. So if you have eight tracks of audio in your DV sequence, you can export four tracks, either as stereo pairs or as channels into the AIFF format. How many tracks are exported is based on the settings in the **Audio Output** panel of your **Sequence Settings** (Figure 8.17). Notice that you can set the **Grouping** to be either **Stereo** mixes or **Dual Mono**. Switch off the **Downmix**, which defaults to −3dB, if you don't want it. When you set multiple track outputs for a DV sequence, you'll get a warning dialog box. Just ignore it.

If you want to export your audio using **Audio to AIFF(s)**, it is important that your tracks be organized and arranged logically—all the narration on a pair of tracks, the music on one or two pairs as needed, the natural sound on as many pairs as needed. Try to avoid jumbling up your tracks, so that you end up with

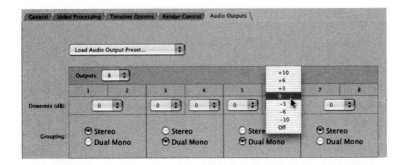

8.17 Audio Outputs Panel

music and natural sound and narration all scattered over the same track pairs.

To export **Audio to AIFF(s)**, select it from the **File** menu, which brings up the simple little dialog box in Figure 8.18. Here you can set the sampling rate, sampling size, and whether you want to export as **Channel Grouped** pairs or as a **Stereo Mix**. Using **Channel Group** will export your tracks as mixed pairs or as distinct mono tracks into separate AIFF files.

Export Audio to OMF

OMF stands for *Open Media Format*, a file format that's widely recognized as an intermediary format for moving audio files between various applications. Exporting to OMF allows you to move your audio tracks as you've laid them out in FCP into a digital audio workstation such as Pro Tools. It works very well, as long as you bear a number of constraints in mind.

To export audio to OMF, select the sequence you want to export, and go to **File>Export>Audio to OMF**.

> **Note**
>
> *Audio to AIFF(s)* uses a file-naming convention based on the sequence name, stereo pairs are mixed into a single file with both track numbers, while mono tracks export each as a separate file as in Figure 8.19.

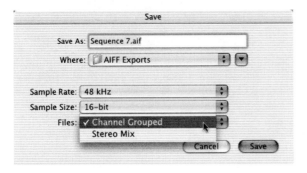

8.18 Audio to AIFF(s) Dialog

8.19 Exported AIFF tracks

OMF Audio Export

Sample Rate: 48 kHz

Sample Size: 16–bit

Handle Length: 00:00:01;00
☑ Include Crossfade Transitions

8.20   Export to OMF Dialog

☆ *Tip*

Audio Sync: When exporting to OMF, it's a good idea to add an audio sync pop at the beginning and end of your tracks. Set a one-frame tone two seconds before the first audio and two seconds after the last audio. Just use the **Generators** to go to **Bars and Tone**, make the single frame, and throw away the video bars. This makes an easy sync point when you bring your audio back into FCP for final output.

This brings up a dialog box that offers you a few choices (Figure 8.20). To be able to use your exported cross fades, you need to be working with Digidesign's DigiTranslator software.

It's important to note that the OMF file does not pass on pans, levels settings, or filters from FCP; all you get are the tracks and media handles. Levels settings and effects are supposed to be added in your audio-mixing software.

After you've exported to OMF, you then have to run OMFTools or DigiTranslator to convert your files into a Pro Tools project.

When you've finished working with your material in ProTools, or whatever audio finishing application you're using, you'll need to export the sound track as an AIFF file and bring it into FCP to marry it with your video.

Batch List

A *batch list* is basically a printout of the contents of a bin. You can only make a batch list when the **Browser** or bin is in List view. Then select **File>Export>Batch List**, choose either **Tabbed** or **Formatted** output, and you're done (Figure 8.21).

The exported batch list will contain everything displayed in the List view columns, and not what's in the selected columns. If you don't want some information in the batch list, use the contextual menu in the bin header to hide the column. Choosing either **Tabbed** or **Formatted**, the list can be opened either in a word processing application or in a spreadsheet application such as Excel, where it is ready to print out (Figure 8.22).

Batch lists are useful for long-form projects. After you have all your material captured and subclipped with notes and comments

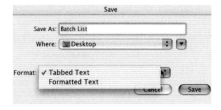

Save

Save As: Batch List

Where: 🖥 Desktop

Format: ✓ Tabbed Text
         Formatted Text
                      Cancel   Save

8.21   Batch List Dialog Box (above)

8.22   Batch List in Excel (right)

	A	B	C	D	E	F	G
	Name	Media Start	Media End	Duration	Capture	Reel	Master Clip
2	Backstage01	00:00:03;11	00:00:16;18	00:00:13;08	Not Yet		3 Yes
3	Backstage02	00:00:16;19	00:00:33;16	00:00:16;28	Not Yet		3 Yes
4	Backstage03	00:00:33;17	00:00:50;24	00:00:17;08	Not Yet		3 Yes
5	Backstage04	00:00:50;25	00:01:04;02	00:00:13;06	Not Yet		3 Yes
6	Backstage05	00:01:04;03	00:01:19;03	00:00:15;01	Not Yet		3 Yes
7	Backstage06	00:01:19;04	00:01:37;29	00:00:09;19	Not Yet		3 Yes
8	Backstage07	00:01:38;00	00:01:48;27	00:00:10;28	Not Yet		3 Yes
9	Backstage08	00:01:48;28	00:02:04;19	00:00:15;20	Not Yet		3 Yes
10	Backstage09	00:02:04;20	00:02:11;12	00:00:06;23	Not Yet		3 Yes
11	Backstage10	00:02:11;13	00:02:20;18	00:00:09;06	Not Yet		3 Yes
12	Backstage11	00:02:20;19	00:02:42;10	00:00:21;22	Not Yet		3 Yes
13	Backstage12	00:02:42;11	00:02:50;25	00:00:08;15	Not Yet		3 Yes
14	Backstage13	00:02:50;26	00:03:01;11	00:00:10;14	Not Yet		3 Yes
15	Backstage14	00:03:01;12	00:03:18;04	00:00:16;23	Not Yet		3 Yes
16	Backstage15	00:03:18;05	00:03:21;10	00:00:03;06	Not Yet		3 Yes
17	Backstage16	00:03:21;11	00:03:28;00	00:00:06;20	Not Yet		3 Yes
18	Backstage17	00:03:28;01	00:03:34;08	00:00:06;08	Not Yet		3 Yes
19							

Batch List

added, printing out a Batch List gives you a hard copy of your bins. You can look it over in those spare moments while you're rendering or waiting for the coffee to brew.

What's great about batch lists is that they work both ways. Because they are just tab-delineated files, you can create them in Word, Excel, or other applications. This way you can log material outside of FCP, such as when you're on the road. Then you can use your list in FCP as a Batch Capture List. Because tab-delineated files are common to many applications, you can move logging lists from one application to another.

EDL

Final Cut Pro can export an Edit Decision List in a variety of common formats (Figure 8.23). CMX3600 is probably the most common carrier, but other systems use other formats. Because an EDL is a text file, you can readily, if laboriously, edit it in any word-processing application. EDLs are the last vestiges of linear systems, an arcane format that is limited to the types and numbers of tracks it can move, and to the types of transitions it will understand, often only dissolves and simple wipes. Sometimes it is the only tool available for moving between different types of edit systems, from offline to online, from nonlinear to linear.

EDLs normally export only one video track. Any additional tracks should be output as separate EDLs. Usually no more than four audio tracks are allowed. Neither effects nor motion information translates into EDLs. Titles do not export. Nested sequences do not export properly either. All in all, EDL export is a very limited format and should be avoided if at all possible.

Remember also that FCP can not only export EDLs, it can also import them from the **File>Import>EDL** menu. This will bring an EDL into the application and lay it out as a sequence ready for batch capture or reconnect (Figure 8.24).

Batch Export

Batch Export is a good, comprehensive interface that allows you to set up a number of different export formats before beginning the export process. You can select a bin, a group of shots, or even a sequence to batch export. Once you've selected **Batch Export** from the **File** menu, the **Export Queue** window will open (Figure 8.25).

EDL Export Options

EDL Title: Sequence 7

Format: CMX 3600

Sorting: Master, Audio Merged

Reel conflicts:
- ☐ Target Video Track Only (V1)
- ☐ Omit Transitions
- ◉ B-Reel Edits
- ○ Pre-read Edits
- ○ Generic Edits

EDL Notes
- ☑ File names
- ☑ Master Comment 4
- ☑ Filters
- ☑ Video Levels
- ☑ Audio Levels
- ☑ Transitions

Master

Start Time: 01:00:00;00 ☑ Drop Frame

Audio Mapping

	None	EDL 1	EDL 2	EDL 3	EDL 4
A 1	○	◉	○	○	○
A 2	○	○	◉	○	○
A 3	○	○	○	◉	○
A 4	○	○	○	○	◉
A 5	◉	○	○	○	○
A 6	◉	○	○	○	○

8.23 EDL Export Dialog (left)

8.24 EDL Import Options (below)

Import Options

Select Preset: DV NTSC 48 kHz

Use this preset when editing with DV NTSC material with audio set to 48KHz (16bit for DV).

Import For

Recapture   Handle Size 00:00:01;00

☑ Make File Names Unique

It's like a bin window, but with special features, mainly the buttons at the bottom. Pressing the **Settings** button brings up an **Export** dialog box (Figure 8.26). Here you have all the usual settings options, like those in the **QuickTime Conversion export** windows. To trim video during batch export, check the box for **Use Item In/Out**.

The only two buttons that are slightly different from QT export are the **Set Destination** button at the top and the **Set Naming Options** button in the middle. **Set Destination** is pretty self-explanatory; it opens up navigation services and lets you pick a location on your hard drives for your material. **Set Naming Options** opens the dialog box in Figure 8.27.

8.25 Batch Export Queue

Export Queue

Name	Type	Status	Base Output Filenan	Length
▼ 🗀 Batch 1	Bin			
▶ 🗀 Clips	Bin			
▼ 🗀 Batch 2	Bin			
🎞 Rough Cut	Sequence	Queued		00:01:30;02
▼ 🗀 Batch 3	Bin			
🎞 Split Edit	Sequence	Queued		00:01:47;20

Export   Settings...   View Exported

8.26 Batch Export Queue (left)

8.27 Set Naming Options (below)

Here you can remove any suffixes or add your own, as well as define the file type. When that's done, just press the **Export** button. Everything queued will be exported as specified in your settings. If your naming convention duplicates with an existing file name, you'll get the error dialog box, which allows you to rename the file you're exporting.

Each set of batches can have different settings of course, so you can use it to set the same material to be exported in different formats, one for MPEG-2 perhaps for DVD creation, and another for Sorenson Video 3 or MPEG-4 for web creation. After exporting, clicking the **View Exported** button will open the clips in separate viewers within FCP. **Batch Export** is in many ways redundant now and has been superseded by the batch capabilities of Compressor.

Summary

We've now gone through the whole cycle of work in Final Cut Pro 4 using its essential editing tools, starting from raw tape material, either analog or digital, capturing, editing, working with audio, transitions, titling, and finally we have returned our finished project to tape. It's been a long journey, but I hope an exciting, interesting, and rewarding one.

Index

Updates

Want to receive e-mail news updates for *Final Cut Pro 4 Editing Essentials*? Send a blank e-mail to fcp4@news.cmpbooks.com. We will do our best to keep you informed of software updates and enhancements, new tips, and other FCP-related resources.

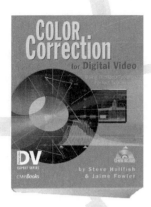

Color Correction for Digital Video
by Steve Hullfish & Jaime Fowler

Use desktop tools to improve your storytelling, deliver critical cues, and add impact to your video. Beginning with a clear, concise description of color and perception theory, this full-color book shows you how to analyze color-correction problems and solve them—whatever NLE or plug-in you use. Refine your skills with tutorials that include secondary and spot corrections and stylized looks.

$49.95, 4-color, Softcover with CD-ROM, 202pp, ISBN 1-547820-201-9

Nonlinear Editing
Storytelling, Aesthetics, & Craft
by Bryce Button

Build your aesthetic muscles with this application-agnostic guide to digital editing so you can make better decisions in the edit bay and in your career. The companion CD-ROM includes a treasure trove of valuable software, image files, tools, utilities, fonts, filters, and sounds.

$49.95, Softcover with CD-ROM, 523pp, ISBN 1-57820-096-2

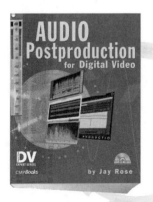

Audio Postproduction for Digital Video
by Jay Rose

Perform professional audio editing, sound effects work, processing, and mixing on your desktop. You'll save time and solve common problems using these "cookbook recipes" and platform-independent tutorials. Discover the basics of audio theory, set up your post studio, and walk through every aspect of postproduction. The audio CD features tutorial tracks, demos, and diagnostics.

$44.95, Softcover with audio CD, 429pp, ISBN 1-57820-116-0

Creating Motion Graphics
with After Effects, Second edition
Volume 1: The Essentials
by Trish & Chris Meyer

Master the core concepts and tools you need to tackle virtually every job, including keyframe animation, masking, mattes, and plug-in effects. New chapters demystify the Parenting and 3D Space features, and a fresh introductory tutorial ensures that even the newest user can get up and running fast.

$54.95, 4-color, Softcover with CD-ROM, 432pp, ISBN 1-57820-114-4

Creating Motion Graphics
with After Effects, Second edition
Volume 2: Advanced Techniques
by Trish & Chris Meyer

Refine your workflow by integrating After Effects with other programs. You'll master the vital details of preparing files for broadcast with an understanding of the technicalities of video and film, as well as tackle advanced animation techniques, Expressions, color keying, and motion tracking with the Production Bundle.

$59.95, 4-color, Softcover with CD-ROM, 432pp, ISBN 1-57820-208-6

Photoshop for Nonlinear Editors
by Richard Harrington

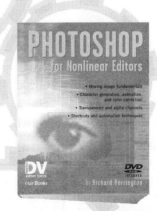

Use Photoshop to generate characters, correct colors, and animate graphics for digital video. You'll grasp the fundamental concepts and master the complete range of Photoshop tools through lively discourse, full-color presentations, and hands-on tutorials. Includes a focus on shortcuts and automation and time-efficient techniques.

$54.95, 4-color, Softcover with DVD, 302pp, ISBN 1-57820-209-4

Final Cut Pro 4 On the Spot
by Richard Harrington & Abba Shapiro

Learn what you need to know—when you need to know it. Packed with more than 350 expert techniques, this book clearly illustrates all the essential methods that pros use to get the job done. Experienced editors and novices alike will discover an invaluable reference filled with techniques to improve efficiency and creativity.

$27.95, Softcover, 236pp, ISBN 1-57820-231-0

Creative Titling with Final Cut Pro
by Diannah Morgan

Create successful and compelling title sequences with Final Cut Pro. Packed with four-color illustrations, explanations, instructions, and step-by-step tutorials, this book teaches and inspires experienced editors to produce work that is a cut above the rest. This book covers not just the "mechanics" of editing, but also the design and methodology behind successful title sequences.

$44.95, 4-color, Softcover, 192pp, ISBN 1-57820-225-6

Available in North America only

Available February 2004

Available March 2004

Using Soundtrack
Produce Original Music for Video, DVD, and Multimedia
by Douglas Spotted Eagle

Discover how Soundtrack can be used to give video projects a professional finish with the addition of custom, royalty-free scoring. Learn the basics of great audio, including advice on recording sound, editing tips, noise reduction tools, and audio effects. Practical tutorials provide hands-on techniques for common tasks that include editing video to audio, editing audio to video, changing the length of a music bed, and mixing dialog with music and sound effects.

$29.95, Softcover with CD-ROM, 256pp, ISBN 1-57820-229-9

What's on the DVD?

The companion DVD for *Final Cut Pro 4 Editing Essentials* includes unedited, raw footage for the tutorial projects, which contain sequences that guide you through the material. The disc contains:

- Over 13 minutes of DV and audio media files
- Six FCP4 tutorial project files
- QuickTime preview movies of all FCP4's 60 transitions
- *Extras* folder with
  - Avid keyboard layout
  - Three column layouts
  - Six Photoshop preset images
  - Replace FCP4 Prefs shareware
  - Free Timecode Calculator